# Child Maltreatment and the Law

Roger J.R. Levesque

# Child Maltreatment and the Law

## Returning to First Principles

 Springer

Roger J.R. Levesque, J.D., Ph.D.
Indiana University
Department of Criminal Justice
302 Sycamore Hall
Bloomington IN 47405
USA

ISBN 978-0-387-79917-9        e-ISBN 978-0-387-79918-6

Library of Congress Control Number: 2008931182

Printed on acid-free paper

9 8 7 6 5 4 3 2 1

springer.com

# Contents

# Part I
# Introduction: The Nature and Limits of Child Maltreatment Law

# Chapter 1
# The Increasingly Curious Response to Children's Harms

The study of child maltreatment has come of age and offers us a tremendous wealth of information. Scientific journals directly dealing with violence against children flourish, and numerous academic books carefully document the nature, causes, consequences, and prevention of a wide variety of harms children suffer (Helfer, Kempe, & Krugman, 1997; Kendall-Tackett & Giacomoni, 2005). In addition and at the behest of the federal government, states now collect unprecedented amounts of information relating to their responses to child maltreatment (Haskins, Wulczyn, & Webb, 2007). Because this information increasingly results in empirically robust findings, leading researchers conclude that we now have gained policy-relevant research that can be harnessed to reform child protection laws and policies in ways more consistent with our empirical understanding of maltreatment and of governmental responses to it (Haskins, Wulczyn, & Webb, 2007). Without doubt, the progress in providing usable knowledge has been phenomenal. However, whether research findings will be used effectively, if at all, remains an entirely different matter.

One perhaps could expect that our legal system would respond to empirical realities rather than popular beliefs or even misperceptions. However, that does not appear to be the typical response. Our legal system frequently does not embrace empirical findings (Levesque, 2006), and even a cursory look at legal responses to child maltreatment, including the commentaries of legal scholars, reveals no exception to the tendency to resist social science research. For example, empirical research reveals that child neglect is the most prevalent form of maltreatment (Levesque, 2002a). Yet, neglect remains neglected: legal responses and commentaries disproportionately focus on, for example, child sexual maltreatment (Levesque, 2002a). Studies also show how broad social forces—cultural, economic, and religious, among others—contribute to child maltreatment (Levesque, 2001). Yet, the everyday life of those administering the legal system tends to focus on individual children, parents, and families (Id.); the legal system even allows social factors, such as religious beliefs, to serve as "excuses" for what would otherwise be deemed maltreatment (Dwyer, 1994). Studies also document well the success of a wide variety of interventions and primary prevention programs (see Klevens & Whitaker, 2007). Yet, the legal system surprisingly moves away from them as it focuses on maltreatment that already has occurred, as illustrated by concern for protecting children from harm and removing them from harmful parents rather than preventing the need for intervention in the first instance (Guggenheim, 2005). To be sure, highlighting the failure to take empirical understandings seriously does not mean that policies do not consider empirical findings: modern laws regulating responses to child maltreatment were spurred by studies of child victimization, such as the battered child syndrome (Helfer, Kempe, & Krugman, 1997). In addition, legal responses for addressing popular perceptions of harms or addressing less-prevalent harms still have their place given the wide variety of harms children suffer. However, the reality appears to be that the legal system and commentators often appear to miss the mark when we consider the focus of laws and well-accepted social science understandings of maltreatment.

A wide variety of reasons help explain the apparent gap between what we know about child maltreatment and legal responses. At bottom, the failure to take basic research findings as seriously as hoped rests on the different ways research and the law approach information and what each deems appropriate and useful evidence. Those who examine intersections between legal responses to social problems and our social science understanding of them describe it as a clash of paradigms and even a culture clash (Levesque, 2006). The apparent clash can be conceptualized in a variety of ways, but a most useful way to do so is to compare normative and empirical approaches to social problems. Empirical research rests on a positivist paradigm, whereas the legal system embraces a normative enterprise. Among other things, empiricists focus on describing what is and why it is that way. Normativists generally focus on what should be, and on ways to design systems that would hold true to rules that produce outcomes that further a normative agenda. As a result, the legal system may not define what is effective, just, useful, and right the same way empiricists might define them. Indeed, some of those goals and outcomes would not even matter much to empiricists. Given how legal systems work and how the social sciences produce evidence, then, it is not surprising that they could focus on different concerns even when addressing the same issues.

The potentially different ways of approaching facts and establishing goals may not necessarily clash, but the reality is that jurisprudence may operate outside of empirical truths. As Supreme Court justices themselves have noted, for example, the battleground for settling constitutional interpretations is constitutional jurisprudence, not scientific facts (Id.). Such potentially strong resistance to empirical research is not limited to jurisprudential approaches to legal interpretations. The legal system also must respond to political realities, such as fiscal considerations, societal values, and even pressures from other countries. As a result, the legal system, with its own set of ingrained values and ways of making decisions, does not always respond well to insights gained from empirical research (Id.). Indeed, the legal system routinely ignores empirical facts that apparently relate to specific concerns but fail to address broader jurisprudential principles and political realities. The legal system is not alone in its resistance; popular opinion often withstands empirical evidence, and those who provide legal commentaries and analyses play a role in efforts that fuel popular beliefs and misperceptions (Jenkins, 1998). In a real sense, the relative utility of research for law reform relating to child maltreatment law simply reflects the broader place of research in our legal system.

Although we may understand reasons for potential divergences between legal responses and our empirical understanding of child maltreatment, these divergences still raise a fundamental concern. Researchers continue to produce important findings, and developmental sciences continue to evaluate policies in increasingly sophisticated and empirically robust ways (see Foster & Kalil, 2005). However, the legal system may not necessarily embrace those empirical truths. Our legal system operates within its own boundaries. Given this reality, those interested in influencing legal responses to child maltreatment must firmly understand the legal regulation of children's lives and engage the legal system's assumptions and rationales. Hoping that the legal system will adjust and embrace empirical findings may not be as fruitful as engaging the legal system on its own terms and addressing its foundational concerns. This is not to say that the social sciences should not challenge the law's assumptions; rather, it is to say that challenging the legal system requires that we understand and respond to its foundations. This text examines those foundations as it explores the laws and values that underlie legal responses to child maltreatment. Our analysis, however, goes even further: After detailing the laws' foundations, we highlight broad legal orientations that would remain faithful to them. Before doing so, however, it is important to understand the law's general response to children's harms and the pressing need to revisit those legal responses so that they could benefit from emerging understandings of the nature of child maltreatment.

## The Law's Peculiar Response to Children's Harms: Its Promise and Limitations

In addressing children's harms, our legal system has developed peculiar responses that can differ remarkably from those for adults' victimizations. If a stranger, acquaintance, or even a family member assaults an adult, society has developed predictable legal machinery that responds to the suffered harms. Most notably, the government has developed a criminal justice system to respond to these types of victimizations. Indeed, in some instances, states require prosecutions even when victims adamantly reject state involvement. Illustrative is the response to battered women, which now includes cases that states increasingly pursue aggressively in the criminal justice system. This aggressive turn does have its critics (Mills, 1999; Morao, 2006). However, there is no doubt that the increasing recognition of violence against women contributed to significant legal reforms marking society's commitment to taking domestic harms seriously. The legal system also has enlisted the use of the criminal justice system to address harms children suffer. When children are maltreated severely enough by their parents or strangers, the legal system pursues criminal remedies (Martell, 2005). The legal system even has enacted reforms that reduce the rights of defendants so that the legal system need not forego criminal justice responses, as evidenced by efforts to address children's particular inabilities (such as their incapacity to testify) and vulnerabilities (their emotional inability to confront alleged offenders) (Levesque, 2002a). However, the use of the criminal justice system to address children's harms constitutes an exception rather than a general rule.

To the surprise of many, legal responses to violence against children typically do not involve criminal law, police, prosecutors or, more recently, even courts. Rather than rely on the criminal justice system, our legal system has seen fit to develop a new system. Our society has developed an entirely different system that deals with the harms children suffer, especially harms suffered at the hands of their parents and family members. Although children's harms may well fit into definitions of crime, the vast majority of cases involving violence against children do not become the subject of prosecutions (see Martell, 2005). Rather than engage the criminal justice system, responses to children's harms now pervasively involve what states typically call the "child welfare system" or "dependency system." This alternative system adopts civil justice approaches. As a result, the civil justice system largely controls when, how, and why the legal system would allow the state to intervene in children's lives to protect them from harm. Given that this system rests on civil statutes and civil case law, this area of law has different purposes and different sets of rationales guiding it than what most of us are accustomed to when we consider the state's intervention in our lives. More recently, the legal trend has been to remove social responses to children's harms out of the legal system altogether. The use of mediation and alternative dispute resolution continues to grow, and they increasingly remove cases involving child maltreatment from formal, adversarial legal responses (Hehr, 2007). No doubt exists that society has deemed fit to develop and support an entirely different system to address children's harms; the vast majority of harms children suffer are not treated the same way as those of adults.

Legally, sound rationales support the need to develop an entirely different system to address children's harms. Given that children (and their caretakers) are in families and are not, in a real sense, independent beings, the law must respond to that reality. The legal response to the recognition that children were worthy of protection from harm required the legal system to adapt to views of children and their place in families and broader society. It was this general recognition that children belonged to their parents that contributed to the development of an approach outside of the criminal justice system. The dual system emerged as the law increasingly viewed children as worth protecting from abusive families while still recognizing that families had the obligation and right to raise their children as they deemed fit, coupled by the reality that children are legally dependent beings. As we will see, these views of children's place in families and society do make considerable sense. We still are left, however, with the reality that the history and current manifestation of child welfare law reveal that children have not been recognized as in need of protections similar to those typically granted to adults. The child welfare system was developed with the dual mission of protecting the rights of parents while engaging in child protection efforts that may infringe on parental rights.

Many benefits emerge from the use of an approach based on the civil justice system. The approach seeks to focus on children themselves. It focuses on families and remedying harms rather than focusing on punishing parents and offenders. This means, for example, that the civil system is one marked by steps that address children's needs (such as safety, stability, and potential reunification with families), something that makes intuitive sense when compared with the criminal justice system's focus on dealing with offenders (such as whether they should be imprisoned or otherwise punished and controlled). In addition to having different goals, the systems have different methods and procedures. The civil system, most notably, permits a high level of discretion and allows for focusing on risks and primary prevention, rather than waiting for more serious victimization needed to obtain responses from the criminal justice system. This discretion permits flexibility, wise decision-making, and a more aggressive identification of cases for intervention even when harms have not occurred.

As we will see, the criminal justice system inevitably must permit discretion, but discretion plays a much less dominant role than it does in civil systems that formally support it by giving those who intervene in children's lives enormous power. All of these characteristics were actually crucial to permitting the development of current legal responses to child maltreatment. These characteristics of child welfare law held the promise that states could assist parents and children in need and only engage the criminal justice system for very extreme cases that could fit, for example, under that system's laws regulating assault and severe harms.

Regrettably, the use of the civil justice system to address children's harms evinces important limitations. Those subject to interventions possess reduced, and in some instances no, rights against the state's interventions. Unlike the criminal justice system, the child welfare system is meant to be remedial and protective, rather than punitive. Because the actions are not labeled as technically punitive, well-established legal principles permit state actions to ignore well-recognized constitutional protections associated with the criminal justice system. These reduced protections range widely, as evidenced by reduced rights in cases involving searches and seizures, the right to counsel, burdens of proof to support intervention, and many others we will examine in the chapters that follow. Importantly, and as we will see even more in the chapters that follow, the effects of reduced rights reverberate and contribute to several other limitations that result from using a civil justice based approach to address children's harms. Most notably, reduced rights leave administrators with considerable discretion. Although discretion may be necessary to protect some children effectively, discretion does come with costs to the extent that it leaves room for considerable bias when case workers intervene. Although it is important not to generalize assumptions about case workers, it is true that the system, for example, evinces bias against minority racial groups (Roberts, 2002; Guggenheim, 2005) as well as other minorities, such as gay and lesbian parents (see Storrow, 2006). Although that bias may be part of laws, the bias continues even when laws do not require differential treatment (Id.). Individuals belonging to certain groups inevitably suffer more intrusions into their personal relationships. Of course, the same charge of biases treatment may be levied against the criminal justice system (Wolf, 2007), as differential treatments may reflect broader institutional commitments. But, even parents not belonging to minority groups have reduced rights when the civil system responds to allegations of victimization, and they have much less access to formal legal protections than they would in the criminal justice system even though the state's intrusion in their personal affairs can be as damaging.

We certainly could enumerate more benefits and limitations to treating children's harms differently, and we will examine more throughout this text. For now, it is important to note that commentators really have not challenged the need for different systems, but they certainly have challenged how those systems respond. Indeed, the child welfare system continues to be the subject of intense criticism. Although it is important to recognize that the system does do much good, especially given the enormous complexities of their tasks and limited resources, critics have made a variety of legitimate claims. Some argue that the system should move toward broader prevention rather than focus so much of its energy on intervening in crises. These commentators, for example, suggest that we must draw strict lines between neglect and abuse and then have law enforcement address severe abuse while social or case workers would focus on neglect (Lindsey, 2003). Others argue that all investigative and coercive aspects of child welfare systems should be conducted by law enforcement; case workers would then be free to respond nonpunitively and better assist troubled families (Pelton, 1989). Some would focus on more aggressive termination of parental rights (Gelles, 1996), whereas others also would do so but highlight the availability of adoption as the most realistic way to deal with current child welfare system crises (Bartholet, 1999). Others champion the need to focus on establishing voluntary, nonpunitive access to help troubled parents (U.S. Advisory Board on Child Abuse and Neglect, 1993). Still others argue for a differential response, one that would have child protective systems involved but have them serve less as investigative agencies and more as resources that assess the needs of families and guide them to formal and informal help from private and public agencies, including the criminal justice system (Waldfogel, 1998). Recent analyses end up offering similar proposals that would further divide the child welfare system from the criminal justice system (Guggenheim, 2005) and that would focus on broader prevention, such as addressing poverty and crafting a child welfare system that focuses on determining specific needs and pointing to resources (Myers, 2006). As we can see, we do not suffer for lack of proposals, all of which agree that the child welfare system needs significant reform.

Criticisms and suggestions for reform all are worthy of close scrutiny, evaluation, and serious discussion. None of them, however, could be undertaken without a clear understanding of the legal rules in which they would operate, and the legal rules that we would need to modify if we were to implement proposals. For example, moving aggressively to sever ties between parents and abused children remains a challenge given, as we will see, the reality that parents have constitutional rights to parent their children as they deem fit and have a right to family privacy that protects them from state intrusions. Similarly, suggesting a response that would remove investigative roles from case workers remains problematic in that, as we will see, they inevitably would have relevant evidence that could be useful to law enforcement. Similar concerns arise for voluntary systems, which could raise problematic and complex legal issues when they would confront abusive situations. Focusing on less-severe forms of abuse in one system and on more-severe forms in another also may be problematic to the extent that maltreatment constitutes a continuum of severity from mild to severe, and such determinations would require, among other things, an investigation and legal rules that would be difficult, if not impossible, to develop and implement. Any of the serious proposals to reshape social responses to child maltreatment, then, require a close examination of legal rules and principles. Regrettably, a clear understanding of legal rules is difficult to attain. Our legal system is exceedingly nuanced and, to complicate matters even more, is undergoing important changes. Indeed, the laws regulating this area increasingly result in conflicting and overlapping legal mandates. These mandates require that they be understood and evaluated in terms of the broader legal principles that have shaped them and also in terms of the breadth of the legal systems in which they operate.

## A Precipitous Rise in Conflicting Legal Mandates and the Pressing Need to Return to First Principles

Reform proposals do not occur in a vacuum; they influence and reflect emerging legal transformations. Because society recognized the need to protect children from maltreatment and the federal government expanded its role in addressing such harms, our legal system has undergone important changes. Some of the most significant changes include those that deal with basic constitutional interpretations of rights as well as how to interpret rights. The changes also include federal legislative mandates meant to influence states' responses to child welfare, as well as a variety of different responses to those mandates. The diversity of mandates leads one to conclude that there actually is not one legal system. Instead, we have a wide variety of legal systems that may or may not work well together. A few examples help illustrate the nature and significance of these approaches to child maltreatment that may produce conflicts.

One of the most illustrative examples of potentially conflicting mandates deals with the increasing recognition of children's rights and the legal system's persistent attachment to parental rights. The simple rule that parents retain their rights as long as they are not abusive becomes quickly unhelpful in practice. How abusive must parents be? Which rights do they lose? When do they lose different rights? How much of a right do they lose when they lose one? Equally problematically for a jurisprudence that would be simple to apply, children increasingly have rights within their homes and outside of them. For example, children now have greater independent rights to services, such as in cases of emergencies, or when they could show that their parents would harm them if they sought their consent, or when they are deemed mature enough (see Levesque, 2000). Similarly, recent Supreme Court cases have revisited the right to privacy, which constitutes one of the most important ways the legal system protects relationships (*Lawrence v. Texas,* 2003); and the Court has revisited the notion of what constitutes children's best interests, the types of relationships a legal system can protect, and when the legal system can seek to protect children's relationships that are, for example, outside nuclear families (*Troxel v. Granville,* 2000). How these recent cases will develop remains to be seen, just as how it remains to be determined how these types of cases will influence the way we differentiate the rights of children from those of their parents.

Yet another area of potential conflict involves the federal system's increasing role in child welfare law. As we will see, the federal government has enacted broad legislative mandates meant to encourage states to develop certain approaches to child welfare law and even criminal law. Yet, numerous state laws conflict with federal mandates. The disparities continue even when states, in theory, are supposed to follow federal mandates or forego significant amounts of federal funds. Some of the clearest instances in which we will see disparities are in the special procedures meant to protect children when they are involved as witnesses in criminal proceedings and in the development of rules of evidence meant to accommodate children's needs. We also will see conflicts when we examine the different state rules that regulate the case plans child welfare agencies are supposed to develop when they remove children from their homes. We even will see differences in such basic responses as the definitions of what constitutes child maltreatment. These potential areas of conflict are likely to continue given that states essentially may not be held responsible if they fail to respond appropriately to federal mandates (see *Suter v. Artist M.,* 1992).

The potential for conflicts also takes the form of cutting edge approaches that seek to combine a wide variety of agencies (including child welfare and law enforcement) into responses to allegations of maltreatment. These efforts take many forms. One of the most popular approaches deals with response teams that respond to allegations of maltreatment. Although such teams clearly have their benefits, they also bring important liabilities when viewed in terms of individuals' rights. As has been demonstrated previously, different legal systems have different rules and different goals; enmeshed systems raise potential conflicts when one system, such as one with a low burden of proof, serves evidence to another one with much stricter mandates. Given the popularity of these trends, it may well be that these issues could be resolved. We still are left, however, with increasingly blurring lines between civil and criminal justice responses. Even the Supreme Court recognizes the blurring of boundaries as it tries to maintain clear distinctions. The Court permits, for example, the use of civil statutes to deal with the failures of the criminal justice system, as evidenced by civil commitment laws used to incapacitate sex offenders who have completed their prison terms imposed by the criminal justice system. The blurring between civil and criminal systems also arises when some parents could be held liable in criminal courts when they follow civil statutes, as evidenced by cases involving religious exemptions to child abuse and neglect laws (e.g., the child welfare system can protect cultural practices and not label them as abusive but then the criminal justice system may still intervene and label the results of those practices criminal). The blurring also arises when our legal system permits intrusive searches of homes and seizures of children from their homes in a way that leading commentators now view as a "child welfare exception" to basic constitutional protections, especially those in the Fourth Amendment (see, most notably, Coleman, 2005). Again, we are left with the reality that legal systems must work with a continuum of maltreatment that may not clearly delineate when actions become abusive for which system, and with the reality that the systems themselves are less than distinct and can be used in a variety of ways to address the goals of other systems.

Potential conflicts also arise when the legal system seeks to remove itself from responding directly to maltreatment. Two examples are illustrative. The first example deals with the privatization of services for children in need. Private charities always have played a dominant role in child welfare responses; indeed, the history of child welfare is one of private humane societies at work (Myers, 2006). Their role certainly still remains, but it continues to change as they increasingly take government supported sources of funds. Concern, in this regard, arises to the extent that individuals have rights against state actions; their civil rights against private groups remain much murkier, if recognized at all. For example, when private organizations play governmental roles, issues inevitably arise in terms of the right of individuals to access those services (Mangold, 1999; Levesque, 2002b). The second example of efforts to remove disputes from formal legal responses involves the increasing use of mediation. Although these efforts vary, they do seek to remove cases from the typical child welfare or criminal justice system and seek to resolve issues by encouraging compliance without coercion. They rest on the belief that the legal system is adversarial and combative and that legal responses produce divisions, misunderstandings, and hostility. Although the use of these alternative approaches continues to increase and gain attention, they too are subject to criticisms levied against, for example, the privatization of social service delivery, e.g., the very intimacy of mediation may facilitate the mediators' projections of their own biases onto the parties (Delgado, 1985), mediation simply may suppress conflict (Abel, 1982) and mediation may foster power imbalances that go ignored (Sinden, 1999). As with existing practices, reform efforts bring their own limitations.

In the chapters that follow, numerous other responses to child maltreatment will reflect the challenges of keeping different systems separate and of engaging the legal system itself, but the above challenges illustrate the emerging need to reconsider trends and mandates. This response requires that we have a clear understanding of legal approaches to child maltreatment, including the values and beliefs that guide them. This text seeks to provide that foundation. In addition to providing that foundation, our discussions reveal that the current status of legal responses has reached a point that we now must identify the broader "first principles" that spur and shape this area of law and consider their continued significance. In the end we will conclude that, even though we may have an increasingly firm grip on what constitutes child maltreatment, our understanding only can guide legal responses if it addresses legal concerns that shape social responses.

## The Chapters Ahead

The next chapter begins our analysis by introducing the legal and political justifications for the most important rule regulating the rights of children: the rights of parents. Because the laws regulating parental authority interweave the bulk of laws affecting children, it is argued that efforts to grasp fully the complete scope of children's rights in legal responses to maltreatment must begin by addressing the nature of parental rights. We find that it makes considerable sense to provide children and their families with barriers to state control and intervention. We further find that this approach to the regulation of family life—one in which the state cedes extraordinary authority to parents—has important consequences, some negative and some positive; but we also learn that this is the foundational rule on which rests the edifice of laws regulating responses to child maltreatment. Thus, regardless of one's beliefs about ways to protect children, this is the rule that we must contend with as we evaluate laws meant to protect children.

Chapter 3 answers the fundamental questions that emerge from a system that attaches priority to parental rights. We begin by asking who legally counts as a "parent" and who, as a result, retains the bundle of rights parents enjoy. To address these questions, we necessarily examine other questions American jurisprudence has raised and answered: What determines parenthood? Does caregiving matter or does a mere biological link suffice? What constitutes suitable parenting? What is the place of parents' own relationships in parenting? What is a family? We explore answers to these fundamental questions through the lens of leading Supreme Court cases dealing with a broad variety of rights that would protect parenting. As we explore the issues raised by these cases, we also consider whether and to what degree a child's perspective about who his or her parents are matters. Our analysis again reveals foundational rules that serious analyses of legal responses to children's harms must address, even regardless of what we think about the proper balance of children's rights, parental rights, and the state's role in fostering healthy development.

Chapter 4 begins our transition from principles and rules regulating the structure of family life to those regulating the internal workings of families. This focus on the actual relationship dynamics themselves is what leads us to center on legal responses to child maltreatment; for what constitutes "child maltreatment" essentially defines the types of relationships states will tolerate as permissible and will define as either healthy or unhealthy. As a result, we begin by analyzing what precisely qualifies as child maltreatment by taking a close look at legal definitions. Our analysis reveals how states tend to focus on similar forms of maltreatment but that what constitutes maltreatment can vary considerably from one jurisdiction to the next. The chapter highlights reasons for the striking lack of uniformity and examines the benefits and limitations of permitting wide diversity. That discussion underscores the need to focus on how legal systems respond to diverse definitions. We find that, at a very deep level, definitions gain significance to the extent that they are the state's gateway into intervening in family life to foster healthy child and adult development.

Chapter 5 details the nature of legal systems that regulate interventions in children's relationships by focusing on laws that address the potential, temporary, or permanent removal of children from their homes. Our analyses focus on the legal principles and mandates that guide decision making processes. To do so, we examine the initial "rescue," when decisions focus on whether to take children from their homes to secure their immediate safety. We then detail how the process involves the provision of services, especially those involving the provision of alternative care. We then focus on how removal can involve the termination of parental rights, a dramatic step that requires states to provide parents and children with considerable protections from potentially erroneous decisions. We find enormous complexity and conclude that we cannot understand components of different legal systems without keeping in mind what, overall, constitutes child protective systems. We also find that we cannot understand what typically constitutes "child welfare law" without understanding the actual and potential role of the criminal justice system. Chapter 6 explores legal issues that arise in criminal justice responses to child maltreatment. These responses are of significance in that they move beyond efforts to deal directly with children's harms and to find a secure and healthy place for individual children. This chapter turns our attention to offenders, to what legal systems do, for example, to those who allegedly have harmed children severely enough that there will not be an effort to preserve relationships. After briefly revisiting the goals of criminal justice responses to victimization, we focus on how states have crafted procedural and evidentiary modifications to address the peculiar needs of child victims when states seek to prosecute cases involving child maltreatment. We then focus on the legal system's efforts to incapacitate offenders as well as contain them by limiting their ability to interact or even see children. Although our analyses provide only a snapshot of the enormous complexity of criminal justice responses to child maltreatment, they do highlight the limitations of these efforts and reinforce the continued need for a different system aimed at addressing children's needs. The analyses also reveal how the use of the criminal justice system serves to highlight how our legal system can take rights more seriously and how our legal system increasingly reveals some flexibility in its jurisprudential responses to maltreatment. These developments, coupled by our understanding of child welfare law, provide us with opportunities to revisit how our legal system can remain faithful to foundational legal principles to address increasingly conflicting and problematic legal responses to child maltreatment.

Chapter 7 examines developments in standards used to determine whether certain types of evidence are adequate enough to be considered in efforts to resolve disputes. Given the central role evidence should play in the resolution of controversies, this certainly constitutes an important area to consider. Our analyses identify important trends toward adopting more consistent and rigorous rules regarding the admission of evidence, including evidence that rests on expert testimony. Despite those trends, we find varying approaches throughout the legal systems that respond to children's harms. After identifying trends, we briefly examine the implications of recent developments. We conclude that, if taken seriously, the developments could help transform legal responses to child maltreatment, that these developments support efforts to return to first principles that should undergird responses to children's harms.

Our last chapter returns to the challenges facing responses to child maltreatment. We begin by highlighting how our analyses reveal that the wide diversity and complexity of child protective systems means that we must address both civil and criminal justice system responses. We then detail the limitations of current approaches to child welfare law. That analysis points us toward potential areas of development, namely the need to take more seriously the expansive ways the law intervenes in family life, reconsider the dominance of informal responses to maltreatment and recognize their failure in protecting some families and children, affirm the foundational principles guiding our legal system's views of basic rights, and develop legal mechanisms that better ensure that systems will recognize and respect those rights. In short, unlike the increasingly popular response that moves our laws addressing child protection further away from a system of laws that embraces formal rights protections, we argue the opposite. We end by reaffirming the need to take more seriously the foundational principles that buttress the laws regulating family life.

# Part II
# The Legal Regulation of Family Life

Part II
The Legal Foundation of Land Use

# Chapter 2
# Families, Child Welfare, and the Constitution

An important line of Supreme Court cases provides the legal foundation for legal responses addressing child welfare. The cases challenge the extent to which the state could regulate family decision-making directly affecting children. The Court has used these cases to build a framework that balances the rights and responsibilities of parents, the needs and rights of children, and the authority and obligations of the state. Given our legal system's pervasive reliance on precedent, we necessarily must examine historical conceptions of the place of children in families and broader society and their influence on recent legal approaches to the regulation of those who control children's environments. Understanding how and why the Court has shaped its responses provides us with the necessary starting point for understanding child maltreatment law.

Great significance is attached to our effort to understand both traditional conceptions and challenges to them. They help us understand the tensions that we must consider when the legal system intervenes to protect children in families. They also play central roles when the legal system intervenes in other locations in which children spend time, such as schools and communities. Of equal importance, these tensions will help us better envision the challenges and opportunities that arise in our efforts to better children's circumstances. To understand this line of cases, we begin our discussion by examining the legal system's assumptions of who should control children's development. We then consider the rationales that support limiting and even usurping the power of those who control children's environments. The first lesson we will learn involves the consequences of having a legal system that relies on tradition, one that does not stray too far away from traditional conceptions of who should control familial decisions. We will conclude that legal responses to family life and child development enormously rely on this deeply entrenched format as they seek to resolve the tension created by efforts to determine the relative power of the state, parents, or children in deciding how to support and direct children's upbringing. Given the law's complexity, our focus, at this juncture, centers on delineating broad parameters that will serve as the foundation for understanding more specific approaches presented in chapters 4–7.

Roger J.R. Levesque, *Child Maltreatment and the Law*
© 2008 Springer Science+Business Media, LLC

# The Rights of Parents to Control Family Life

The Supreme Court developed a parent–child–state constitutional framework when it considered when the state could intervene in families without violating fundamental constitutional principles. The initial cases emerged during the first half of the twentieth century. Although often not directly dealing with the family itself, the cases did articulate who would control the right and responsibility to raise children. As a result, the cases deal with the rights of parents or legal guardians to exercise authority and control over the upbringing of their children in the face of state laws limiting that authority. Although these cases may appear quite dated, they still provide the foundational rationales that guide current laws and were reaffirmed recently in even more direct and forceful language that protects the rights of parents to raise their children as they see fit.

In *Meyer v. Nebraska* (1923), the Supreme Court overturned the conviction of a parochial school teacher who had violated a state law requiring the teaching of all subjects in the English language until the eighth grade. Although the case dealt with the right to work (teach), the Court took the opportunity and to reason that it also was dealing with the rights of parents to guide their own children's upbringing by engaging others to instruct their children. The *Meyer* Court discussed the statutes as infringing, in part, on the right "to marry, establish a home and bring up children" (p. 399). The Court appropriately noted that "[c]orresponding to the right of control, it is the natural duty of the parent to give his child education suitable to their station in life; and nearly all the states, including Nebraska, enforce this obligation by compulsory law" (p. 400). The Court also recognized the state's rights and duties to improve the quality of its citizens, physically, mentally, and morally, but it reasoned that it also must respect individuals' fundamental freedoms. The Court used a description of Plato's ideal commonwealth, where the wives of guardians are to be common, and their children are to be common, and no parent is to know his own child, nor any child his parent. The Court cited extreme state control to assert that some limit of state power must be assumed, and to conclude "that any legislature could impose such restrictions upon the people of a State without doing violence to both letter and spirit of the Constitution" (p. 402). The Court wanted to make clear that the State should not go too far in standardizing its children, that our society seeks to respect diversity that could be best protected through refraining from intervening in family life, especially parents' decisions to control their children's development. Importantly, the child's corresponding right to learn German did not play a significant role in the case's outcome. Similarly, although the Court considered the state's interest in having English become the primary language for all children reared in Nebraska, it ignored children's interests in becoming successfully integrated into their society. Under *Meyer*, the Court considerably limits the child's place in the triangle of parental, state, and children's rights and obligations. *Meyer* stands for the legal rule that parents and the state share the burden of childrearing, and the state fulfills its duty when it limits its imposition on parents who are thought as the appropriate locus of control over children's lives.

Two years later, in *Pierce v. Society of Sisters* (1925), the Court further developed the jurisprudence that limits state intervention into the parent–child relationship. *Pierce* deemed unconstitutional a state law that had required children to attend only public schools. *Pierce* was not initiated by parents challenging the law in an effort to stop the state from requiring them to send their children to public schools. Rather, private parochial schools run by the Society of Sisters had challenged the law. The Court's inquiry noted well how the religious group provided resources complementary to those of the state.

> [The Society is] an Oregon Corporation, organized in 1880, with power to care for orphans, educate and instruct the youth, establish and maintain academies or schools, and acquire necessary real and personal property. It has long devoted its property and effort to the secular and religious education and care of children, and has acquired the valuable good will of many parents and guardians. It conducts interdependent primary and high schools and junior colleges, and maintains orphanages for the custody and control of children between eight and sixteen. (*Pierce v. Society of Sisters,* 1925, pp. 531–532)

The Court went further and described the duties performed by this private provider as "a kind of undertaking not inherently harmful, but long regarded as useful and meritorious. Certainly there is nothing in the present records to indicate that they have failed to discharge their obligations to patrons, students or the State" (p. 534). Following this reasoning, the Court was unwilling to support an arbitrary law requiring a public education in the absence of claims that there was anything wrong with a private education.

Although *Pierce* directly dealt with a dispute between a corporation and the state, the *Pierce* Court went further and reasoned that the case must be resolved in a manner that recognizes the rights of parents (including those acting as parents) and their duty to their children and the state. The Court held that Oregon could not require children to attend public schools because that requirement would interfere with private schools' ability to sustain their businesses and would obstruct parents' right to educate their children in the manner they deem fit. The Court enlisted *Meyer* to reach this conclusion.

> Under the doctrine of Meyer v. Nebraska, we think it entirely plain that the Act of 1922 [mandating that children attend public schools] unreasonably interferes with the liberty of parents and guardians to direct the upbringing and education of children under their control … The child is not the mere creature of the State; those who nurture him and direct his destiny have the right, coupled with the high duty, to recognize and prepare him for additional obligations. (pp. 534–535)

This oft-cited language recognizes an exchange of rights and duties between parents and the state on children's behalf. The case rested on the need to address the parent–child–state triangular balance. Although these cases did not directly involve claims from parents, the Court would accept this doctrinal framework as *Pierce*'s contribution to constitutional jurisprudence. Although the Court did acknowledge the presence of children as a third party, the Court gave children only a tangential role that focused on the child's right to influence the parent's decision, as opposed to an independent right to have specific interests or desires considered as a separate constitutional matter. The question of whether children have an independent interest in attending schools that meet their own various educational and social needs not only went unanswered, it went unasked. The interests at stake were those of the parents and their social need to guide the development of their children.

The 1972 case of *Wisconsin v. Yoder* confirmed *Meyer* and *Pierce*'s place in the jurisprudence that regulates the place of children in family life. In this case, Amish parents had been convicted under a Wisconsin law that required children's attendance at school until the age of 16 years. The parents argued that sending their teens to school past the eighth grade violated their Amish beliefs and lifestyle. The Supreme Court agreed with the parents. Its reasoning relied on the parent–child–state balance established in its earlier cases. The Court declared, in relevant part:

> There is no doubt as to the power of a State, having a high responsibility for education of its citizens, to impose reasonable regulations for the control and duration of basic education. Providing public schools ranks at the very apex of the function of a State. Yet even this paramount responsibility was, in Pierce, made to yield to the right of parents to provide an equivalent education in a privately operated system. There the Court held that Oregon's statute compelling attendance in a public school from age eight to age 16 unreasonably interfered with the interest of parents in directing the rearing of their offspring, including their education in church-operated schools. As that case suggests, the values of parental direction of the religious formative years have a high place in our society. (*Wisconsin v. Yoder*, 1972, pp. 213–214)

The Court worked within a balance of rights and responsibilities between parents and the state to further develop the triangular doctrinal framework. The framework developed an approach to rights and duties on behalf of, but not owed to or by children.

The *Yoder* case became legendary for the manner in which the majority did not explicitly consider children's own, individual rights. Only one lone dissent questioned the extent to which courts should ignore children's rights. The dissent criticized the majority for framing the issue as parent versus state without directly dealing with either the free exercise or educational rights of the involved teenage children. According to the dissent, the religious freedom issue did not solely involve, as the majority professed, whether parents should have the right to direct their children's religious upbringing as they saw fit but also whether those children should have the right to pursue the religious tenets of their own choice. The dissent argued that the children were "persons within the meaning of the Bill of Rights" (p. 243) and, as such, the Court had an obligation to consider their right to forego state-mandated educational requirements that conflict with their religious beliefs. The same argument for inclusion of children's individual rights could have been made when framing the state's interest. Instead of asking only whether the state could constitutionally require all children to obtain a certain level of education, the Court could have considered whether children have a unique liberty interest in becoming educated, regardless of their parents' wishes. Both of these modes of analysis, however, escaped any serious discussion by the majority. Instead, the Court essentially left children invisible as it focused on allocating the rights and responsibilities of parents and the state toward children.

Although one reasonably could have argued that the above cases were not clearly parental rights cases in that they often involved other claims, the Supreme Court recently affirmed the line of cases and framed them as authority for establishing parents' fundamental right to control their children's development. In *Troxel v. Granville* (2000), the Court squarely faced—arguably for the first time—the question of the scope of the parents' constitutional right to control the upbringing of their minor children separate from any other constitutional claims. *Troxel* involved a mother's attempt to limit her children's visitation with their paternal grandparents. The mother, Granville, had never married the children's father, the father had allowed a relationship with his parents and children to develop, but the father died and his parents wanted to continue their relationships with their grandchildren. The grandparents invoked the state of Washington's visitation statute that would become the center of controversy for the manner it broadly permitted any person to petition the superior court for visitation rights of any child at any time and gave the court discretion to order visitation if it found that visitation would be in the child's best interests. Given even our cursory look at jurisprudence in this area, we can discern that, on its face, the statute permitted considerable interferences in parents' right to control their own children's upbringing. Nevertheless, the case provided the Court with an important opportunity to revisit this area of jurisprudence and consider, for example, developments in conceptions of children's rights and the changing role of the state in fostering child development.

The Supreme Court struck down the Washington statute on the grounds that it unconstitutionally interfered with the fundamental right of parents to raise their children as they see fit. The Court held that the Constitution does not permit a state to infringe on the fundamental right of parents to make child-rearing decisions concerning the care, custody, and control of their children, simply because a state judge believes a "better" decision could be made. The Court reasoned that, because the statute did not require that the child's guardians first be deemed unfit, the state had not rebutted the presumption that the parents were acting in their child's best interests. The failure of a lower court to hold that parents are failing as parents rendered unwarranted the Court's independent judicial analysis and decision of what is best for the child. This holding essentially rejects the substitution of a judge's opinion that a particular child would be better raised in a situation a trial judge prefers. A court cannot arbitrarily interfere so directly in parental decision making regarding who can build a relationship with their children. The *Troxel* Court held that a public judge must afford adequate deference to parental childrearing by granting "special weight" to decisions made by parents, holding that "the problem here is not that the Washington Superior Court intervened, but that when it did so, it gave no special weight at all to Granville's determination of her daughters' best interests" (*Troxel v. Granville,* 2000, p. 69). The Court returned to the presumption that parents act in the best interests of their children as it held that the Fourteenth Amendment due process clause requires states to give special weight to parents' determination of their child's best interest. Importantly, *Troxel* did not merely cite *Meyer*; *Troxel* relied on *Meyer* as the foundational precedent for "perhaps the oldest of the fundamental liberty interests recognized by this [U.S. Supreme] Court . . . the fundamental right of parents

to make decisions concerning the care, custody, and control of their children"
(p. 65).

The plurality opinion rejected the Washington Supreme Court's absolutist interpretation of parental rights. This was emphasized by one justice who would have
upheld the Washington Supreme Court's reasoning as well as its judgment. Accepting a more robust definition of parental rights under the due process clause, the
justice agreed with the Washington Supreme Court that the state statute was unconstitutional on its face in that it authorizes any person to petition at any time and a
judge to order visitation based upon a "best interest of the child" standard that places
virtually no limits on the judge's discretion. He concluded:

> Meyer's repeatedly recognized right of upbringing would be a sham if it failed to encom-
> pass the right to be free of judicially compelled visitation by "any party" at "any time: a
> judge believed he "could make a 'better' decision" than the objecting parent had done. The
> strength of a parent's interest in controlling a child's associates is as obvious as the influ-
> ence of personal associations on the development of the child's social and moral character.
> Whether for good or for ill, adults not only influence but may indoctrinate children, and a
> choice about a child's social companions is not essentially different from the designation of
> the adults who will influence the child in school. Even a state's considered judgment about
> the preferable political and religious character of schoolteachers is not entitled to prevail
> over a parent's choice of private school. (pp. 78–79)

Another concurring opinion agreed with the "Court's recognition of a fundamental
right of parents to direct the upbringing of their children resolves this case" (p. 80).
However, this opinion strongly hinted that, had the parties argued it, it would be appropriate to overturn all of the Court's substantive due process cases on the grounds
that the due process clause does not authorize judicial enforcement of unenumerated
rights. Together and despite some disagreements, these opinions supported parental
rights claims.

Three justices dissented for a variety of important reasons. One found no support
in the Supreme Court's case law for the Washington Supreme Court's claim that
the federal constitution requires a "showing of actual or potential harm to the child
before the court may order visitation over a parent's objections" (pp. 85–86). Although he did not doubt "that parents have a fundamental liberty interest in caring
for and guiding their children, and a corresponding privacy interest—absent exceptional circumstances—in doing so without the undue interference of strangers to
them and to their child" (p. 87), he, like the plurality, would likely support a more
carefully drawn third-party visitation statute. Another dissent argued that the Constitution did not recognize a protected liberty right to direct the upbringing of one's
children. Another justice agreed that case law has developed in a manner that recognizes that the custodial parent has a constitutional right to determine, without undue
interference by the state, how best to raise, nurture, and educate the child; however, the justice reasoned that the cases do not indicate whether the parental right
must be protected by the legally distinct best interest or harm standard. This dissent
suggested that a best interest standard might be constitutionally acceptable in some
third-party visitation cases brought by individuals with significant pre-existing relationships with the child. This view would grant considerable power to children's interests, one that goes beyond the right to have their lives controlled by their parents.
These three dissenting views reveal important nuances that lead to the conclusion,

as we will see more below, that we can no longer view parental rights as absolute, with at least one justice not viewing the Constitution as recognizing parental rights at all.

The dissents' views highlight the point that the decision should not be interpreted too broadly. Most notably, whereas the Washington Supreme Court had held that, as a matter of federal constitutional law, parents have a right to deny third-party visitation with their children and that, absent a showing of harm, or potential harm, to the child, the state cannot interfere with that right, the U.S. Supreme Court's plurality declined to decide whether the due process clause mandates a harm, or potential harm, threshold. Rather, the plurality opinion found the constitutional violations to be in the specific applications of this "breathtakingly broad" statute. The Court suggested a much more limited parental right by finding constitutional flaws in the reasoning of the lower court. The parental right the Court protects is the right of a fit, custodial, parent to enjoy the law's presumption that parents act in the best interests of their children. The fit, custodial parent's determination of her/his children's best interest must be given special weight by placing the burden of proof on the third-party seeking visitation, rather than by arbitrarily displacing the parent's determination whenever disagreements arise between a state judge and the parent as to the better decision.

Together, the above Supreme Court decisions determined and continue to shape the wide parameters of the parent–child–state relationship. And those parameters still are the subject of important challenges. Yet, at least three important conclusions could be drawn from Supreme Court jurisprudence. First, somewhat unexpectedly, the cases that would influence the development of child welfare law actually did not deal directly with children. Rather, they dealt with disputes between parents and the state. Although the interests of additional parties were present in several cases, the Court does not go out of its way to recognize children's place in the legal system. Second, the cases stand for a line of family law cases developing a framework for analyzing parent, child, and state rights and responsibilities in the face of state intervention or infringement. Third, although the parties were intimately involved in the cases and in the lives of the children affected by the challenged laws, the decisions are accepted as precedents for a family law jurisprudence that operates as though only parents, children, and the state were involved in the cases or hold rights and duties in the lives of children. The cases tend to ignore the influences of people and social forces, including those related to the legal system, outside of families that affect child development and that constitute children's environments. To the extent that they are recognized, the state confers on parents broad rights to control their children's exposure to them.

## Justifying State Intervention in Families

The cases we just have examined have long been considered key to understanding the nature of laws regulating families. Although American case law clearly protects parental authority in most aspects of childrearing—creating a private realm of family life that the state should not enter—our legal system appropriately refused to recognize parental discretion as an absolute. Parental discretion must yield when its exercise interferes with the state's interests and, occasionally, when it interferes with the children's own, independent interests. As expected, a long line of cases now deals with the extent to which the state can interfere in families to usurp parental roles. In a real sense, these cases ensure children a more direct voice in decisions affecting them. As we will see, however, there still remains a tendency to dichotomize legal concerns as though they involved parental and state interests. As a result, the cases we explore reveal the extent to which we can envision the nature of rights and responsibilities in ways other than the deeply ingrained approach.

The leading Supreme Court case recognizing the limits of parental rights is *Prince v. Massachusetts* (1944). This case involved the right of Jehovah's Witness parents to raise their children in accordance with their religious beliefs. Sarah Prince had been convicted of violating the Massachusetts child labor laws after she had allowed her niece, for whom she was the legal guardian, to distribute religious publications on the street at night and in her company. In upholding the conviction, the Court invoked the constitutional rights of parents: "It is cardinal with us that the custody, care and nurture of the child reside first in the parents, whose primary function and freedom include preparation for obligations the state can neither supply nor hinder" (p. 166). Nevertheless, "these sacred private interests, basic in a democracy," were outweighed by "the interest of youth itself, and of the whole community, that children be both safeguarded from abuses and given opportunities for growth into free and independent well-developed men and citizens" (p. 165). Citing empirical research on the effects of child labor, the Court asserted that a "democratic society rests, for its continuance, upon the healthy, well-rounded growth of young people into full maturity as citizens, with all that implies" (p. 168). In the same vein, the Court concluded: "Parents may be free to become martyrs themselves. But it does not follow that they are free, in identical circumstances, to make martyrs of their children before they have reached the age of full and legal discretion when they can make that choice for themselves" (p. 170). The *Prince* Court identified limits to parental authority aimed at reducing the power of parents to foster values inconsistent with children's growth into independent democratic citizens. In contrast to the earlier decisions, here the Court sustained a powerful role for the state in inculcating democratic values and fostering healthy human development over the objection of parents and guardians.

The *Prince* Court, for the first time, best articulated the state's dual *parens patriae* and *police power* interests in children's development, and how the state balances those interests against the rights of parents to control their children's upbringing. The state's police power interest justifies regulations that seek to secure generally the comfort, safety, morals, health, and prosperity of the society as a whole, thus permitting the regulation of children and families when doing so is deemed necessary to promote the general welfare. The distinction between two subtypes of police power justifications is of particular relevance to our discussions of state intervention with troubled and troublesome youth. The first subtype of policies is justified by public safety-oriented purposes and seeks to regulate the conduct of particular individuals who present a danger to others so as to protect society from this danger. Clearly, our criminal justice system and law enforcement apparatus are in place primarily to further these police power goals. In the case of juveniles, government intervention in the lives of youth who endanger the public by committing violent acts would fall under this subtype of the police power. The police power, however, extends to all aspects of the public welfare; it is not limited solely to restricting the dangerous conduct of some for the protection of others. Given that children are the future adult citizens of our nation, society deems their socialization and positive development as critical to the well-being of the rest of us in society, and perhaps even to our democratic form of government. Thus, the socialization-oriented dimensions of the police power, as exercised in relation to children, authorizes considerably broad governmental intervention including, but not limited to, state requirements for school attendance and prohibitions against child labor. The state's *parens patriae* power (translated literally as "parent of the country") refers to the traditional role that the state has played, much like a guardian or benevolent parent, in safeguarding and serving those who cannot protect their own interests because of incapacity or youth. When dealing with children, the state's *parens patriae* power authorizes its regulation of children and their families, for the purpose of protecting the children's welfare so as to guard society's general interest in children's well being. Thus, under this limited power, the state may pursue ends that would be impermissible under the police power because they may be unrelated to any harm to third parties or to the public welfare.

Although the *parens patriae* and police power justifications for regulating children's lives are theoretically quite distinct, both sets of interests justify many regulations of children's and families' lives. To the extent that an intervention authorized by the police power seeks to further the common good by promoting the child's healthy development into well-educated, productive, and well-adjusted adults, that intervention also may be justified under the *parens patriae* power, in that such positive development is likely to be in the children's own best interests as well as those of their community. Furthermore, the convergence of these two sets of justifications in particular contexts allows the state to forge some of its most expansive interventions in the lives of children and families, such as universal compulsory education, child labor restrictions, and the development of state-based child welfare and juvenile justice systems. Together, these state powers can be quite expansive, and our legal system places a duty on courts to ensure their legitimate use.

The *Prince* decision also gains significance for the manner it reexamined Supreme Court precedents. The Court adopted the view that, in *Pierce v. Society of Sisters* (1925), it had sustained the parents' authority to provide religious with secular schooling, and the child's right to receive it, as against the state's requirement of attendance at public schools. It also interpreted *Meyer v. Nebraska* (1923) as holding that children's right to receive teaching in languages other than the nation's common language are guarded against the state's encroachment. It also noted that the state has a wide power that permits it to limit parental freedom and authority in matters affecting children's welfare. The *Prince* Court focused on the limits of state and parental control over children, thereby obscuring the holding in the earlier cases, which included rights and duties of other rights holders, namely teachers, schools, and private providers. By relying on a narrow, three-party holding in *Meyer* and *Pierce*, the *Prince* Court further established the parent-child-state framework for considering liberty rights and concurrent duties.

The Court would revisit *Prince* in *Wisconsin v. Yoder* (1972). In *Yoder*, the Court noted that states clearly are empowered, under *parens patriae* powers, to "save" children from themselves or their Amish parents by requiring an additional 2 years of compulsory formal high school education. The Court reasoned, however, that, if the state did require additional state-run education, the state would largely influence, if not determine, the religious future of children. Even more markedly than in *Prince*, then, this case involved the fundamental interest of parents, as contrasted with that of the state, to guide the religious future and education of their children. Despite the possible interest in obtaining an education to both shape one's healthy development and safeguard our civic duties, the Court sided with parents. The Court found that the intervention did not affect children's health and did not pose a significant burden on society. These cases would lead to a fundamental challenge faced by legislatures and child welfare officials. Those who intervene in families need to determine what types of harms to individual children and society constitute the ones worth infringing on parental rights in the hopes of properly addressing alleged harms.

The parent–child–state framework has important implications for efforts that seek to determine the permissible extent of interventions as well as, equally importantly, whether there should be any intervention at all. *Santosky v. Kramer* (1982) is illustrative. The *Santosky* case began with a determination by a New York state social agency that the Santosky parents had, for four-and-a-half years, both been neglecting and abusing three of their children. When the state determined that the children were in danger of "irreparable harm," it ordered proceedings to determine whether to terminate legally and permanently the Santosky's parental rights. Similar to most states, New York divided the termination hearings into two stages: one stage sought to ensure the due process rights of parents in determinations of the parent's fitness to raise their children and the other sought to determine the best interests of the child. In *Santosky*, the state had met its threshold burden at the first, "fact-finding," stage. The state had shown by a preponderance of the evidence both that it had (a) provided the parents ample opportunity and assistance in rehabilitating their parental relationship with their children, but that, despite doing so, (b) the parents still had failed to improve adequately their familial situation. Thus, the Santoskys' case was headed to the second, "dispositional" stage, in which the court would make a final decision as to whether or not termination of their rights would, in fact, be in the children's best interests. Before that hearing, however, the Santosky parents challenged the constitutionality of the preponderance of the evidence standard at the fact-finding stage. Although this evidentiary standard is used in most civil cases, the Santoskys argued that the critical and fundamental interests of parents required greater safeguards—especially in the context of termination. Because the taking of one's children is so traumatic and damaging to a parent, the Santoskys argued that the law must take extraordinary steps to ensure the justness of such a decision. The state countered that the legislature had already determined that there were adequate procedural measures to protect the parents' due process rights of parents and that the standard needed to be lowered to deal more effectively with child maltreatment. Having lost in all lower courts, the Santosky parents then appealed to the U.S. Supreme Court.

The *Santosky* Court relied on our now familiar line of cases, beginning with *Meyer*, *Pierce*, and *Prince* to demonstrate historical recognition of parental rights.

> Freedom of personal choice in matters of family life is a fundamental liberty interest protected by the Fourteenth Amendment. The fundamental liberty interest of natural parents in the care, custody, and management of their child does not evaporate simply because they have not been model parents or have lost temporary custody of their child to the State. Even when blood relations are strained, parents retain a vital interest in preventing the irretrievable destruction of their family life. If anything, persons faced with forced dissolution of their parental rights have a more critical need for procedural protections than do those resisting state intervention into ongoing family matters. (*Santosky v. Kramer*, 1982, p. 753)

The Court used this framework to invalidate the use of the preponderance of the evidence standard. The Court determined that because the harm to the parental interest from termination is so "grievous," as well as "permanent," and because there is such a strong societal preference to err on the side of keeping families "united," the interests of the Santosky parents were deemed to be "greater" than the interests of the Santosky children (Id., pp. 756–759). The majority thus held that the "only" way to ensure that the greater status of parents—and thus to properly reflect "the value society places on individual liberty" (meaning the liberty of the Santosky parents) —was the clear and convincing evidentiary standard (Id., p. 756). In contrast, the "preponderance" standard was said only to afford parents an equal status with children and, therefore, it was declared to be constitutionally intolerable.

The implications of framing the parent–child–state framework in a way that presumes parental fitness also were obvious in a now famous case involving the state's failure to intervene appropriately despite strong evidence of child maltreatment. In *DeShaney v. Winnebago County Department of Social Services* (1989), the Court declined to find a state duty to protect a child who was in the custody of his father, rather than in state custody, when the child had suffered permanent serious injury at the hands of his father. The Winnebago County Department of Social Services had been repeatedly informed of incidents of abuse and the risk of further abuse, but the agency had removed and returned the young child from his father's care. The Court reasoned that the state's right to intervene, investigate, and monitor the situation did not implicate a duty to protect the child who remained in his father's care. In accordance with the parent–child–state framework developed in the *Meyer–Pierce–Prince* line of cases, the state had not assumed the custodial right and therefore did not hold the accompanying duty to protect the child. The right of control had been left to the father, and the child could not support a liberty claim for denial of a duty to protect based on the father's acts of private violence. Both *Santosky* and *DeShaney* reveal the extent to which the need to protect private families influences the state's actions on behalf of children involved in the dependency system.

We will certainly consider in the next chapters the types of harms the law deems worth intervening in families to protect children. It is important to highlight at this point, however, that raising constitutional questions about the meaning and parameters of childhood has resulted in a murky, inconsistent jurisprudence of childhood. The Court—and the legal system more widely—continues to view children as vulnerable and naive. *Yoder*'s preference for the rights of parents and the communal rights of the Amish community over individuals' claims nicely illustrates this trend. Also illustrative is *Parham v. J.R.* (1979). *Parham* involved a class action challenge to a Georgia law permitting the voluntary commitment of children, by their parents or legal guardians, to a state mental hospital if a physician agreed with the admission. The Court upheld parents' right to commit their children to state psychiatric inpatient hospitals. The Court even did so despite evidence that children's interests may well conflict with those of parents as well as hospital staff. The Court summarized the legal presumption toward the rights of the family in the following manner:

> Our jurisprudence historically has reflected Western civilization concepts of the family as a unit with broad parental authority over minor children. Our cases have consistently followed that course and asserted that parents generally have the right, coupled with the high duty, to recognize and prepare their children for additional obligations. Surely, this includes a "high duty" to recognize symptoms of illness and to seek and follow medical advice. The law's concept of the family rests on a presumption that parents possess what a child lacks in maturity, experience, and capacity for judgment required for making life's difficult decisions. More important, historically it has recognized that the natural bonds of affection lead parents to act in the best interests of their children. As with so many other legal presumptions, experience and reality may rebut what the law accepts as a starting point . . . That some parents may at times be acting against the interests of their children . . . creates a basis for caution, but is hardly a reason to discard wholesale those pages of human experience that teaches us that parents generally do act in the child's best interests. (*Parham v. J.R.*, 1979, pp. 602–603)

In rejecting the claim that a formalized, fact-finding hearing was needed in such cases, the Supreme Court reasoned that parents, not children, possess the maturity required to make difficult decisions and that there was no reason to reject the traditional presumption that the parents act in their children's best interests. Legal doctrine tells us that the family is the parents' private realm to control, that the law and the state may not unnecessarily invade parental decisions and assure parents the flexibility to act on their children's best interests.

In other contexts, the law provides that children may be granted rights generally accorded to adults if the children involved can demonstrate their maturity. The leading case in this area is *Bellotti v. Baird* (1979). *Bellotti* involved a class action challenge to Massachusetts' abortion law that prohibited an unmarried minor from obtaining an abortion without the consent of both parents. If the parents refused to give consent, the minor could seek permission from a judge who may give his consent "for good cause shown" (*Bellotti v. Baird*, 1979, p. 625). In this landmark decision, the Court recognized the right of mature minors to make medical decisions absent parental input. Under *Bellotti* and its progeny, minors are able to consent to an abortion without "blanket" parental involvement because a state may not grant a third-person absolute veto power over a patient's abortion decision. Indeed, minors must be afforded the opportunity to appear before a neutral, detached decision-maker to seek an abortion free from parental involvement. That case required a female minor seeking abortion without parental involvement to convince a court that she was mature enough to undergo an abortion or, if not able to prove adequate maturity, to prove that abortion was in her best interest. Although this case often is deemed as highly liberative and as granting adolescents their own rights, the approach actually does not grant adolescents the rights adults enjoy. By giving the power to judges, it is clear that even the cases that seem to provide children with independent rights tend to limit those rights. A minor wishing to exercise her independent right to abortion must nevertheless seek judicial assistance when an adult need not do so.

In still other contexts, lawmakers have redefined large groups of children for various legal purposes as entitled to rights granted adults in similar situations. Although lawmakers may be viewed as having widely redefined children as autonomous individuals in certain contexts, a close look reveals a considerable lack of autonomy and rights. Most notably, *In re Gault* (1967) is known as the classic, watershed case that extended constitutional protection to children involved in delinquency proceedings. That case involved a 15-year-old Arizona boy who allegedly had made a prank phone call to a female neighbor while he was on probation for "having been in the company of another boy who had stolen a wallet from a lady's purse" (*In re Gault,* 1967, p. 4). The local sheriff had taken him into custody without notifying his parents that he was under arrest. His parents did not even receive a copy of the formal charge document until a later hearing. During those hearings, the complainant never appeared, and the court made no record of the hearings. The juvenile court judge sentenced Gault, in effect, to a 6-year sentence for an offense he would have had to pay a fine between $5 and $50, or imprisonment in jail for not more than 2 months. Given that Arizona did not provide a right to appeal in juvenile delinquency cases, the *Gault* family appealed to the U.S. Supreme Court. The Court held that Gault's due process rights had been violated because he was not given adequate notice of the charges, he was deprived of his right to counsel, he was unable to question the complainant, and he was forced to testify against himself. Yet, the child's right were actually secondary to those of their parents and hardly were uniquely their own. The *Gault* Court wrote "if the child is delinquent—the state may intervene. In so doing, it does not deprive the child of any rights, because he has none" (p. 17). If we look more fully at that section, we better understand how *Gault* expresses the concept of the state as the ultimate guardian and protector. In a recapitulation of the history of the juvenile justice system, the Court recited the basic philosophy that, "[i]f [the child's] parents default in effectively performing their custodial functions—that is, if the child is 'delinquent'—the state may intervene. In doing so, it does not deprive the child of any rights, because he has none. It merely provides the 'custody' to which the child is entitled" (p. 17). Even *Gault*, often viewed as the leading children's rights case that heralded a juvenile rights revolution, reflected the Court's major concern of exerting control over children; under law, children are always in some form of custody.

That children always are in some form of custody, including in the custody of the state, may end up reducing their rights. Constitutional challenges to children's being wrongly in foster care are illustrative, as evidenced by *Lehman v. Lycoming County children's Services* (1982). In that case, a mother's rights to her three children were terminated simply because she was mentally retarded. Her attorneys appealed based on a writ of *habeas corpus*—a petition seeking relief on the grounds that they are unlawfully detained. To prevail on a *habeas corpus* claim, petitioners must show that the state has the individual in its custody in violation of the Constitution. In addition, habeas corpus law requires a showing that the challenged "custody" subjects the individual to restraints not shared by the public generally. The Supreme Court dismissed the case. It ruled that children in state-supervised foster care are not in custody that is protectable by habeas corpus because children are always in some form of custody. The Court reasoned that foster care was not sufficiently distinguishable from the kind of custody to which children ordinarily are subjected when raised at home. The Court found this even though state officials make every decision about the children's lives, including where they will reside, as well as educational and medical choices. Importantly, the same argument was used to reject claims that juvenile delinquents were unlawfully in state custody in violation of the federal constitution when it was alleged that state judges were sending juveniles to jail arbitrarily as a form of punishment even when they posed no danger to others and were likely to return to court for trial (Schall v. Martin, 1984). More recently, the Court would return to the custody metaphor to find that adolescents had reduced rights in schools, as highlighted by cases in involving drug testing (*Board of Education v. Earls,* 2002) and student speech (*Morse v. Frederick,* 2007). Juvenile rights have not fared well over the past generation despite the resounding victory announced in *In re Gault.*

## Conclusions: Why the Law's Assumptions About Children and Families Matter

In moving toward a better understanding of how the legal system conceives the rights of children and the rights and obligations of those responsible for them, it is important to understand the law's assumptions and keep them in mind as we consider their implications when laws are applied. Our look at Supreme Court jurisprudence regulating the relative legal power of family members and the state's role in child welfare reveals foundational principles and assumptions. These are worth highlighting given that, as we will see, legal responses to child maltreatment law must respond to them.

Our government generally has relied first on parents to guard, secure, and provide for children's welfare. Twentieth century constitutional jurisprudence shields parental autonomy from state interference except where state intervention is necessary to achieve a compelling state interest. Our legal system generally views as compelling the protection of children's welfare, either under *parens patriae* or police power theories. This view means that a Court's scrutiny of regulations that allow for intervening in the family will focus on whether the means chosen by the state are sufficiently narrow to the extent that they further the state's interests and do not unnecessarily infringe on recognized rights. This approach has considerable intuitive appeal: parents tend to view children as "theirs" and children tend to view parents as "theirs." Of equal importance, having parents take care of families makes considerable sense given the costs, abilities, and resources that a state would need to allocate if it sought to raise children. As the *Meyer* Court rightly recognized, our system of government and visions of child rearing rest on a vision of family life that views parents as children's primary caretakers.

It was only in the year 2000, in *Troxel v. Granville* (2000), that the Supreme Court first squarely addressed the rights of parents to control their children's upbringing as an independent parental right (not one, for example, also dealing with the religious right to control one's children's destiny). When confronted directly and only with a parental rights claim, a majority of the Court did recognize an independent parental right protected by the Constitution, but at least one justice did not view the right as fundamental. This recognition gains significance to the extent that, as we have seen, defining a right as fundamental or not determines the extent to which the legal system should protect it. Relatedly, not all agree on the extent to which parental rights must be protected if they are to be recognized: some would require a parent to be deemed unfit before a judge could intervene while at least one justice would not; only one dissenting justice openly recognized that individuals outside the family may have recognizable rights to a relationship with children who are under the control of their parents, and only that justice seemed to recognize the possible rights children could have to relationships outside their homes. The beginning of this century, then, leaves open the possibility that the Court may well support a more flexible approach to parental rights.

It may well be true that the Supreme Court's latest statement on the resolution of family disputes allows for considering that conflicts of interests may exist in families. However, this would not be new. We already have seen that the Court, in *Bellotti v. Baird* (1979), recognized the need to offer children ways to protect their rights when a potential conflict between the rights of parents and those of their mature children exists. We have seen that cases addressing children's rights by limiting the power of parents and the state reveal that even the cases that seem to provide children with independent rights tend to limit them. In the end, it certainly does seem that children do not have very strong independent rights to make decisions that affect them; they tend to be under the control of parents or those acting on behalf of the state. Children certainly do not have robust rights when they are under the control of their parents.

The limits of children's and parental rights, and reasons for them, reveal well the justifications for intervening in the first instance. The state's *parens patriae* and police powers provide powerful and legitimate reasons for intervention. The intervention may be in children's interests, but it does not mean that those interests, or children's own individual interests, for that matter, should control the outcome of specific situations. Having determined that parents have the right to control their families and now having determined that the state may intervene and take over that control when parents fail still leaves us with considerable terrain to cover. We need to understand more specifically the circumstances that will help determine if, when, and how a state will intervene. Legally, this determination means that we need to understand better the legal system that has emerged to ensure that interventions in families respect the principles and assumptions that merely guide the specific development of the rights of parents and their children as well as the state's obligations.

Although presuming that parents are fit does make sense, this particular allocation of authority between the parents and state leaves us with considerably important dilemmas and challenges, especially as the child welfare system adapts to changing realities. Most notably, if the state must assume some responsibilities for children, and if those responsibilities are growing with an increased recognition of the need to protect children, it becomes rather difficult for the state to discharge those responsibilities when society still considers childrearing a private responsibility. The dominant solution ever since the early nineteenth century has been to allow the state to intervene directly into childrearing only when families are considered to have failed and the state must act on the child's best interests to respond to an actual or threatened harm. Yet, the reality is that state regulations infuse family life, even when against parents' best wishes, and there are now more reasons for the state to intervene in families. In reality, the family is far from private and outside the state's control than suggested by the leading cases that formed this area of jurisprudence. The state has grown much, and the state influences families much more than it did even a few decades ago. Changes in the nature of the state challenge established versions of families and the manner society regulates them. Before examining the implications of the legal system's assumptions for legal responses to child maltreatment, it is important to turn to other sets of assumptions—those that guide the law's views of proper parents and families, views that largely will dictate the protection they receive from the state.

# Chapter 3
# Suitable Families and Parents in Law

We have seen that parents retain the right to control their children's upbringing and that the legal system still wields the power to limit those rights to further the interests of specific children or broader society. Those conclusions still leave much to be considered. Understanding the rights of parents and their families requires understanding the law's view of what constitutes the type of familial relationships deemed worth protecting. As might be expected from our previous discussion, the legal system asserts a vision of the family itself, and that vision helps shape who the law recognizes as part of a family and as able to seek and maintain claims to children.

Understanding the extent to which certain relationships are recognized and privileged over others is of considerable significance to our understanding of laws that guide how states can intervene in families to protect children from harm. As we will see in later chapters, the extent to which relationships gain legal recognition shields them from state intervention and provides individuals with rights that states must respect when they intervene in the name of child protection. The nature of individuals' rights involved in these situations largely will dictate the legal system's response. Most notably, for example, parents need to be able to assert a claim to a child if they wish to have any legal influence on that child's development. In addition, certain family structures or parents may be defined as presumptively inappropriate, a status that legally renders them both unfit to raise children and unworthy of legal protection. Similarly, even if not defined as presumptively unfit, some parents may well need to ensure that they act as parents before the law deems them as parents and worthy of protection from efforts to infringe on the relationships they have with children. Likewise, individuals who accept parental roles, even with the state's financial support, may not be deemed parents and, thus, they have few legal claims to protect their relationships with those they consider their children. This wide variety of limits reminds us of the law's immense power to regulate intimate relationships and underscores the need to examine quite closely what type of relationships the law deems worth protecting from intervention.

Later chapters will focus on how the law regulates relationships and reveal how laws vary considerably depending on which state children, parents, and those

Roger J.R. Levesque, *Child Maltreatment and the Law*
© 2008 Springer Science+Business Media, LLC

deemed legal guardians find themselves. This chapter reveals that those variations do not occur in a vacuum. General legal rules have emerged, and the Supreme Court's jurisprudence regarding family structures and functions sets the parameters for those rules. This chapter explores these general rules that guide how the legal system generally approaches family life and determines what types of relationships are worth protecting. Equally importantly, we explore the law's assumptions and rationales for protecting certain familial relationships. Likewise, we consider the legal principles themselves that provide the legal foundation for people's claims—the constitutional protections the Court deems important in shaping and recognizing the extent to which the law must protect relationships. Together, these analyses will reveal a tension between protecting traditional views of what constitutes appropriate relationships and recognizing more diverse forms of relationships important to children. In the end, we will find little movement away from the manner our legal system continues to trumpet the traditional, marital and nuclear family as the family form most worthy of the law's protection.

## Recognizing A Traditional View of Family Life

A look at Supreme Court cases regulating family life reveals the law's assumptions about families as well as the place the law views families as occupying in civil society. The cases highlight how our legal system views marriage as the foundational intimate relationship on which to build all other relationships and structures—be they familial, social, or political. Additionally, these cases collectively stand for the notion that marriage is the fundamental and preexisting core for other Constitutional protections for certain family structures as well as kinship-related functions like procreation. The earliest cases outlined broad principles that retain their currency. The Court uses early cases in many of its subsequent decisions that consider whether certain adults have claims to children. Even when the Court addresses rapid changes in family structures and intimate relationships, it necessarily returns to earlier cases and their images of family life. Given the significance of these precedents to family jurisprudence, understanding the law's approach to family life necessarily requires a brief tour of leading cases and the rationales the Court found persuasive enough to offer certain relationships more protection than others. As we will see, these leading cases rest on a traditional view of families and their proper place in society.

The Court's first two cases dealing directly with the structure of families reveal a narrow view of families, one based on marriage that the state controls. The Court began its project of describing and circumscribing families in *Reynolds v. United States* (1878). *Reynolds* was the first case to test the validity of a federal law that had made polygamy a criminal offense. Reynolds, a polygamous Mormon, chose to contest his conviction under the statute by challenging the law's constitutionality. In arguments before the Supreme Court, the case touched on several issues, but the case is best remembered for being one of the earliest cases to examine closely the First Amendment's Free Exercise Clause. Reynolds argued at his trial that he was a

Mormon and that, as a Mormon, one of his core beliefs was that polygamous marriage was a "duty" of Mormon men (*Reynolds v. United States,* 1878, pp. 161–162). He requested jury instructions that would tell the jury that his religious obligations meant that he could not be convicted for actions his religion did not view as a crime. The trial court refused, and Reynolds was convicted. The Supreme Court upheld Reynolds' conviction. A unanimous Court recounted that polygamy had "always been odious among the northern and western nations of Europe" and that until the Mormon Church was established, it was mainly confined to "the lives of Asiatic and of African people" (p. 164).

The Court then outlined the history of the crime of polygamy in England and how statutes outlawing the practice had been enacted in at least one former colony before the adoption of the Bill of Rights. Marriage was a civil contract, the Court argued, and was the "most important feature of social life. Upon it society may be said to be built, and out of its fruits spring social relations and social obligations and duties, with which government is necessarily required to deal" (p. 165). Viewed in this manner, the government had an overriding interest in maintaining that certain types of marriages were impermissible. Because Congress had a legitimate rationale for proscribing marriage laws, the Act was indeed constitutional. The only question remaining was whether Reynolds (and, by extension, all Mormons) could claim that the law was inapplicable because it violated the First Amendment Rights to the free exercise of his religion. Framing the issue as whether the Mormons were asking to be exempted from a law, the Court ruled that "Laws are made for the government of actions, and while they cannot interfere with mere religious belief and opinions, they may with practices" (p. 166). Mormons could believe that polygamy was necessary for entry into the Kingdom of Heaven, but they could not act on those beliefs without risking imprisonment at the hands of a society that the Court viewed as threatened by polygamy's very existence. The state's interest in marital monogamy would trump religious freedom. The language placing the structure of marriage at the center of civilization and within the state's control would gain increasing significance as it would serve to guide the Court's development of the manner it envisioned families and their importance to individuals and civil society.

Ten years after deciding *Reynolds,* the Court again exalted the position of marriage in U.S. family structures, but it did so in a way that again highlighted the power of the state to control it. In *Maynard v. Hill* (1888), descendants challenged a law, passed by the Oregon House of Representatives, that granted their father's divorce from their mother. They argued that their father had left them and their mother in Ohio with the intention of going to California under a promise to them that he would either return or send for them within 2 years, and that in the meantime he would send them the means of support. He left them without such means, and never afterwards contributed anything for their support. Instead, he settled in Oregon and acquired donated land as a married man. His marriage, at this point, was of significance because it allowed him to qualify for the land. Not long after settling, however, he requested that the legislature pass a law that would grant him a divorce, even though his wife was not given notice, had never acquiesced, and had never consented to the divorce. The legislature granted the father's request. The father then quickly remarried and, upon his death, part of his land went to his second wife's family. The descendants of the first wife, who would acquire a significant amount of land donated by the Territory of Oregon to their father if the divorce were void, argued that Oregon had no power to grant the divorce. The Supreme Court repeated *Reynolds'* rhetoric as it held that a state legislature had the power to regulate divorce. After finding such legislative power the historical practice in England and the colonies, the Court re-iterated its view of marriage's foundational place in society and society's power to regulate it:

> Marriage, as creating the most important relation in life, as having more to do with the morals and civilization of a people than any other institution...is an institution, in the maintenance of which in its purity the public is deeply interested, for it is the foundation of the family and of society, without which there would be neither civilization nor progress. (*Maynard v. Hill*, 1888, pp. 205, 211–212)

Rather than seeing marriage as a simple contract, the Court viewed it as "a social relation, like that of parent and child, the obligations of which arise not from the consent of concurring minds, but are the creation of the law itself; a relation the most important, as affecting the happiness of individuals, the first step from barbarism to incipient civilization, the purest tie of social life and the true basis of human progress" (pp. 212–213). *Maynard* clearly claimed marriage's fundamental role not just for families but also for individual development and civilization. By sweeping marital contracts under its control, the state confirmed the societal significance of marriage. As with *Reynolds*, the Court would again use *Maynard* as a powerful base on which to analyze many of its family law cases. As we will see, even when not directly cited to, the views espoused in *Maynard* echo throughout jurisprudence regulating the structure of family relationships.

    While *Reynolds* and *Maynard*'s pronouncement of marriage's place in family life and society may be interpreted as relics and rhetoric, important twentieth and twenty-first century cases reveal that those perceptions of marriage still play a pow-erful role in substantive rights determinations. Although the Court would exalt the significance of marriage to family life in myriad ways, three lines of cases are par-ticularly illustrative. These illustrations are quite important to consider given that they involve early as well as more recent cases that make use of well-recognized and well-developed constitutional doctrine. Even though these cases deal with con-cerns that sometimes arise outside of marital relationships and outside of traditional family relationships, they do reveal that the early views exalting marriage's place in family and community life retain their power.

## The Right to Control Procreation

The first way that the Court has exalted the significance of marriage in determining the extent to which it would protect family relationships from state intrusion was in the manner the Court enlisted marriage to describe the individual right to control procreation. The leading case in this area is *Skinner v. Oklahoma* (1942). The case involved Mr. Skinner, who was convicted of stealing chickens. Because it was his third conviction, he was set for castration under an enhanced penalty statute that provided for the sterilization of persons convicted of two or more crimes "amounting to felonies involving moral turpitude" (p. 536). The Court invalidated the statute on equal protection grounds because the statute distinguished between individuals convicted of embezzlement and those, like Mr. Skinner, who had been convicted of larceny. The Court was not persuaded that there was a valid distinction between the two groups of offenders. In reaching its conclusion, the *Skinner* Court emphasized the importance of procreation, stating that, "we are dealing here with legislation which involves one of the basic civil rights of man" (p. 541). Although *Skinner* has come to be remembered as the first case to establish that procreation is a fundamental right, the Court had linked that right to marriage. The Court held, for example, that "marriage and procreation are fundamental to the very existence and survival of the race" (p. 541). By linking marriage to procreation in this manner, the *Skinner* Court tied procreative rights directly to the formal institution of marriage as it highlighted the place of marriage in family life and procreation.

The *Skinner* Court certainly made only implicit links between marriage and procreation, but the link would be one that the Court would reiterate in subsequent decisions. Most notably, the Court tied marriage and procreative rights very explicitly in the landmark case best known for recognizing the Constitutional right to privacy. That case, *Griswold v. Connecticut* (1965), involved a challenge to Connecticut's laws banning the use of contraceptives. Griswold, the Executive Director of the Planned Parenthood League in Connecticut, and Dr. Buxton, a professor of medicine at Yale Medical School, were found guilty of counseling married persons to use contraceptives. The Court's plurality opinion held that the law unconstitutionally intruded on the right of marital privacy and the Constitution's protection against the government's invasion of the sanctity of home and privacies of life. The Court famously found that a constitutional right to privacy existed in the "penumbras" of the various guarantees of the Bill of Rights that "give [it] life and substance" (p. 484). In reaching its decision, the Court declared that marriage is "intimate to the degree of being sacred" and "an association that promotes a way of life" (p. 486). Importantly, the Court reasoned, deciding what is a fundamental personal right requires following an orderly inquiry:

> In determining which rights are fundamental, judges are not left at large to decide cases in light of their personal and private notions. Rather, they must look to the "traditions and [collective] conscience of our people" to determine whether a principle is "so rooted [there]...as to be ranked as fundamental." The inquiry is whether a right involved "is of such a character that it cannot be denied without violating those 'fundamental principles of liberty and justice which lie at the base of all our civil and political institutions'...." "Liberty" also "gains content from the emanations of...specific [constitutional] guarantees" and "from experience with the requirements of a free society." (pp. 493–494)

The *Griswold* Court, then, emphasizes the critical point that established principles must guide constitutional decision-making, not unrestricted personal discretion and biases. By raising and applying these principles, the Court found unacceptable the failure to protect marital privacy. The failure to protect decisions within marriage, the Griswold Court argued, would permit the state to regulate the future use of contraception, including compulsory birth control. Such control by the state could lead to the undesirable result of decreeing that "all husbands and wives must be sterilized after two children have been born to them" (pp. 496–497). The Court saw both scenarios as unacceptable invasions of marital privacy. Thus, in *Griswold*, the Court again signaled its high regard for marriage as it used marriage's high value to protect conduct within it. The Court, however, did recognize that this right to privacy does not automatically invalidate all state laws regulating this area. The Court concluded that such regulations must pass muster under strict scrutiny review and held that any regulation that imposes a burden on the right to procreate can be justified only by compelling state interests and only if the regulation is narrowly drawn to express only those interests. Following this approach, the Court struck down the law because it held that the contraceptive ban had not met this heightened standard of scrutiny because it was narrowly tailored. In essence, the Court found that the state may have an interest in limiting access to contraceptives, but that the state would need to further that interest in ways that infringe less on people's rights to family privacy.

As much as it recognizes and protects the right to procreate within families, the Court clearly has not envisioned the right as something states must actively support. The most illustrative example of this limit on the right to control procreation involves state policies that seek to limit the size of families by capping the number of children for whom a family on public assistance can receive state support. The leading Supreme Court case in this area is *Dandridge v. Williams* (1970). In *Dandridge*, Maryland welfare recipients challenged the Maryland maximum grant regulation (family cap policy) as a violation, in part, of the Equal Protection Clause. The families claimed that the regulation illegally "capped" the size of a family at six members and, in effect, "denies benefits to the younger children in a large family" (p. 476). The Court held that the regulation complied with federal mandates regulating the disbursement of welfare funds because the family cap policy did provide some assistance to all qualified families; the Court also found no violation of the Equal Protection Clause given that Maryland's conduct was reasonable and justified by the need to move individuals from welfare to the workforce, equalize the welfare recipient and the worker, and encourage family planning. This decision lends support to the view that states can impose limits on family size without fear that their decisions will be subjected to rigorous judicial scrutiny. Thus, a state's decision not to provide support can essentially preempt a poor family's decision to bear a child. This approach is consistent with traditional understandings that cast constitutional rights in essentially negative terms that view the government as having negative obligations to refrain from certain acts as opposed to affirmative obligations to act, provide or protect. It is this orientation that justifies viewing the right to be free from state interference in making familial decisions or in forming relationships as falling within the zone of protected privacy that the state cannot enter. The state cannot enter the private realm of family life at least without a good cause given, as we have seen, that the right of privacy most manifestly is not absolute and that the state need not actively support families' private decisions.

When dealing with adults, the legal system certainly aims to protect intimate relationships outside of marriage, but the Court is often quick to analogize those relationships to marital and adults' family relations. For example, the Court expanded *Griswold*'s reach as it revisited the right to privacy, specifically in terms of the right to contraceptives, to relationships outside of marriage and outside of families. The major case after *Griswold* to address this issue was *Eisenstadt v. Baird* (1972). In *Eisenstadt*, Baird was convicted of an offense under Massachusetts state law for giving away a package of Emko vaginal foam, a contraceptive, at the close of his lecture on contraception to a group of students at Boston College. At the time, it was against the law to give away any article used for the prevention of conception. Only married persons were eligible to obtain contraceptives, and they could get them only from doctors or pharmacists by prescription. The social policy behind this law was to promote marital fidelity, deter premarital sex, and prevent the transmission of sexual diseases. The constitutional attack focused on the state's scheme of control and distribution. The Supreme Court held that the legislative aims were unreasonable and that the statute, in its effect, was a prohibition on contraception *per se*. Viewed from this perspective, the law was unconstitutional because it violated the rights of single persons under the Equal Protection Clause of the Fourteenth Amendment. At least with respect to contraceptives, the Court found that the rights of unmarried persons equaled those of married people. In its reasoning, the Court linked nonmarital relationships to marital ones, and this link provided the necessary rationale to find the state intrusion impermissible. *Eisenstadt* was very clear when it cited to *Stanley*, a case we will examine below, to hold that the right of privacy includes the right of the individual, married or not, to be free from unwarranted government intrusion into matters so fundamental as the decision to bear or beget a child and start a family. The Court's need to analogize relationships to familial ones reveals how familial bonds do set the standard.

The Court similarly has expanded the right to relationships outside of families—it expanded the reach of constitutional protections again by equating those relationship to those in families. Most notably, the Court, in *Lawrence v. Texas* (2003), recently overturned criminal sodomy statutes proscribing consensual adult sexual conduct. In *Lawrence*, police in Harris County, Texas entered Lawrence's home in response to a report of a weapons disturbance. The police found him engaged in anal sex and the prosecutor charged him under Texas' same-sex sodomy statute. Although the Court did not expressly recognize a fundamental right to engage in intimate relationships, the majority engaged in a careful review of the deeper meaning and import of earlier judicial and legislative pronouncements on sodomy regulations. A slim majority of five made the rare leap to reject *stare decisis* and overruled *Bowers v. Hardwick* (1986). In *Bowers*, the Court had applied "rational basis" review because it found that there was no fundamental right to homosexual sodomy, and it upheld a Georgia sodomy statute under that test. Under this standard of review, given that the right in question was not fundamental, the state had needed to provide only a rational reason to infringe on that right. *Lawrence* expressly rejected an asserted historical tradition against same-sex relations, a major premise on which *Bowers* rested. That analysis led the Court to conclude that the states were acting too arbitrarily. The Court's opinion, however, is famously ambiguous because it fails to mention the magic words—privacy, fundamental right, and compelling interests—that would help to situate the case in the Court's established substantive due process framework, which applies either strict scrutiny or a more rational basis approach, to determine the law's constitutionality.

The Court was evasive in its determination of the nature of the right involved. The valued liberty interest that *Lawrence* asserted was emphatically something, as the Court put it, "more far-reaching" than "a Particular sex act" (pp. 565, 567). The *Lawrence* Court repeatedly returned to family and emotional commitment to others in explaining the defect in the Texas sodomy law. Sexual conduct, the Court noted, "can be but one element in a personal bond that is more enduring" (p. 567). The Court directly analogized same-sex intimacy with marital intimacy, saying that viewing the right to form same-sex relationships merely as "the right to engage in certain sexual conduct demeans the claim the individual put forward, just as it would demean a married couple were it to be said marriage is simply about the right to have sexual intercourse" (p. 567). Having traced the Court's past affirmation of "constitutional protection [for] personal decisions relating to marriage, procreation, contraception, family relationships, child rearing, and education," the *Lawrence* Court concluded that "persons in a homosexual relationship may seek autonomy for these purposes, just as heterosexual persons do" (p. 574). The Court viewed the relationships as worthy of respect because it found connections between homosexual activity and the construction of intimate family lives essentially like those of heterosexuals. Following this reasoning, non-heterosexual relationships deserved protection because they were like heterosexual, married relationships. But how much of that protection they would get remained to be determined.

It remains to be seen whether the Court will transfer this type of evaluation to other contexts. The contexts that most likely come to mind may well be same-sex relationships and parent–child issues in those relationships. Individuals generally are free to avoid or create intimate sexual relationships as well as parent–child relationships outside of marriage. The cases leave unsettled, however, what will be the nature of those individuals' rights to children. In terms of our interest in how the law treats children, this clearly is the more relevant concern. Those cases, which we now turn to, deal with rights to children born outside of wedlock and, it turns out, actually do privilege marriage.

## Claims to Children Outside of Marriage

The cases dealing with adults' rights to children born or being raised outside of marriage constitute the second line of cases that has exalted marriage's place in family life. Those cases emerged when the Court addressed unmarried fathers' rights to their children. When the Court decided *Stanley v. Illinois* (1972), it issued the first of several important decisions that would eventually decide the scope of Constitutional protection to be granted unmarried fathers. *Stanley* involved an unwed father who lived intermittently with the mother of his three children for 18 years. When the mother died, his children were temporarily removed. In such situations, Illinois law made children of unwed mothers state charges and allowed fathers to petition for custody, adoption, or guardianship. Divorced, widowed, and separated fathers, however, were not deprived of their children absent proof of unfitness, which the state had the burden to show. The state's interest was to protect the mental and physical welfare of children and the community, and to strengthen the child's family ties whenever possible, removing him from his parents only where the child's welfare or public safety required it. Although this group of family members previously had been granted only meager protection, the Court found that the law inappropriately discriminated against unwed fathers. The *Stanley* Court held that by denying an unmarried father a hearing on his fitness as a parent before the initiation of adoption proceedings, yet extending it to married parents whose custody is challenged, the state had denied him equal protection guaranteed by the Fourteenth Amendment. Although it did not conduct an historical analysis, the Court did reiterate language from previous decisions that "emphasized the importance of the family" and "the integrity of the family unit" (p. 375 ). As the Court extended Constitutional protection to a parent not within the confines of a traditional marital family, the Court took an important step toward expanding its previously narrow notion of American family life, noting that the law has not refused to recognize those family relationships not legitimated by a marriage ceremony.

*Stanley,* however, was not as expansive as some would have hoped. The case itself was not that expansive to the extent that the Court still allowed states to treat unwed and wed fathers differently. It would be permissible for the state to assume that wed fathers, but not unwed fathers, are fit to care for their children. This would mean that the state could require unwed fathers to demonstrate their fitness whereas the married father would be assumed to be fit and avoid intrusive legal proceedings. In addition to the case itself, the cases that would follow would highlight the higher value placed on marriage and would approve of significant limits on unmarried fathers' rights.

The first leading case that followed *Stanley* and highlighted the limits of unwed fathers' rights was *Lehr v. Robertson* (1982). In *Lehr,* an unwed mother broke up with the father of the child and married someone else after the child was born. Although the natural father had lived with the mother before the birth and visited her in the hospital when the child was born, his name did not appear on the birth certificate, and he provided no support. When the child was older than 2 years of age, the stepfather, unbeknownst to the natural father, petitioned to adopt the child. The natural father filed a paternity action in another county. Meanwhile, the adoption court ordered the adoption after searching the registry and finding no one listed. Only then did the father learn of the adoption petition. He petitioned to stop the adoption pending the determination of his paternity action, but the court denied his claim because it had already ordered the adoption. The Court found the New York law abundantly clear. New York required an adoption petitioner to give notice to fathers who had been: adjudicated as fathers, identified on the birth certificate, identified by the mother in a sworn statement, married to the mother before the child was 6 months old, or had lived openly with the child and the mother. Fathers not fitting any of these categories had to file with New York's putative father registry to receive notice of the adoption. In this case, the father had not filed with the putative father registry simply because he had not known about the registry. The father petitioned to nullify the adoption, arguing that it was obtained in violation of his due process and equal protection rights. The trial court denied his petition, and the New York higher courts upheld the denial.

The Supreme Court held that where a putative father had not established a substantial relationship with his child, failure to give him notice of the pending adoption of that child did not violate either his due process or equal protection rights. The Court confirmed that, in its eyes, "parental rights do not spring full blown from the biological connection between parent and child. They require relationships more enduring" (p. 260). According to the *Lehr* Court, where an unwed father actually steps forward and demonstrates a "full commitment to the responsibilities of parenthood" in the form of contributing to the rearing of the child, "at that point it may be said that he '[acts] as a father toward his children' " (p. 261). Thus, in *Lehr,* we see the Court actively delineating who is and who is not a parent to a child; the Court defines parenthood by what that "potential" or theoretical parent does or does not do and whether that behavior accords with assumptions of what constitutes a "true" parent.

Although the *Lehr* case adopted a functional approach rather than a formalistic one that would focus on biological links, the Court somewhat retracted from the approach in what has since become another leading case in the Court's family jurisprudence, *Michael H. v. Gerald D.* (1989). Indeed, it is in this case that the Court retracts even more to move beyond formal biological links between father and child to focus on the formal structure of the family as a whole to determine the grounding of parental rights. In *Michael H.*, the undisputed biological, unmarried father (Michael H.) conceived a child (Victoria) with Carole D., who was married to Gerald D. at the time of conception and throughout the litigation. From the time of her birth until the time Carole finally reconciled with her husband, Michael actively parented Victoria, living with her and her mother at various points, providing financial support, and affirmatively holding her "out as his own" child (pp. 113–115). Michael clearly satisfied *Lehr*'s combined biological and active-parent requirements. Importantly, Victoria also asserted an interest in continued visitation with her father. In passing, the Court held that the child did not even have a due process right to maintain a filial relationship with both "fathers" despite that child's request to do so. The Court continued and upheld the constitutionality of the state statute that created a presumption that a child born into a marriage is a child of that marriage, regardless of actual genetic parentage and, apparently, regardless of the relationship between the children and their biological fathers. The Court saw no reason to reject a state law's presumption that paternity derives from the marital father.

The Court's ruling in *Michael H.* certainly is of significance, but so is the Court's reasoning. The plurality found that Michael had failed to prove that his "liberty interest" in parenting Victoria was one so "deeply embedded within [society's] traditions" as to be a fundamental right worthy of substantive due process protection (p. 120). The plurality characterized Michael's interest as that of an adulterous parent. The Court proceeded to examine the historical basis for the claim and found historical support for presuming disrespect for the claim of a biological father in Michael's position. The plurality also returned to the Court's earlier unmarried fathers' rights cases and reasoned that those cases rested on "the historic respect—indeed, sanctity would not be too strong a term—traditionally accorded to relationships that develop within" what the Court neatly named "the unitary family" (p. 123) and thus not on the notion that parenting, in and of itself, was "deeply embedded" in tradition. A unitary family, the Court explained, is "typified, of course, by the marital family, but also includes the household of unmarried parents and their children" (n.3). Focusing on the requirement of co-residence and adopting a functionalist approach, the plurality noted that *Stanley* involved an actively engaged, if nonmarital, father who also co-resided with his children and their mother for 18 years. The Court's reasoning suggests a loosening of the biological leash for adult/child kinship ties in the manner the Court privileged a mere social parent (a stepfather) over a biological (although also social) father. The case also suggests that the Court was privileging marriage. The facts of the case and cases that would follow, however, reveal well that the Court was not necessarily privileging a social parental relationship; instead, it was promoting the marriage relationship over genetic parental ties.

In *Michael H.*, the focus on historical acceptance of appropriate relationships was the subject of important concurrences and dissents. A concurrence noted that enduring family relationships may develop in unconventional settings, drawing this conclusion from *Stanley* and *Lehr*. This approach would not foreclose the possibility that a constitutionally protected relationship between a natural father and his child might exist. A powerful dissent agreed with this position and another concurrence when it challenged the plurality opinion's exclusively historical analysis. The dissent especially challenged the focus on adulterous parents rather than on parenthood more generally and rejected the suggestion that the Court's prior cases supported its "cramped vision of the family" (*Michael H.*, 1989, p. 157). The dissent concluded by rebuking the plurality's view that it is "tradition that alone supplies the details of the liberty that the Constitution protects" (p. 157). As we now know, the dissent's view may assist in our understanding of principles and contribute to doctrinal development, but it does not control. In *Michael H.*, the historical analysis was determinative, and it did not give way to recognizing what the majority viewed as nontraditional family arrangements.

Although it may have been thought that the Court would move away from traditional stereotypes of mothers, fathers, and what constitutes appropriate relationships, the Court recently agreed that children's relationships with their mothers are established at birth and that children's relationships with their fathers could be limited by the father's post-birth conduct and relationship to the mother. In *Miller v. Albright* (1998), the Court was faced with a challenge to Section 1409 of Title 8 of the U.S. Code, which governs citizenship requirements for children born to U.S.

citizens overseas. Compared with families with a father married to a child's mother, fathers of illegitimate children born overseas must take additional steps if they wish their children to gain U.S. citizenship. The requirements in 1409 impose those additional burdens. To be fully accepted as a father, a father must have proved his blood relationship with the child by clear and convincing evidence, have had U.S. citizenship at the time the child was born, and have agreed in writing to provide financial support to the child. A father also must legitimate the child before the child is 18 years of age by performing one of three acts: legitimate the child under the laws recognized under that jurisdiction, acknowledge paternity in writing under oath, or establish paternity by adjudication in court. In contrast, the mother of an illegitimate child born overseas is specifically exempt from these requirements under 1409(c) and, as such, a child born out of wedlock to a U.S. citizen mother acquires citizenship at birth, provided that the mother had a U.S. citizenship at the time of the birth and had been in the United States for a continuous period of one year before the birth. In *Miller*, the Court rendered a splintered opinion that rejected Miller's challenge to differential treatment, a challenge based on an alleged violation of equal protection rights. The Court found no equal protection violation in a challenge to this gender disparity that determined the statutory privilege of citizenship by virtue of *jus sanguinis* ("right of blood"), which provides the basis for citizenship by virtue of being the descendants of citizens. Among the rationales used to support its claim, the Court accepted the important and real difference inherent in the birthing event. Because of this difference, the birth itself establishes the mother's legal relationship, while the father's legal relationship depends on his post-birth conduct. A few years after *Miller*, the Court again, in *Nguyen v. INS* (2001), ruled that mothers and fathers could be treated differently when their children are born overseas. The Court again came to this conclusion based on the difference between mothers and fathers. The Court stated that the opportunity to develop "real, everyday ties providing a connection between child and citizen parent and, in turn, the United States ... inheres in the event of birth in the case of a citizen mother and her child, but does not result as a matter of biological inevitability in the case of an unwed father" (p. 2056). As *Miller* and *Nguyn* demonstrate, the limited expectation of unwed fathers remains as prevalent in the immigration context as it is in the domestic custody setting. The disparate treatment of unwed fathers is a logical byproduct of the law's preference for marriage. By placing no similar evidentiary demands on wed fathers, the statute encourages the unity of a married man, wife, and child while creating obstacles for the unification of an unwed man and his child.

A most recent and striking example of the lack of constitutional protection granted to parents who are outside of marriage involves noncustodial parents. *Elk Grove Unified School District v. Newdow* (2004) is illustrative. In *Newdow*, a father claimed that the recitation of the phrase "Under God" in the U.S. Pledge of Allegiance at his daughter's public school violated both the First Amendment and his fundamental rights as a parent to determine her religious upbringing. What was thought of as a potentially far-reaching First Amendment religious freedom case quietly fizzled as the Court decided it as a case turning on parental rights. The Court held that the father lacked standing to bring the claims, and it grounded that conclusion in Newdow's limited rights under state law as a noncustodial parent. Although Newdow was nominally granted "joint legal custody," the custody decree specified that the girl's mother, with whom she lived, would have final control over her upbringing, making Newdow a de facto noncustodial parent. The Court viewed Newdow's parental status as defined by California's domestic relations law. The Court accepted that "state law vests in Newdow a cognizable right to influence his daughter's religious upbringing" and that "the state cases create a zone of private authority within which each parent, whether custodial or non-custodial, remains free to impart to the child his or her religious perspective" (p. 16). But California law did not grant Newdow, as a noncustodial parent, "a right to dictate to others what they may and may not say to his child respecting religion" (p. 17). Because state law assigned that authority to the girl's mother as the custodial parent, Newdow could not object to the alleged state-sponsored religious indoctrination of his daughter on the ground that it violated his own constitutional rights as a parent. By tying the scope of enforceable parental authority under the Constitution to the generosity of a particular custody order, the Court in Newdow seemed not to allow for constitutional parenting rights beyond those provided under state law. Following *Newdow*, if state law declines to confer a particular parenting prerogative, the noncustodial parent has no basis to object under the Constitution. Although *Newdow* is illustrative, it should not be overread to extinguish the constitutional rights of noncustodial parents. However, the Court clearly stated the rule: a noncustodial parent's status weakens the parental interest, so much so that claims to guiding a child's upbringing beyond the custodial parent's family (such as in schools) falls outside the scope of fundamental constitutional protection.

In light of cases we already have discussed, the above cases are quite illustrative. As we already have seen in education-related decisions decided long before the string of unwed fathers' rights cases, the Court had recognized the right to control one's children. *Meyer v. Nebraska* (1923) and *Pierce v. Society of Sisters* (1925) arguably stand for the proposition that (biological) parents have the right to control their (biological) children. In unitary families and in most circumstances, the familial interests are superior to states' interest in those same children. With the arrival of the 1960s, the Court earnestly engaged the question of the Constitution's protection of kinship rights and relationships. When it did address these issues, the Court ended up privileging unitary families. There have been important developments that lead to granting constitutional protection to the parenting interests of noncustodial parents, but the developments have not been as encompassing as hoped by many. The Court continues to qualify the potentially broad victories of noncustodial parents. Most notably, the general rule that arises in father's rights cases is that the most important factor in determining whether a genetic father will be entitled to constitutional protection of his parental rights is his relationship with the mother. Unwed fathers prevail, for example, where the evidence suggests an implicit agreement with the child's mother to share parental rights. In short, the Court gives more protections to unitary families, to families that act unitarily, and those that do not ask much from the government.

## The Right to Marry

The third instance in which the Court has exalted the place of marriage in family life occurred when the Court addressed the matter in terms of the right to marry. We already have seen in education-related decisions turned into leading parental rights cases that the Court has long noted the high value placed on the right to marry. Most notably, in *Meyer v. Nebraska* (1923), the Court held that the right to study the German language in a private school was part of a much broader liberty interest: "Without doubt, [liberty] denotes not merely freedom from bodily restraint, but also ... the right ... to marry, establish a home and bring up children ... " (p. 399). This recognition may well be viewed as, again, rhetorical. But, the Court eventually did recognize the right to marry as a fundamental right directly protected by the U.S. Constitution. The Court first did so in *Loving v. Virginia* (1967). In that case, a married couple was prosecuted under a Virginia law that banned interracial marriage. The Lovings, who were married in Washington, DC, but had moved to Virginia, pleaded guilty to the charge. The trial judge sentenced them to 1 year in jail but suspended the sentence for a period of 25 years on the condition that the Lovings leave the state and not return to Virginia together for 25 years. The couple found both options unacceptable and appealed to the Supreme Court. The Court declared the statute unconstitutional. Borrowing from earlier opinions, specifically the ones dealing with procreation, the Court recognized the fundamental right to marry by stating that "[m]arriage is one of the 'basic civil rights of man,' fundamental to our very existence and survival" (p. 12 [quoting *Skinner v. Oklahoma*, 1942, p. 541]). Given the great significance attached to marriage, the state could not prevail on the claim that preventing miscegenation justified its infringement.

The *Loving* case is of considerable significance for the manner the Court reasoned how the Constitution protected marriage. Despite *Reynolds* and *Maynard*'s strong rhetoric about the importance of marriage to civilization, the Court had yet to rule that marriage itself was a fundamental right deserving robust constitutional protection. It was only in the 1960s, in *Loving*, that the Court arguably established marriage as a fundamental right when it concluded that Virginia's antimiscegenation statute violated both the Equal Protection and Due Process clauses of the Fourteenth Amendment. In its analysis of Virginia's equal protection argument, the Court flatly rejected the State's purported rationale for the statute–to "preserve racial integrity of its citizens, to prevent corruption of blood, a mongrel breed of citizens, and the obliteration of racial pride" (p. 7). The Court also rejected the argument that the state was not discriminating in that it was treating all races similarly. Borrowing some of the language from the Court's polygamy case, *Reynolds v. United States* (1878, p. 11), the Court held that distinctions based on ancestry are "odious to a free people ... founded upon the doctrine of equality." Following this line of reasoning, a race-based classification, such as an antimiscegenation statute, categorically violated constitutional protections.

The finding that a race-based categorization for marriage violated the fundamental principles of equality was not surprising. The Court, however, went further and briefly addressed the case under the Fourteenth Amendment's Due Process Clause.

The Court held that "these statutes also deprive the Lovings of liberty without due process of law in violation of the Due Process Clause of the Fourteenth Amendment. The freedom to marry has long been recognized as one of the vital personal rights essential to the orderly pursuit of happiness by free men. Marriage is one of the 'basic civil rights of man,' fundamental to our very existence and survival" (p. 12). To support its claim, the Court engaged in an historical discussion. It noted that, at the time *Loving* was decided, 16 states prohibited and punished marriages on the basis of racial classifications. At least with respect to those states that still had antimiscegenation statutes, one could argue that the tradition of penalizing interracial marriage was of somewhat long-standing historical pedigree. According to the Court, "penalties for miscegenation arose as an incident to slavery and have been common in Virginia since the colonial period" (p. 6). Thus, one interpretation of *Loving* is that the Court overturned the statute despite both possible historical practices in accordance with its mandate, and even with current practices and laws mirroring anti-miscegenation practices. This would be consistent with the perspective of the Fourteenth Amendment's enactment as a protection for minorities against majoritarian tyranny. It also is consistent with a view that contradicts the perspective that the Due Process clause narrows its focus to existing legal protections to prevent future generations from lightly casting aside important traditional values when there exists some explicit protection for the interest, or at least not a prohibition of it. Alternatively, *Loving* could be seen as an Equal Protection case, on the grounds that the Court's separate Due Process Clause analysis (finding that marriage is a liberty interest) cannot stand on its own without reference to the race-based statute at issue. The Court's own opinion suggests that this might be the case when it explains its Due Process holding:

> To deny this fundamental freedom [to marry] on so unsupportable a basis as the racial classifications embodied in these statutes, classifications so directly subversive of the principle of equality at the heart of the Fourteenth Amendment, is surely to deprive all the State's citizens of liberty without due process of law .... The Fourteenth Amendment requires that the freedom of choice to marry not be restricted by invidious racial discrimination. (p. 12)

Although the decision may have different interpretations, it is clear that *Loving* identified two potential constitutional grounds for protecting the right to marry and, even though the footing may be unclear, *Loving* arguably establishes the right to marry as fundamental.

Since *Loving*, the Court has continued to recognize marriage as a fundamental right protected under the U.S. Constitution. The Court's second right-to-marry case, *Zablocki v. Redhail* (1978), decided more than 10 years after *Loving*, does take the fundamental right to marry outside of a race-based context, although possibly leaving the right still constrained by other factors. In *Zablocki v. Redhail* (1978, p. 375), the Court considered the constitutionality of a Wisconsin statute that prevented any "Wisconsin resident having minor issue not in his custody and which he is under obligation to support by any court order or judgment" from obtaining a marriage license without first obtaining a court order. To acquire a court order, the statute required an applicant to submit proof of compliance with his or her child support obligations and, further, to convince the court that any child covered by the support order would never become a ward of the state. The Court held that a state statute that requires court approval in order to marry when the applicant is a noncustodial parent owing a support obligation to his or her child violates the Due Process and, possibly, Equal Protection clauses of the Fourteenth Amendment. Under Wisconsin's statutory scheme, economic status determined eligibility to enter into lawful marriage. Again echoing (and at times quoting) the flowery dicta of its earliest family cases of *Reynolds* and *Maynard* and its later decisions in *Loving* and *Griswold*, among others, the Court held that:

> [T]he freedom to marry has long been recognized as one of the vital personal rights essential to the orderly pursuit of happiness ... [it is] fundamental to our very existence and survival ... the most important relation in life ... the foundation of family and society, without which there would be neither civilization nor progress ... fundamental to survival of the race ... a right of privacy older than the Bill of Rights ... [and] intimate to the degree of being sacred. (pp. 383–384)

In recognizing that "the right to marry is of fundamental importance for all individuals" (p. 384), the Court acknowledged its previous decisions, which consistently characterized marriage as a fundamental right, describing marriage as "the most important relation in life" (quoting *Maynard v. Hill*, 1888, p. 205) and "fundamental to the very existence and survival of the race" (quoting *Skinner v. Oklahoma*, 1942, p. 541). The Court then held that the challenged Wisconsin statute interfered directly and substantially with the right to marry and was unconstitutional. By citing to its earlier substantive due process cases, the Court found the decision to marry on the same level with other matters of family life that it had previously held were protected liberty interests, such as procreation, childbirth, child-rearing, and family relationships. In so doing, the Court appears to have expanded the right to marry into a protected liberty interest in a context other than where an invidious classification scheme exists, be it race-based or otherwise (with the "otherwise" in this case being poverty).

More recently, in *Turner v. Safley* (1987), the Court addressed the right to marry in the penal setting. The *Turner* Court struck down a prison regulation limiting all Missouri inmates' right to marry by conditioning that right on the receipt of the prison superintendent's approval. Because the Court was dealing with the prison setting, the Court approached its analysis in light of the need to be responsive both to the policy of judicial restraint regarding prisoner complaints and to the need to protect constitutional rights. Despite the application of rights within a system founded on and perpetuated by restrictions, the Court elevated the status of marriage on the spectrum of fundamental rights by insulating it from restriction; the Court maintained that the sanctity of the right to marry overrode the state's interest in prison security. Thus, the Court legitimized the fundamental right to marry by emphatically granting it to criminals—a class of citizens whose liberty interests the state already has curtailed severely. In striking down a prison regulation that prohibited inmates from marrying unless there were compelling reasons for them not to marry, the Court followed and extended *Zablocki*. The Court applied *Zablocki* even though the prison setting is distinctive usually calls for a measure of judicial deference. In fact, the Court went beyond its previous decisions to delineate some of the foundations of the right to marry. It said that marriages, by inmates as by others, "are expressions of emotional support and public commitment" (p. 95). The Court emphasized that these are "important and significant aspects of the marital relationship" (p. 96). It added that marriages are often recognized as having spiritual significance and that marital status often is a prerequisite for a number of material benefits, including property rights, government benefits, and less-tangible advantages.

These conclusions underlay the Court's position that, even in prisons, the right to marry must be respected unless the state produces highly compelling reasons to interfere with such a right. Importantly, the *Turner* Court did not specify whether the right to marry rooted in substantive due process (as *Loving* suggested) or in the fundamental rights branch of equal protection doctrine (as *Zablocki* did). For purposes of reaching its conclusion, the Court did not have to choose between its decisions' two possible sources. The Court simply ruled that, taken together, the elements of marriage that remain even during incarceration are sufficient to form a constitutionally protected marital relationship in the prison context. It would be fair to read the Court as treating marriage as it does other privacy rights, in a way that suggests considerable protection through the involvement of substantive due process.

Together, the *Loving*, *Zablocki* and *Turner* decisions support the proposition that the right to marry stands on a similar footing as liberty interests found by the Court in some of its other substantive due process decisions, such as those dealing with procreation or parental control of their children's upbringing. The Court's language in these cases reifies marriage; the Court extols marriage's virtues as the central driving force (natural, legal and social) for civilization and the continuation of the species. Indeed, even when one actually may not be able to live with the spouse, marriage's benefits are deemed so great that the Court would protect the right to marry for those who would have been severely deprived of most civil liberties. By exalting marriage, the Court exhibits the high value it places on the need to protect unitary families, especially those with married adults.

# Hesitating to Protect Children's Ties Outside of Nontraditional Families

The Court has adopted a more expansive definition of family, most notably in its series of cases addressing kinship ties other than those between spouses or biological parents and their biological children. In some instances, the Court has done so in dicta while ultimately sublimating the expanded family to the biological one. In others, the Court has granted the protection to the nonbiological or nonmarital family. In a third set of cases, the Court expanded its notion of kinship ties when it addressed Constitutional questions surrounding adult intimate relationships. These new lines of cases highlight important movements in the Courts' responses to changing family structures. As a rule, however, these cases again reveal that nontraditional "family" relationships receive reduced protections, if they receive protections at all.

The Court squarely faced issues regarding the rights between adult family members and their children in the context of what would become a leading child welfare case. The case, *Smith v. Organization of Foster Families for Equality and Reform* (O.F.F.E.R.) (1977), directly dealt with the rights of non-nuclear, nonmarital family members that constituted a foster family. In *Smith*, a group of foster parents challenged New York's procedures for removing foster children from their homes. The foster parents argued that they had a protected liberty interest entitling them to a hearing before a child's removal from their foster homes. In support of this claim, the foster parents pointed to the psychological bonds established between foster parents and foster children in their care. Drawing on a "psychological parent" theory developed by leading psychologists at the time, the class of foster families argued that these bonds established the foster family as a "psychological family...[and] that [a] family...has 'liberty interest' in its survival as a family" (p. 839). In essence, the foster families argued that they were the functional equivalent of "natural" families.

The *Smith* Court addressed the foster families' claims by centering on the definition of family and the connection between biological ties and kin ties. The Court framed the question before it as follows: "Is the relation of foster parent to foster child sufficiently akin to the concept of 'family' recognized in our precedents to merit similar protection?" (p. 842). The Court recognized that children in foster placements often lose contact with biological parents when placed in foster care, and that children often develop deep emotional ties with their foster parents. The Court further noted that, although "the usual understanding of 'family' implies biological relationships," "biological relationships are not [the] exclusive determination of the existence of a family" (p. 843). The Court also explained that "the importance of the familial relationship, to the individuals involved and to the society, stems from the emotional attachments that derive from the intimacy of daily association as well as from the fact of blood relationship" (p. 844). The Court admitted that "no one would seriously dispute that a deeply loving and interdependent relationship between an adult and a child in his or her care may exist even in the absence of a blood relationship" (p. 844). In so doing, the Court noted the possibility of children developing deep ties with nonbiological, foster families comparable with those in biological, natural families; and it further recognized that foster families can serve the same role as biological families in terms of socializing functions. Despite these significant concessions, the *Smith* Court concluded that foster parents' state-created contractual rights lose out to the conflicting liberty interests of biological parents. The Court considered the appropriateness of a broader notion of family, recognized it as a reality but, in the end, refused to grant foster families precedence over natural families.

Although not fully recognizing the rights of unrelated individuals' claims to children and rejecting a more expansive view of what constitutes families, the Court would revisit the issue when required to focus again on the functions rather than forms of families. The Court did so in, most notably, *Moore v. City of East Cleveland*

(1977). It would be in *Moore* that the Court would adopt what arguably is its broadest view of what constitutes a family in law, a family worthy of legal protection. *Moore* involved a challenge to a city ordinance that adopted a narrow view of families in the manner it allowed only nuclear family members, essentially a couple and their dependent children, to live together. A grandmother who had allowed her grandson to live with her challenged her *criminal* conviction under the statute. The Court held that the zoning ordinance could not restrict cohabitation between grandparents and other relatives. The Court stated its rationale for this broader conception of family as follows:

> Ours is by no means a tradition limited to respect for the bonds uniting the members of the nuclear family. The tradition of uncles, aunts, cousins, and especially grandparents sharing a household along with parents and children has roots equally venerable and equally deserving of constitutional recognition. . . . Even if conditions of modern society have brought about a decline in extended family households, they have not erased the accumulated wisdom of civilization, gained over the centuries and honored throughout our history, that supports a larger conception of the family. (pp. 504–505)

While reaching this unusual result that granted Constitutional protection to a nonnuclear family, the Court simultaneously reaffirmed its previous decisions that "the Constitution protects the sanctity of the family precisely because the institution of the family is deeply rooted in this Nation's history and tradition" (p. 503). Thus, despite an apparent broadening of what the law deems as constituting a family, the Court made clear that it still adhered to a central definition of family as rooted in biology (blood), adoption, or marriage. However, in reaching its ultimate decision, the Court focused again on the functions rather than forms of families, emphasizing economics, "mutual sustenance," and need for a "secure home life" (p. 505). In *Moore*, then, the Court seems to recognize that the importance of the "extended family" in American society requires it to protect extended families from state interference when those families essentially take a nuclear form and function.

The Court's most recent iteration of Constitutional protections of adult/child family relationships, *Troxel v. Granville* (2000), involved children's ties to grandparents and tested the reach of *Moore, Lehr* and *Michael H.* in the context of children's ties to their grandparents. The family quarrel at the center of *Troxel* emerged from tragedy. Brad Troxel and Tommie Granville shared a romantic relationship and had two daughters outside of wedlock. After separating from Granville, Brad moved in with his parents, and Tommie retained custody of the two girls. The grandparents often saw the girls during visits with their father in their own home. After Brad had committed suicide, his parents continued to see the girls regularly. However, after Tommie informed the Troxels that she wished to reduce the amount of time the girls spent at their home, the grandparents balked at the new restrictions and took legal action. The Troxels filed a petition for court-ordered visitation under two state statutes, both of which gave legal standing to nonparents.

The Supreme Court held that the statute that allowed a family court to order visitation rights for "any person" if "visitation serves the best interest of the child" violated the mother's substantive due process right to make decisions concerning the care, custody, and control of her children (p. 57). Citing to its previous decisions on parental decision-making authority and autonomy, the *Troxel* Court held that the primary role of parents was established as an "enduring American tradition" reflecting "western civilization concepts of the family as a unit with broad parental authority over minor children" (p. 66). Apart from validating the principle that parents have the right to raise their children without governmental interference, the Court did little to define what types of families would qualify for this privacy protection. Invoking *Meyer*, *Pierce*, *Prince*, and *Parham v. J.R.*, the Court determined that the Washington statute disregarded the traditional presumption that parents act in the best interests of their children. The Court explained that this presumption precludes a parent from being placed in the position of disproving that visitation would be in the best interest of her daughters. Instead, the Court required deference to a parent's determination of her child's best interests. The Court declined to define what level of deference would be required and did not explain whether this presumption applied equally to all parents. However, the Court strongly implied that such deference would control in the absence of a finding that a parent was unfit. Yet, the Court had closely considered the changing demographics of the American family life, as it nonetheless characterized grandparents as third parties who could gain visitation privileges to promote children's welfare if they actually had assumed parental responsibilities.

Although appearing to think in an expansive way about the family and calling for greater recognition of children's liberty interests in preserving intimate relationships, even the dissenting opinions held traditional families in greater regard than other families. For example, one dissent presented an argument on the scope of parental autonomy that is difficult to distinguish from the majority's; he argued that parental rights are not dictated by biology but depend on "some embodiment of family" (p. 88). Another dissent did not move away from privileging traditional families either. That dissent expressed concern that the majority's decision swept too broadly in establishing harm to the child as the controlling standard in every visitation proceeding. Commenting that "the conventional nuclear family ought not establish the visitation standard for every domestic relations case," the dissent cited to *Moore* to point out that many persons other than biological or adoptive parents assume caregiving roles associated with families (pp. 98–99). Although revealing support for nontraditional families, the dissent actually presented a narrow argument. In the end, the plurality and one dissent evidenced strong support for traditional families. Granville had remarried and provided her daughter with a traditional nuclear family, it was that family that the Court now granted the highest level of deference possible. Ultimately, then, the Court declined to define the precise scope of the parental due process right in the visitation context; but it did highlight the significance of marriage.

It would be unwise to wager that the Court would expand visitation rights to individuals outside of families. The Court already recognizes that families of divorce produce reduced parental rights for those who do not secure custody. We already have witnessed the effects of this approach in *Newdow*. The Court evinces reluctance to credit seriously the constitutional rights of non-custodial parents.

Ultimately, these cases reveal something of broader significance about constitutional rights of family privacy generally, including the rights of custodial parents and parents in intact or "unitary" families. Courts have not been receptive to the argument that a sate can infringe on parental rights in the name of acting on children's best interests. As we have seen, the Supreme Court, in leading cases like *Meyer v. Nebraska* (1923) and *Pierce v. Society of Sisters* (1925), has held that parents have a fundamental constitutional right to raise their children without state interference. State actions that sharply limit the child-rearing role of either parent, substantially burden that right, triggering strict judicial scrutiny. And, under strict scrutiny, the state must show some "compelling interest," such as imminent harm to the child, to justify its intervention. Arguments that the state is acting on the "best interests" of children, for example, remain insufficient.

Our analysis of Supreme Court jurisprudence reveals that the contours of the concept of "family privacy"—of the right of family members to be free from state intrusion—really have yet to expand and respond more deliberately to social changes in family life. There now exist many types of social arrangements that many view as families, but they have yet to align well with those that the Court bestows with strong privacy protection. While aware of these changing demographics, the Court still envisions nuclear families as archetypes of family life. Despite the many landmark privacy cases that have been decided since *Meyer* and *Pierce*, cases that revolutionized the concept of family privacy by recognizing individual autonomy rights, the law of family privacy remains focused squarely on the defense and promotion of nuclear, heterosexual families.

## Conclusions: On Defining Family Ties Worth Protecting

For more than a century, the Supreme Court directly addressed the interface between families and the Constitution. In its earliest and even most recent cases, the Court has enlisted grand rhetoric about families in general and marriage in particular to bolster its decisions on such diverse topics as legislative power, education, polygamy, contraception, adults' sexual relations, divorce, unwed parenthood, citizenship, religion, and attachments to children. Although these sweeping statements about family and marital life are not always necessarily crucial to the outcome of those cases, the rhetoric infuses decisions and guides outcomes that are now supported by combinations of equal protection analysis, substantive due process doctrine, and the general concept of privacy. The Court's "family" cases reveal the struggle to come to terms with a wide diversity of family forms and a variety of ways to offer protection to the forms deemed worth protecting.

Although several different conclusions can be drawn from our review, four are particularly important to highlight. First, the Court hesitates to innovate in its views of families deemed worth protecting from intrusions from state actions. The Supreme Court only rarely moves away from its dual definitional parameters of family ties: marriage and consanguinity (blood ties and adoptions that end up equivalent to blood ties). When the Court does move in such directions, the outcomes of the Court's decisions becomes quite less predictable. In some instances, the law's protections remain strong, apparently as equal in force to those involving marital relationships. For example, in *Eisenstadt v. Baird* (1972), the Court protects nonmarital couples' right to use contraception. In other instances, the Court agrees with the need to adopt broader views of family life but ultimately offers those more inclusive views little protection. For example, in *Smith v. O.F.F.E.R.* (1977), the Court references the bonds that nonbiological foster families can establish but ultimately decides that such bonds must lose out against the potential rights of parents. In yet other instances, the Court takes a middle ground. Thus, we find that, in *Moore v. City of East Cleveland* (1977), the Court protects non-nuclear families' rights in the housing context and appears to take a broader view of families. Finally and, in some instances, the rights of natural parents lose out against those simply presumed to be parents. The cases dealing with unmarried fathers' rights offer the starkest example of this possibility. The Court ultimately holds, for example, in *Michael H.*, that marriage trumps any biological or genetic connection between parent and child. These cases do reveal the Court's willingness to expand its notion of Constitutional protection of conduct within intimate adult relationships that do not fit within the announced blood and marriage parameters. But, even with this apparently more broad view of families viewed as worthy of legal protection, the Court tightly clings to the belief that only blood (and adoption) and marriage establish family ties worth protecting.

Second, the cases that suggest a more expansive view of families worth protecting primarily involved adults' familial decisions and leave uncertain the place of children in those families. For instance, cases such as *Griswold*, and even moreso *Eisenstadt*, unequivocally supported the rights of family members (in *Griswold* as family members and in *Eisenstadt* as separate individuals) to make intimate familial choices without state interference. Those decisions and others that followed altered the shape of domestic jurisprudence as they ensured the right of adults to design and negotiate the terms of their familial relationships. The cases support the position, now widely reflected in state laws regulating adults in families, that adults' autonomous individuality continues when they form families. This position supports the notion that adults may freely construct their own domestic relationships within a fairly wide range of options. Regrettably, these decisions fail to explore the implications of this approach for cases involving children born to or socialized by adults free to make domestic choices. Constitutional cases that do involve the right to parent–child relationships outside of traditional family structures still do not rest on a coherent jurisprudential base. For example, the Court's reliance on substantive due process in cases involving disputes about children, even in cases like *Troxel v. Granville* (2000) that focus primarily on adults' comparative rights to relate to and control children in families, has not resulted in a set of decisions with consistent understandings of parent-child relationships. *Troxel* is especially telling because the plurality opinion invokes at least three different, often contradictory, models of the parent–child relationship: the individualist model of family, the nuclear model of family, and the model of family as an extended network of loving kin. As these cases reveal, the Court's efforts to craft a jurisprudence of parent–child relationships that would recognize independent rights produces a much less coherent response to family matters than the Court's cases that involve adults within families.

The legal system's ability to envision and support adults' rights moreso than those of children is not surprising. Society broadly understands adults as relatively autonomous individuals, even in domestic settings, and thus increasingly has regarded adults as appropriate recipients of individualistic constitutional rights. No similar consensus has emerged with regard to children. In many contexts, the Court—and the legal system more broadly—continues to view children as vulnerable, naive, and as inappropriate recipients of individual rights. In other contexts, lawmakers permit courts to grant children rights generally accorded to adults if the children involved can prove their maturity. In still other contexts, lawmakers have redefined large groups of children for various legal purposes as entitled to rights granted adults in similar situations. The legal system remains unsure in its views of children and, as we will see in the next several chapters, how to protect their rights.

Third, our analysis of "family" cases reveals the Courts' consistent tendency to enlist conclusory statements about what constitutes our Nation's tradition and history. The use of history and tradition to define the scope of a Constitutional right is certainly neither necessarily unprincipled nor unprecedented. Yet, such determinations may vary depending on the sources used; and those variations may contribute to unrecognized injustices. For example, the Court's kinship cases often reify historical practices over current kinship practices. The Court obviously produces this result when it follows a general doctrinal rule that limits the scope of substantive due process to historical practices. Yet, in two cases, *Loving* and *Lawrence*, the Court faced the unusual situation of supporting a minority of states that had rejected the protection for relationships with complex social histories. In *Loving*, the Court specifically noted that the antimiscegenation statutes at issue had deep roots dating back to the colonial period and that only sixteen states had enacted antimiscegenation statutes with, 15 years earlier, a total of 30 states having had such provisions. Similarly, in *Lawrence*, the Court addressed the rapid transformation of the legal regulation of sodomy in the preceding decade and a half. In both *Loving* and *Lawrence*, the Court decided not to uphold historical practices even though those practices supported the challenged statutes. These are important developments. These cases can be seen as normative (they imagine the way families should be) rather than merely descriptive and reproductive of historical practices. Further, in both *Loving* and *Lawrence*, the Court rejected current practices reflected in some state statutes and adopted a more contemporary view of accepted social practices and beliefs. Notably, however, these two impressive cases do not deal with families with children. When cases do deal with children, the Court appears quite less reluctant to move away from perceptions of what constitutes traditional families worth the highest protection from state intrusion and control. Children do not necessarily fit well in emerging visions of family life.

Finally, the Supreme Court's family cases reveal an apparent shift in its ways of assessing the state's ability to intrude in people's rights and the extent to which they must have sound reasons to do so. Two approaches appear to be developing, and those approaches differ depending on whether we are dealing with unitary (married, heterosexual) or nontraditional families. The approach that guards unitary families follows the more traditional view of rights as it deems them fundamental and requires states to overcome a high burden to justify its laws that infringe or aim to interfere in family life. Of course, saying that the state's action would trigger high constitutional scrutiny is not the same thing as saying that the state's action would be unconstitutional. Privacy rights, like other individual rights under the Constitution, can be overcome by sufficiently strong public interests. Importantly, however, the approach places on the state the burden of justifying its choices. This approach, then, identifies whether a family is traditional and, if it is, the approach grants it considerable protection. It is this approach, which has become known as a strict scrutiny analysis, that originated in family cases and has since been transported to many areas of constitutional jurisprudence dealing with rights the Court deems fundamental to our very existence.

Another approach seems to guard non-traditional families. In this context, the law withholds formal recognition and triggers much less judicial scrutiny of state invasions of familial relationships. As a result, when dealing with nontraditional families, strict scrutiny tends not to be the appropriate judicial test. A long line of family-privacy cases, from at least *Moore* through *Troxel,* reveals the Court's intent to apply a more flexible form of scrutiny. In *Moore* and *Zablocki*, the Court moved from the usual language of "compelling" interests and "narrow tailoring" in describing the type of review governing the Court. In its place, the Court substituted ambiguous language. In *Troxel*, the Court moved even more clearly away from strict scrutiny in the course of striking down the state court's order of grandparent visitation. All but one of the Justices agreed that the visitation order burdened the mother's fundamental rights as a parent. Nevertheless, the plurality did not suggest that such orders must be justified by "compelling" state interests. Rather, it held that trial judges must give some unspecified "special weight" to a parent's reasons for objecting to contact with a nonparent (p. 69). *Troxel*'s omission of a strict scrutiny analysis strongly signaled a more flexible accommodation of the contending family interests at stake. The Court's *Lawrence* decision further confirms the Court's commitment to a flexible approach. The *Lawrence* plurality recognized the idea of emergent rights, recognizing that there are some legal restrictions, while perhaps not yet elevated to the status of fundamental rights, that nevertheless are entitled to the Court's heightened solicitude because of enduring traditions or their close association with already protected rights. Together, these cases certainly reveal movement toward greater protection, but the supporting rationales and jurisprudential standards supporting those rationales render the foundation for such a movement less than obvious.

The Court has grappled with many issues that eventually have shaped its jurisprudence of family life. The jurisprudence certainly is not complete and it clearly adapts to fit emerging concerns. Yet, existing views of what constitutes a family, the proper functions of families, and rationales for protecting those views necessarily influence the law's response to families and relationships that fail to provide children with appropriate environments. Given the centrality of these views, efforts to engage in legal reforms must take them seriously. We now turn to current legal responses to child maltreatment. We do so with the hope of using our understanding of legal rules to shape more effective legal responses to children suffering maltreatment at the hands of those entrusted with their care.

# Part III
# Legal Responses to Child Maltreatment

# Chapter 4
# Defining Maltreatment and Permitting Startlingly Broad State Intervention

As discussed in previous chapters, the state reserves for itself the power to intervene in children's abusive relationships and circumstances. One of the most significant aspects of this power includes the mandate to define the contours of maltreatment. As expected, defining what constitutes child maltreatment obviously plays an important role in addressing it. Definitions set the threshold for gaining state jurisdiction, which then guides the state's intervention. The significance of this mandate, however, has not produced an easy consensus about what constitutes the types of maltreatment worthy of state intervention. A look at definitions reveals that they are notable for the diverse forms of circumstances and events they regard as maltreating, the different ways legal systems approach similar forms of maltreatment, and the pervasive lack of guidance they provide those who rely on them to intervene in children's lives. As important as they are, existing definitions reveal a myriad of ways to define maltreatment and, by doing so, provide states with enormous power to interfere in families. Despite a lack of uniformity in identifying what precisely constitutes maltreatment, statutes permit all states to intervene in a very wide variety of situations that may be deemed maltreating; they permit intervention regardless of whether the maltreatment is minor or severe, or of whether the child is at risk for harm versus actually harmed. This chapter focuses on this set of tools that states have at their disposal to intervene and address the maltreatment of children.

## Challenges to Definitional Uniformity and Clarity

Before examining definitions and their use in more detail, we must consider why the immense diversity and lack of consensus continue in what one most likely would have expected to have been the easy task of defining when children are being maltreated. Achieving definitional clarity and consensus remains elusive, and several factors account for the deep attachment to the wide variety of definitions of what constitutes maltreatment. For now, however, it is important to highlight three related

Roger J.R. Levesque, *Child Maltreatment and the Law*                    61
© 2008 Springer Science+Business Media, LLC

challenges that continue to foster a lack of standard, universally accepted definitions. As we will see, those challenges inevitably complicate responses to maltreatment much beyond determinations of definitions that permit interventions in families and other situations in which children are maltreated by those entrusted with their care.

The first factor that contributes to the lack of definitional uniformity deals with the reality that the concept of child maltreatment addresses an exceedingly complex phenomenon. Abusive events and circumstances can take a wide variety of forms, as do the extent of their harms and their risks. As a result and possibly except for extreme forms of maltreatment, what constitutes conditions worthy of formal state intervention actually remains contentious. Several examples illustrate the broad range of complexities that continue to foster controversies. Some view certain actions as abusive, whereas others accept those same actions as beneficial to children, as revealed by continued controversy involving parents' use of corporal punishment and, more recently, yelling to correct children's behaviors. Not everyone agrees that an offender's intent should matter: some would not hold parents responsible if a child were harmed accidentally, although others would be more willing to hold parents accountable if such harms stemmed from parental neglect (which raises the question of what constitutes parental neglect). Some may not agree that parents' social circumstances should excuse certain harms they inflict on their children, such as when family poverty contributes to illnesses as a result of a lack of appropriate medical care. Some are more willing to use controversial moral standards to define harm, such as parents' involvement in same-sex relationships or criminal behaviors that may not directly cause harm to children. Others find maltreatment even in the absence of documentable harms; they would encourage intervention because a harm could be assumed, such as when parents permit their teenage children to engage in consensual sexual activities that nevertheless constitute statutory rape. Cultural and religious differences also contribute to disagreements, e.g., some would hold parents responsible for failing to provide medical services despite cultural explanations for not providing them, whereas others would urge that religious and cultural freedom excuses the parents' behaviors. Some would have the legal system focus on the risk of harm, rather than actual harm, such as when families place their children at risk for delinquent behavior. Some would disagree about whether the availability of social services should matter, such as when services are available but parents do not avail themselves of them, or when children are harmed even though parents sought and would have accepted preventive services. Others suggest that some forms of maltreatment simply have too wide a range of possibilities that could count as abusive, with no clear point at which something becomes abusive, whereas others would have the legal system retain the broadest power to intervene even in situations that many would not view as inherently harmful, such as in instances involving emotional maltreatment and mental injury. (Would a slight injury suffice, especially if the child is very vulnerable? Should the vulnerability of a child matter given that some children are resilient and apparently better able to endure what some would deem psychologically abusive?) Challenging difficulties like these considerably complicate matters and most likely will continue to hamper efforts to develop more precise, commonly accepted definitions of child maltreatment.

The second primary factor that accounts for lack of definitional uniformity and other definitional problems derives from the pervasive lack of consensus about the scope and overall policy framework for addressing maltreatment. Most notably, important disagreement centers on determining the most appropriate balance between the rights of parents and the state's interest in child protection. As we already have seen, the legal system grants states the power to intervene in abusive situations. However, that agreement remains a far cry from a consensus that would include details of the nature of situations that would constitute circumstances requiring intervention. Agreeing that the state holds the power to intervene also does not necessarily bring us closer to an agreement about the intervention itself. Determining the appropriate extent and nature of interventions in child maltreatment cases still remains a highly contentious exercise. For example, it would seem reasonable to suggest that minor harms would warrant less intrusive interventions and that serious harms would require more aggressive and invasive intrusions. Regrettably, what constitutes minor versus serious harm is more problematic to determine than one would think. In addition, even if we could reach consensus about a specific harm, disagreement may then center on the intrusiveness of the intervention meant to address it. The temporary removal of children from their homes, for example, may be seen as a relatively unobtrusive measure that provides the state with the needed opportunity to evaluate the risk of harm to children. Yet, such removals could be quite intrusive and damaging to family relationships, as could temporary removals of a parent from a family. Indeed, this area of law is fraught with examples of well-meaning state intrusions eventuating in more damage than the harm the interventions were meant to address. The absence of a broader consensus guiding this area of policymaking ensures that variations will continue.

The third reason for diversity and failure to agree on basic definitions deals with the existence of multiple legal systems and sources of law. Legal responses to child maltreatment potentially involve several systems. These systems, ranging from the dependency system, criminal justice system, and family court system to the juvenile justice system, establish legal worlds onto themselves. These systems have different goals and social purposes that shape the development of legal rules guiding their responses, and the state has developed procedures with specific references to the different systems' goals and purposes. Remarkably, this diversity exists even though the systems often wield overlapping jurisdictions. Sources of law contribute yet another layer of diversity to these differences. In the United States, law is generated from three primary branches of government (the executive, judicial, and legislative branches) that themselves may operate in any of several levels of government (the federal, state, and local levels). For example, the federal constitution broadly sets forth the structure of government and articulates a range of substantive and procedural rights for persons, rights that typically are framed as limiting governmental authority that infringes on these rights. State constitutions operate similarly, but they cannot contravene the federal constitution. Legislatures enact statutes, also known as codes, that guide how courts regulate administrative agencies (such as those charged with providing child welfare services). Courts interpret and apply regulations, statutes and constitutions, and contribute to the development of what is known as case law. In turn, that type of law often influences the development of statutes, regulations and interpretations of constitutions. To varying degrees, different areas of law, including those that target child maltreatment, reflect an interplay between legislative, administrative, and judicial systems, and between federal and state levels of governments. This interplay currently results in having state legislative mandates largely promulgating laws addressing child maltreatment, although important federal legislative and constitutional mandates also do influence this area of law. Together, these many layers of diversity, especially diversity permitted by federal and state levels of government, foster a lack of definitional consistency in our society's overall response to child maltreatment.

## The Diverse Definitions of Child Maltreatment

Given the complexities and challenges we have identified, we necessarily start our investigation of legal responses by briefly examining the ways our legal systems approach definitions of child maltreatment. To do so, we begin with an analysis of broad federal mandates that set the standard on which states now operate. We then examine states' general approaches to defining child maltreatment and, when doing so, reveal considerable diversity within some broad, agreed upon categories as well as some definitions peculiar to each state. Given that civil systems largely control this area of law, we necessarily focus on civil systems' definitions; but, we do, where relevant, note criminal laws. We also will find that several states apparently do not differentiate between civil and penal definitions. Our conclusion briefly summarizes major themes that emerge from our analyses of definitions and highlights their significance to understanding legal responses to child maltreatment, which, in turn, lays the foundation for the next chapters.

Both federal and state laws define what encompasses child maltreatment deemed appropriate for state intervention. The federal government defines crimes and offenses for which it could have sole jurisdiction (such as child trafficking, child prostitution, and distributions of child pornography across state lines), but the major source of definitions derives from civil statutes that provide a minimum standard for states to follow. States wishing to receive federal funds to support their responses to child maltreatment must incorporate these federal definitions into their own responses to child maltreatment. Given the vastness of the federal governments' financial incentives, reliance on the federal government would seem like an effective way to encourage consensus and achieve uniformity in approaches to child maltreatment. The federal government's approach, however, often is incomprehensive, lacks detail, and leaves considerable discretion to states. In this section, we examine the federal statutes designed to guide states and then examine trends in states' efforts to define child maltreatment. Although we do find some broad commonalities, we also find considerable variations.

## *The Federal Government's Approach to Defining Child Maltreatment*

A wide variety of federal laws address and define child maltreatment, but the *Child Abuse Prevention and Treatment Act (CAPTA)* (1974) is the federal legislation that provides minimum standards for the definition of child maltreatment; and that standard is the one that states incorporate into their statutory definitions. Congress originally enacted CAPTA in 1974, but it has since amended it several times. Currently, the statute is entitled the Child Abuse Prevention and Treatment and Adoption Reform General Program (2007) to reflect a move toward encouraging adoption. We will see, in the next chapter, how the move toward encouraging adoption has reshaped legal responses to maltreatment. For now, that shaping is illustrated by the statute's numerous goals that now supplement the original statute's mandates.

CAPTA's several goals reveal the impressive breadth of the federal legal system's involvement in shaping legal responses to child maltreatment. The statute provides the source for federal funding to states in support of prevention, assessment, investigation, prosecution, and treatment activities. In addition to supporting the entire range of states' potential responses to child maltreatment, the statute also provides grants to public agencies and nonprofit organizations for demonstration programs and projects. Additionally, the act identifies the federal role in supporting research, evaluation, technical assistance, and data collection activities. Furthermore, the act established the Office on Child Abuse and Neglect as well as the Child Welfare Information Gateway, which provide a variety of technical resources and information to shape legal and policy responses to child maltreatment. Most importantly for our immediate concerns, the statute also sets forth a minimum definition of child abuse and neglect.

Two of CAPTA's provisions provide definitions: 5106g and 5106i. The main section, 5106g, defines a "child" as a person who has not attained the age of 18 or, except in cases of sexual abuse, the age specified by the child protection law of the state in which the child resides. The statute then continues and defines "child abuse and neglect" to mean, at a minimum, "any recent act or failure to act on the part of a parent or caretaker, which results in death, serious physical or emotional harm, sexual abuse or exploitation, or an act or failure to act which presents an imminent risk of serious harm." The focus on action or inaction reflects the effort to include neglectful actions, typically described as the failure to act. The statute, however, does not describe what would constitute serious physical or emotional harm, nor does the statute describe what would be serious harm, something that would be important to understand given that children at imminent risk for it would be deemed maltreated. Unlike for other major forms of child maltreatment, the statute specifically defines sexual abuse. It defines the term as including " (A) the employment, use, persuasion, inducement, enticement, or coercion of any child to engage in, or assist any other person to engage in, any sexually explicit conduct or simulation of such conduct for the purpose of producing a visual depiction of such conduct; or (B) the rape, and in cases of caretaker or inter-familial relationships, statutory rape, molestation, prostitution, or other form of sexual exploitation of children, or incest with children." Although sexual abuse appears defined more specifically, it is important to note that what qualifies as rape, molestation, etc., remains far from obvious and varies considerably from one jurisdiction to the next. The federal mandate that directly addresses child maltreatment, then, offers a broad approach that provides few specifics.

The above terms have been the ones used most commonly to describe the types of child maltreatment that would require state intervention. More recently, however, the federal government has delineated an additional form of maltreatment, one dealing with medical neglect. This newer provision of the federal statute defines the term "withholding of medically indicated treatment" as meaning "the failure to respond to the infant's life-threatening conditions by providing treatment (including appropriate nutrition, hydration, and medication) which, in the treating physician's or physicians' reasonable medical judgment, will be most likely to be effective in ameliorating or correcting all such conditions." The statute further provides that the withholding of treatment does not include instances in which the treatment would be contrary to the "treating physician's or physicians' reasonable medical judgment." The statute then includes a list of circumstances that would render prolonged treatment futile, ineffective, and inhumane. These important amendments reveal an unusual commitment in that it clearly delineates who determines whether actions are maltreating—the treating professionals; and those who make such determinations are not state officials we typically would associate with determining what qualifies as child maltreatment under particular statutory provisions (i.e., child welfare case workers, prosecutors, police, judges, juries, etc.).

In addition to the above amendment, congress has amended the federal statute by offering a rule of construction, § 5106i. This rule is unusual in that it too provides for circumstances that the federal government explicitly does not view as necessarily maltreating. The provision states that the act shall not be construed "(1) as establishing a Federal requirement that a parent or legal guardian provide a child any medical service or treatment against the religious beliefs of the parent or legal guardian; and (2) to require that a State find, or to prohibit a State from finding, abuse or neglect in cases in which a parent or legal guardian relies solely or partially upon spiritual means rather than medical treatment, in accordance with the religious beliefs of the parent or legal guardian." The statute also requires states to avail themselves of the authority to permit the state child protective services system to pursue legal remedies to intervene and provide for a child when the care or treatment is necessary to prevent or remedy serious harm to the child or to prevent the withholding of medically indicated treatment from children with life threatening conditions. The statute further finds that, except with respect to the withholding of medically indicated treatments from disabled infants with life-threatening conditions, the state will retain the sole discretion to make case by case determinations. These amendments soften the federal government's support for the parental right of refusal to provide medical care by taking a more neutral stance on religious exemptions. States no longer must recognize a religious exception to be eligible for federal funds under the statute, an approach that leaves states free to choose whether to recognize religious exemptions.

As we can see, the federal statute provides only a floor, one that entrusts states with considerable flexibility. This flexibility derives from the extent to which mandates remain far from straightforward. For example, the mandates are both specific and vague. The statute's approach to medical neglect is quite specific. Yet, the statute does not define what would constitute harm, let alone serious harm, for the purposes of defining other forms of maltreatment. The mandates also are broad yet narrow in scope. By including emotional harm, the statute allows for moving in directions that potentially would include a wide variety of situations given that all forms of maltreatment necessarily result in emotional harm. Yet, the focus on imminent harm to define actions that place children at risk of harm is quite restrictive; the focus on imminent risk complicates efforts to include forms of maltreatment that may appear minor now but have long-term effects (such as educational neglect and some forms of medical neglect). The federal mandates also are quite limited in terms of who can be held responsible for maltreatment. The mandates focus, for example, on parents or caretakers; this focus provides a limitation to the extent that it is not always entirely clear, under law, who qualifies as caretakers. As a result, for example, the statute could permit the exclusion of siblings and those with attachments to family members but who are not deemed responsible under law. The definition of children also is potentially quite limiting; for forms of maltreatment other than sexual abuse, the statute leaves it to the states to denote the age at which one qualifies as a child for specific forms of maltreatment. As a last example of the statute's flexibility, the statute does not take a position on excuses to a variety of maltreating circumstances. The statute does address religious or spiritual "excuses" for not providing medical treatment, but it falls remarkably short of addressing the religious and cultural issues necessarily involved in many other forms of maltreatment. Nor does the statute address caretakers' abilities, such as their financial circumstances, to evaluate accusations of child neglect requiring resources caretakers simply may not have through no fault of their own. The failure to address more fully possible excuses and justifications does not mean that the statute prohibits their use, nor does it indicate permitting them. By pervasively failing to address religious, cultural, and other social issues, federal mandates do not guide state legislatures, and state variations could persist. As even a quick look at federal mandates reveals, then, states retain considerable flexibility in their efforts to define and respond to child maltreatment.

## *The States' Approaches to Defining Child Maltreatment*

Although potentially influenced by federal mandates, each state has enacted its own definitions of child maltreatment. The most common sources of definitions are those that link to child abuse and neglect reporting statutes. By doing so, these definitions determine the grounds for state intervention to protect children from harm by using what the state has developed into a child protection system. It is those statutes that link closely to the federal mandates. It also is those statutes that are more in a state of flux as they respond, among other things, to federal mandates and the changing recognition of the need to address child maltreatment through a variety of means. In addition to those statutes, states have penal statutes that guide their criminal justice systems' responses, which the civil, child welfare provisions were meant to complement to ensure more effective child protection. As a result, the criminal/penal statutes most likely have a much longer history and deal with what most would deem as more extreme forms of maltreatment. Together, these statutes provide states with a considerable amount of flexibility and options to address situations and circumstances that harm children or place them at risk. Emotional maltreatment arguably remains the most contentious form of maltreatment, even though the vast majority of states formally delineate it as a separate, identifiable form of maltreatment. Definitions vary considerably; see Appendix A for citations. Some states approach definitions of emotional maltreatment in a very straightforward fashion. These states simply declare that abuse includes mental injury, emotional abuse, or another term that they use to define emotional maltreatment. For example, the state of Connecticut finds that "Abuse includes emotional maltreatment" whereas Delaware notes that "Abuse includes emotional abuse" and Michigan states that "Child abuse includes mental injury" and Mississippi declares that an "abused child includes emotional abuse or mental injury." Missouri and New Mexico adopt a similar approach that does not provide much guidance to those entrusted with implementing the statutes. Other states simply do not include psychological maltreatment as a distinct category, such as Georgia and Washington. Arguably, those states have other provisions that would allow for addressing emotional abuse by, for example, addressing it as the result of another recognized form of maltreatment like physical abuse. This approach is similar to those of states that neither explicitly include or exclude it; e.g., Alabama finds that "abuse includes non-accidental injury," which could allow for including emotional injury, and Nebraska simply defines abuse very broadly: "Abuse or neglect means knowingly, intentionally, or negligently causing or permitting a minor child to be placed in a situation that endangers her mental health." Rather than permit so much flexibility, other states explicitly do define mental injury and limit it, for example, to injuries that can be evidenced by symptoms, and sometimes symptoms that must be documented by qualified experts (see Alaska, Arizona, Iowa, Pennsylvania, and South Carolina). This focus on observable symptoms (such as depression, withdrawal, severe anxiety), including when statutes do not dictate who must make the determination, seems to be the most dominant approach; see, for example, Arkansas, California, Colorado, Florida, Hawaii, Maryland, New Hampshire, North Carolina, Oregon, Rhode Island, South Dakota, Tennessee, Texas, and Wisconsin.

Other states limit what would qualify as maltreating to those situations that would be determined "serious" abuse, injury or endangerment (Alaska, Arizona, California, Indiana, Maine, North Carolina, Pennsylvania) or "substantial" impairment, injury, or risk (Colorado, Florida, Hawaii, Idaho, Illinois, Minnesota, and Ohio) or "severe maltreatment" (Montana) or "protracted impairment" (New York). A number of states adopt both approaches, and find that the maltreatment must be "observable (or discernable) and substantial" harm or impairment (Nevada,

Oregon, South Carolina, and Tennessee) or "observable and material impairment" (Texas); others simply require one or the other (Illinois requires "impairment or substantial risk of impairment" and Wyoming requires "observable or substantial impairment").

Kentucky, Minnesota, Oregon, South Dakota, Tennessee, and Wyoming explicitly find that evaluations of mental injury must be viewed with due regard to the child's culture, and some of those states include the need to consider the child's age (Kentucky, Minnesota, and Wyoming); a few other states explicitly consider age or developmental age (Alaska and Pennsylvania). Some states define psychological maltreatment as the major aspect of child maltreatment, as they define the harm of various forms of maltreatment in terms of emotional harms or injury (Massachusetts, New York, and North Dakota). Finally, only a few states explicitly provide an age for which the statutes apply, and that age is universally set at 18 (see Massachusetts, New Jersey, North Carolina, Pennsylvania, and Virginia).

All states directly and explicitly address physical abuse. As expected from our previous discussions, however, states do not do so uniformly. See Appendix A for citations. One of the most important ways states approach physical maltreatment is to define it as constituting harm or threat of harm through non-accidental physical injury (see, e.g., Alabama, Alaska, Arkansas, California, Connecticut, Georgia, Hawaii, Illinois, Iowa, Kentucky, Michigan, Minnesota, Mississippi, Missouri, Nevada, New Hampshire, New Jersey, New York, North Carolina, North Dakota, Ohio, Oklahoma, Oregon, Pennsylvania, Texas, Utah, Vermont, Virginia, Wisconsin, and Wyoming). Although the focus on injury inflicted by other than accidental means would seem an important distinction, several states actually do not specify that physical injury (and sometimes including the risk of injury or harm) must be nonaccidental (see, e.g., Arizona, Indiana, Kansas, Louisiana, Maine, Maryland, Massachusetts, Montana, Nebraska, Rhode Island, South Carolina, South Dakota, Washington, and West Virginia). Some focus on whether the physical injury can be justifiably explained (Colorado, Delaware, Idaho, Oregon); and some include similar provisions in addition to recognizing abuse when nonaccidental (Texas). Rather than focus on whether the actions can be justified, other states explicitly delineate the factors to consider in determining the significance of injuries, such as Arkansas and Florida, both of which similarly require evaluations in light of the following factors: the age of the child, any prior history of injuries to the child, the location of the injury on the body of the child, the multiplicity of the injury, and the type of trauma inflicted.

Many states, in addition to providing specifics about accidental injuries (or not), provide nonexclusive lists of specific harms that would indicate physical injury or risk of physical harm, such as Michigan's listing of brain damage, skull or bone fracture, subdural hemorrhage or hematoma, dislocation, sprains, internal injuries, poisoning, burns, scalds, and severe cuts. For statutes that provide similar lists, see Hawaii, Idaho, Massachusetts, Montana, Nevada, New Mexico, Washington, Wisconsin, and Wyoming. Rather than (or in addition to) focusing on the results of actions, some states provide examples of specific actions that, depending on circumstances, may constitute physical abuse. For example, the state of Arkansas views as abusive the striking of a child aged 6 or younger on the face or head and the shaking a child aged 3 or younger. Minnesota provides a similar list, because it includes any of the following that are done in anger or without regard to the safety of the child: throwing, kicking, burning, biting, or cutting a child; striking a child with a closed fist; shaking a child younger than 3 years of age; striking or other actions that result in any nonaccidental injury to a child younger than 18 months of age; unreasonable interference with a child's breathing; threatening a child with a weapon, as defined by law; and striking a child younger than 1 year of age on the face or head. Unlike what we have seen for emotional maltreatment, only one state, Tennessee, includes a provision that provides for the need to have a qualified expert find that the actions have caused or reasonably could be expected to cause severe negative effects, such as "severe psychosis, severe neurotic disorder, severe depression, severe developmental delay or retardation, or severe impairment of the child's ability to function adequately in the child's environment." As these provisions demonstrate, all states may recognize child physical maltreatment, but that recognition varies considerably.

Several states explicitly permit what is popularly known as corporal punishment. States do so by permitting reasonable discipline or actions (Arkansas, Minnesota, Mississippi, and Missouri) or prohibiting "cruel" or "excessive" corporal punishment (California, Connecticut, Florida, Illinois, Nebraska, Nevada, New Jersey, New Mexico, North Carolina, North Dakota, Rhode Island). South Carolina does include, as abusive, injuries resulting from excessive corporal punishment, but it is the state that provides the most detail as to the type of corporal punishment or physical discipline it would exclude, that which "is administered by a parent or person in loco parentis; (ii) is perpetrated for the sole purpose of restraining or correcting the child; (iii) is reasonable in manner and moderate in degree; (iv) has not brought about permanent or lasting damage to the child; and (v) is not reckless or grossly negligent behavior by the parents." Almost surprisingly, one state, Ohio, potentially leaves considerable discretion to those imposing corporal punishment, as it finds that "A child exhibiting evidence of corporal punishment or other physical disciplinary measure by a parent, guardian, custodian, person having custody or control, or person in loco parentis of a child is not an abused child." Rather than excluding physical discipline, Georgia permits it "as long as there is no physical injury to the child." Notably, the remaining states do not address directly issues of corporal discipline or punishment, a failure that again reveals the diversity of ways states approach child maltreatment.

Statutes defining physical maltreatment also delineate the required personal characteristics of victims and of those who maltreatment them. Only a small handful of states explicitly provide an age for which the statutes generally apply, and that age is universally set at 18 (Alaska, Indiana, New Jersey, New York, North Carolina, Pennsylvania, Tennessee, and Virginia); the vast majority simply use the term child, which may or may not be defined by other statutes. States evince much more variety when it comes to defining who, for the purposes of gaining state jurisdiction over the circumstances, qualifies as abuser. A few states find that abuse may be the action of a (or any) person (California, Florida, Louisiana, and Washington), whereas many states simply provide no such specifics in their statutes defining physical maltreatment (Alaska, Arizona, Colorado, Connecticut, Idaho, Kansas, Massachusetts, Michigan, Nebraska, Nevada, New Hampshire, Oregon, Utah, Wisconsin, and Wyoming). Others limit the category of abuser to a parent, custodian, or guardian (Illinois, New Mexico, Ohio, South Dakota, and Texas) whereas some extend it to those responsible for the care, custody, and control of the child (Delaware, Georgia, Hawaii, Iowa, Kentucky, Maine, Minnesota, Missouri, Montana, New Jersey, North Carolina, and Tennessee), or simply to a person responsible for the child's health, safety, or welfare (Oklahoma, Rhode Island, South Carolina, Vermont, Virginia, West Virginia), and some extend that category to "a relative" (Tennessee). Some states extend the reach to persons responsible for the child's care or support, whether or not legally obligated to do so (Mississippi) while others explicitly limit such obligations to persons legally responsible for the child's care (New York). Some states extend the category beyond those responsible for a child's care to include any household or family member (Maryland) or any individual residing in the home or a paramour of the child's parent (Illinois); Arkansas stands alone in the manner it specifically extends it to foster parents including, but not limited to, an agent or employee of a public or private residential home, child care facility, public or private school, or any person legally responsible for the juvenile's welfare (but excluding the spouse of a minor). Finally, one state simply labels them "a perpetrator" (Pennsylvania). These provisions help highlight that those who commit abuse differ because we are dealing with different systems; the focus on parents and caretakers directly relates to traditional child welfare, while the focus on other family members and others outside the immediate family reveals a broadening of what would constitute child maltreatment.

Chid neglect constitutes another well-recognized form of child maltreatment; see Appendix A for citations. Typically, the law defines neglect, like negligence, as the failure to act and it does not consider an individual's intent as a prerequisite to holding them responsible for their failures. State statutes defining child neglect pervasively adopt this approach, as the language of statutes addressing neglect highlight the irrelevance of intentional or unintentional aspects of harm. As long as the harm or risk of harm exists as the result of certain inadequacies in the child's environment, the state may view the child as neglected. For example, Alaska defines neglect as meaning "the failure by a person responsible for the child's welfare to provide necessary food, care, clothing, shelter, or medical attention for a child." Most states follow a similar approach to the extent that they too focus on the failures of those who care for the children (Idaho, Iowa, Kansas, Arkansas, Colorado, Delaware, Kansas, Louisiana, Maryland, Michigan, Minnesota, Missouri, Montana, New Jersey, New York, Oregon, Pennsylvania, Rhode Island, South Carolina, Tennessee, Texas, Vermont, and Washington). Some states focus less on the failure, which may be active or inactive, and frame neglect in terms of the "inability" or incapability (Arizona and Kentucky), "negligence" (Alabama and California), or the neglect, refusal, or fault (Mississippi, Nevada, Ohio, West Virginia, Wisconsin, and Wyoming) of parents, caretakers or others entrusted with the care of the children. Others focus on caretakers' knowingly, intentionally, or negligently causing the situation (Nebraska). Other states simply focus on the status of the child and their need for care (or their lack of care) rather than on the apparent actions or inactions of those who care for them (Connecticut, Hawaii, Illinois, Indiana, Maine, North Carolina, North Dakota, and Oklahoma). As expected, some focus on both, the condition of the child and the caretakers' actions or inactions (New Hampshire, New Mexico, and South Dakota). Finally, some states do not elaborate much on what constitutes neglect; they simply find that abuse or neglect means that the child is being neglected (Georgia, Massachusetts, and Utah).

Statutes addressing child neglect also tend to delineate other factors, although they vary widely in how they address them. We have seen that some states focus on circumstances, rather than the actions or inactions of individuals who would have placed the children in neglectful situations. Statutes that do focus on the actions or inactions of individuals typically focus on parents, guardians, custodians or other officially designated caretaker or person responsible for the child (Arkansas, Colorado, Delaware, Georgia, Idaho, Illinois, Iowa, Kansas, Kentucky, Louisiana, Maryland, Michigan, New Hampshire, New Jersey, New Mexico, New York, North Carolina, North Dakota, Ohio, Rode Island, South Carolina, South Dakota, Tennessee, Texas, Vermont, West Virginia, and Wisconsin); other states simply provide that neglect can be the result of the action or inactions of "persons responsible" for children (Alaska, California, Iowa, Maine, Minnesota, Mississippi, Missouri, Nevada, Vermont, Washington, and Wyoming). Some do not mention individuals in their provisions dealing with neglect and rather focus on the environment, home or the child's living conditions (Alabama, Connecticut, Florida, Hawaii, Indiana, Massachusetts, Montana, Nebraska, Oklahoma, Oregon, Pennsylvania, and Utah). States' provisions relating to child neglect tend not to define what age makes a child eligible for protection; only Indiana, Massachusetts and New York explicitly mark the age (and all use 18), whereas some use the term juvenile (Arkansas and North Carolina). Rather than use a clear age limit, some states allow the use of the child's age, in addition to other factors, to determine the relative appropriateness of the care provided to the child (Arkansas, Florida, Kentucky, Minnesota, and South Carolina).

States sometimes provide lists of actions or circumstances deemed neglectful. Those that do so include deficiencies relating to basic necessities such as food, care (for some deemed supervision), clothing, shelter or medical attention (Alabama, Alaska, Arizona, Arkansas, California, Colorado, Florida, Hawaii, Idaho, Indiana, Iowa, Kentucky, Louisiana, Maine, Michigan, Minnesota, Mississippi, Missouri, Montana, Nebraska, Nevada, New Jersey, New York, North Dakota, Ohio, Oklahoma, Oregon, Pennsylvania, Rhode Island, South Carolina, Tennessee, Texas, Vermont, West Virginia, and Wyoming). However some statutes also include, for example, pregnant mothers' use of illegal substances or unlawful exposure of a child to a controlled substance or a parent's use of controlled substances (Arkansas, Illinois, Indiana, Massachusetts, Minnesota, North Dakota, Rhode Island, South Dakota, and Washington) or situations where another child from the same household has been maltreated (Colorado and North Carolina), or the child's abandonment (Arkansas, Colorado, Connecticut, Illinois, Nevada, New Mexico, New York, North Carolina, North Dakota, Oklahoma, South Carolina, South Dakota, Vermont, and Wyoming), or injury to the child's morals (Connecticut, Mississippi, North Dakota, Ohio, and Tennessee). Although neglect does not typically focus on the intent of those who place children at risk, several states explicitly find that the caretakers' financial or other inabilities (sometimes including lack of available services) can negate the finding of certain types of neglect (Arizona, Arkansas, Iowa, Michigan, Mississippi, New Hampshire, New Jersey, North Dakota, Rhode Island, South Carolina, Washington, West Virginia, and Wisconsin).

As we have noted previously, child maltreatment also falls under the jurisdiction of the criminal justice system. States' penal codes address child maltreatment in a variety of ways. Indeed, many of the forms of maltreatment enumerated in this chapter can be prosecuted if the circumstances were severe enough to cause serious harm or risk of harm to children. Unlike the statutes that were developed as part of the civil, child protection systems, penal statutes vary even more in how they approach child maltreatment. We can, however, identify general themes and trends; see Appendix A for citations. The most encompassing way that states address the criminal aspects of child maltreatment is through their child endangerment statutes; half the states take this approach (Alaska, Arkansas, California, Delaware, Hawaii, Illinois, Iowa, Kansas, Kentucky, Maine, Massachusetts, Minnesota, Missouri, Montana, Nevada, New Hampshire, New Jersey, New York, Oregon, Oklahoma, Pennsylvania, Tennessee, Texas, Utah, and Wyoming). These statutes generally define endangerment as recklessly or with criminal negligence subjecting a child to a substantial risk of harm, with the harm varying from undefined actions that injure children's physical and emotional health to specific actions from parents (such as abandonment the failure to provide medical care) and to the neglect or the sexual abuse of children. Other states address these issues by focusing on prohibitions against contributing to the delinquency of a minor, dependency of a minor, and/or child in need of services (such as through, for example, neglect). Such statutes hold adults, typically parents and other caretakers, for placing children in situations that render them in need of state intervention. States that take this approach include Alabama, Alaska, Arizona, Arkansas, Delaware, Florida, Louisiana, Maine, Mississippi, Montana, New Mexico, North Carolina, Kentucky, Ohio, Vermont, and Virginia. Notably, most of these statutes are separate from endangerment statutes, although some states (such as Delaware, Maine, Montana, and Ohio) include similar provisions into their statutes dedicated to child endangerment. Rather than use this approach, some states have statutes that focus on cruelty to children (Georgia, Louisiana, Rhode Island, and Vermont) and some have statutes that focus on criminal child abuse (often in addition or included in child endangerment statutes): Arizona, Colorado, Florida, Kansas, Michigan, Missouri, Nebraska, New Mexico, North Carolina, North Dakota, Oklahoma, South Dakota, Tennessee, and Utah. These latter provisions are quite important to the extent that they tend to include a wide variety of harms; for example, these statutes tend to define child abuse broadly, such as the intentional infliction of physical or mental injury upon a child, with several including acts of omission. Other states take even broader approaches as they include, for example, impairing the morals of children (Connecticut, Delaware, Louisiana, New Jersey, and Wyoming).

It is important to emphasize that penal statutes dealing with endangerment and contributing to the dependency of minors address issues relating directly to neglect. They include omission or failure of a duty to protect children among the lists of prohibited behavior. States use these statutes to punish not only the perpetrators of abuse, but also any person who fails to fulfill his or her duty to protect a child from abuse. Under most statutes, those subject to punishment for omission are limited to parents, guardians or other persons having care, custody or control of a child. By criminalizing omissions, these statutes have the effect of creating affirmative duties for parents to protect their children from acts of abuse and neglect, as well as from risks of harm. It also is important to note statutes creating other criminal acts against children, such as reckless conduct, involuntary manslaughter, contributing to the deprivation of a minor, or cruelty to children. These latter statutes, however, may not create liability for criminal negligence specifically directed towards a child, may require proof of malice (an evidentiary standard that is difficult to meet in cases relating to breach of a custodial duty) and, especially relating to prohibitions of contributing to the deprivation of a minor, the provisions tend to be limited to parents or guardians, and not others who have custody and control of a child. But, overall, it is difficult to argue that the criminal justice system cannot reach very deeply into families and address child maltreatment.

One last form of maltreatment addressed by all states is sexual abuse. As expected, great variation exists; some states refer in general terms to sexual abuse, while others specify various acts as sexual abuse. See Appendix A for citations. Although civil provisions contain language relating to sexual abuse as, for example, a definition of child abuse, the more specific definitions are found in penal codes. Several states simply define child abuse as meaning sexual abuse, exploitation, molestation, mistreatment, or sex offense as defined by penal law; among these states, those that provide more specifics include the commission or omission of the person responsible for the child's care (Alaska, Arizona, California, Connecticut, Delaware, Hawaii, Illinois, Iowa, Kansas, Maine, Michigan, Missouri, New Jersey, New Mexico, New York, North Dakota, South Carolina, South Dakota, Virginia, and Wyoming). Other states take the approach of delineating specific forms of sexual abuse. Thus, some refer to penal statutes for defining offenses but some also provide examples of what sexual abuse includes, such as child pornography (Alabama, Arkansas, Hawaii, Idaho, Kentucky, Louisiana, Mississippi, Nebraska, Nevada, New Mexico, Oklahoma, Rhode Island. and Washington). Criminal statutes contain a wide variety of offenses, including rape, prostitution, sexual contact, masturbation, incest, sodomy, debauchery, public indecency and unnatural or perverted sexual practices. This wide variety of offenses can be defined differently and include different categories of individuals, such as children below a certain age for certain offenses and individuals with different relationships with the child. Arkansas, for example, lists sex offenses as perpetrated by a person 10 years of age or older to a person younger than 18 years of age. Tennessee defines some categories of abuse as the unlawful sexual abuse, molestation, fondling or carnal knowledge of a child younger than 13 years. States that have minimal ages in their statutes directly relating to sexual abuse, however, generally set the age of 18 as the upper limit for victimization (Alaska, Arkansas, Indiana, Kansas, New Jersey, North Carolina, Pennsylvania, and Virginia). The manner states define sexual maltreatment, then, also allows for considerable variability.

A review of the statutes reveals another area of variation worth considering: explicitly recognized exemptions and excuses for what otherwise would be deemed maltreatment. See Appendix A for citations. The most frequently mentioned exemption involves statutes that exclude religious or spiritual treatments as a basis for not finding neglect. Several states include an exemption from prosecution for endangering the welfare of a child for parents who withhold certain aspects of medical treatments from their children due to their religious beliefs, but those exemptions typically do not bar prosecutions if the children remain seriously harmed or die: Alabama, Alaska, Arizona, Arkansas, California, Colorado, Connecticut, Delaware, Florida, Hawaii, Idaho, Illinois, Indiana, Iowa, Kansas, Kentucky, Louisiana, Maine, Maryland, Massachusetts, Michigan, Minnesota, Missouri, Nevada, New Hampshire, New Jersey, New York, North Dakota, Ohio, Oklahoma, Oregon, Pennsylvania, Rhode Island, South Dakota, Tennessee, Utah, Vermont, Virginia, Washington, West Virginia, Wisconsin, and Wyoming. In addition to permitting criminal prosecutions when serious harm still results from alternative medical approaches, the neglect statutes that have these exemptions tend to be worded in ways that still permit intervention: the alternative approach may not, in and of itself be grounds for neglect, but courts still may order medical services for children who may be harmed if they do not receive the services. States, then, provide important immunities, but those immunities vary and are far from certain.

In addition to immunities that seek to accommodate for religious and spiritual differences, statutes provide many other often ignored exemptions. Arguably the most common exemption includes those that permit physical punishment. As we already have seen previously, several states define abuse as not including reasonable and moderate physical discipline of a child administered by a parent or legal guardian which does not result in an injury, with some states taking Ohio's approach that simply does not view evidence of corporal punishment or other physical disciplinary measures as signs of child abuse. We also have seen previously that determinations of neglect can take into consideration, in at least a dozen states, the financial abilities of parents. In addition to these justifications for what would otherwise be deemed maltreatment, three states explicitly require that those who intervene to determine the presence of abuse to take into account cultural differences: Colorado requires those investigating reports of child abuse shall take into account accepted child-rearing practices of the culture in which the child participates; both South Dakota and Tennessee require evaluations of emotional harm or mental injury to discern the impairment in the child's ability to function within the child's normal range of performance and behavior, with due regard to the child's culture. In addition, we already have seen above that considerations for a child's culture also figure in determinations of whether a child can be considered emotionally maltreated. The vast majority of states, then, provide parents with considerable exemptions when they fail to provide their children with levels of care for which other parents would be deemed as maltreating their children.

As our brief review reveals, considerable diversity marks states' approaches to defining child maltreatment, and those differences are embedded in important similarities. For example, some states define child abuse and neglect as a single concept, whereas others provide separate definitions for physical abuse, neglect, sexual abuse, and/or emotional abuse. Some states permit what could be deemed justifications and excuses for certain forms of maltreatment, and those vary in terms of what they could permit relative to the caretakers' actions or inactions as well as in terms of the system (civil or criminal) involved in addressing what would otherwise be deemed maltreatment. States, then, greatly vary in the level of specificity, nature, breadth, scope and severity of harm required for the threshold for state jurisdiction. This diversity continues despite a federal mandate that delineates key types of maltreatment to help clarify the jurisdictional scope of laws addressing child maltreatment.

## Conclusions: The Costs and Benefits of Definitional Diversity

Our legal system, broadly defined, recognizes similar forms of child maltreatment, but great diversity distinguishes that recognition when we consider more specific legal systems. The federal and state legal systems differently approach this general form of maltreatment, and states define it in a myriad of ways. We have seen that many reasons account for that diversity and that the wide variation gains significance to the extent that it guides how states will intervene to protect children from harm, including whether states will intervene at all. Although many reasons account for the diversity in approaches, the diversity raises the need to consider its attendant costs and benefits and determine whether it indicates a need to reconsider society's legal responses to child maltreatment. This evaluation appears especially warranted given that the federal government has sought to foster and guide reform and that the states have had ample opportunities to develop responses and consider a variety of approaches. In the end, the issue for us to consider is whether the approach has set our legal systems on the right track to offering children and families protections from harms the state should address and from the harms the state may create when it fails to intervene appropriately. As expected, the issue is far from straightforward; the diverse ways to define (and subsequently approach) child maltreatment come with both advantages and disadvantages.

The typical benefits of permitting diverse approaches to defining legal mandates that address complex and contentious problems are well known, and those benefits do emerge in the context of efforts to address child maltreatment. Most notably, the lack of definitional agreement and precision makes considerable sense when it reflects the reality that our society lacks a consensus in how best to respond to child maltreatment. The lack of precision permits flexibility and allows for accommodating states' responses to specific needs. These needs vary as much as definitions do, but they tend to include the availability of resources for state-sponsored and charitable programs, the willingness to obtain resources to support programs, particular values relating to children's needs, as well as the overall manner a particular state has structured its legal system. At a very deep level, this flexible approach reflects our federalist system at its best. This approach allows for experimenting with different responses that then can be embraced more widely once their relative effectiveness can be evidenced; the approach also, of course, points us toward directions we should not take when we realize that the approaches lack effectiveness or otherwise fail to reach stated goals. Equally importantly, the flexibility, especially when it takes the form of vague laws that permit different interpretations, allows for individualized responses for different situations with different needs rather than inappropriately forcing predetermined responses. This individualized approach comports well with the popular belief that people should be treated as individuals, a belief that resonates with our legal system's broader appeal to individualized justice. These all are important points to consider. But, although these potential benefits comport with ingrained ideals, the reality for us to consider is whether current legal responses in fact further those ideals. We only can undertake such an analysis once we have examined laws guiding intervention after potential maltreatment has been identified, an undertaking we will take in the next three chapters.

For now, it is important to note that, as much as ideals serve important functions in shaping societal responses, many difficulties can arise in any system of individualized justice that permits diversity in ways to approach daunting societal issues. Individualized and discretionary systems leave room for egregious discrimination when those who implement laws wrongly treat similar cases quite differently. Lack of consistency also means that legal systems may lack a general sense of predictability. Among other concerns, lack of predictability increases the risk of fostering injustice. Most notably, for example, the failure to define problems consistently and in broadly understood ways leaves individuals without notice that their actions are problematic. This failure is especially troublesome in a legal system with vague statutes that permit a wide variety of state interventions. This, in turn, becomes increasingly problematic when legal systems rely on nonexperts to administer laws, such as when individuals who are not experts in child maltreatment are required to report their suspicions of maltreatment and could be held criminally responsible if they failed to do so. Even the implementation of laws by experts, however, may be problematic when experts lack the guidance, training, supervision and other needed supports to abide by appropriate mandates, a list of needs often attributed to causing the recurring failures in systems responding to high demands with only limited resources. Those limitations may be even more problematic when the legal system does not allow ready recourse for harms that would occur when the implementation of mandates fails: as we will see, the law generally grants immunity to those who implement laws as long as they act within their discretion. Lack of consensus and tolerance of variety in legal mandates, then, certainly runs the risk of hampering their effective administration.

Determining how to balance the costs and benefits of legal approaches to social problems inevitably turns into a normative concern open for debate. That is, how the law should address child maltreatment is something that our legal system leaves in the hands of many institutions, with the legal system drawing broad parameters in hopes that rigorous debate and clear thinking will lead to just responses. In this sense, the difficulties of balancing many concerns in responses to child maltreatment are far from unusual. All legal responses to complex problems require us to weigh the relative advantages of consistency over difference, and of flexibility over rigidness. Although these challenges may be common, systems do differ in the extent to which they permit variety. Regrettably and as we have seen, laws addressing child protection are marked by a wide variety of ways they approach child maltreatment. Our legal system tolerates great diversity in the ways states define child maltreatment.

Given the wide diversity of potential systems that can claim jurisdiction over children's maltreatment, legal responses to child maltreatment most likely exacerbate both the benefits and costs that typically associate to a wide variety of definitions. The variety of systems that may address child maltreatment gains particular significance to the extent that they define similar actions differently and even use similar terms differently. If one steps back and looks at the place of the immense diversity across and within systems, one finds that the legal system has developed ways to address these issues. Most notably and as case law and statutes themselves in this area often reveal (see Levesque, 2002a), the concept of "reasonableness" serves as the overriding standard on which to evaluate the appropriateness of the state's actions in response to allegations of maltreatment. The reasonableness standard often is used by the state, most likely child welfare caseworkers or police, to evaluate whether actions were abusive. Judicial evaluations also use the standard to evaluate actions by the state and individuals. Reasonableness, then, prominently figures in determining whether to deem caretakers' actions as causing or risking abuse as well as in assessing the appropriateness of the state's actions when its child protective systems respond. The legal system uses this standard for the simple reason that it must rely on the discretion and relative power of those who administer statutes and of the judges who oversee their actions. As one may have expected, however, this approach does not eliminate problems altogether and may leave much to be desired. What remains potentially problematic is the extent to which what constitutes reasonableness may vary considerably from one legal system to the next such that, for example, reasonable actions in a child welfare system may not be reasonable enough for the criminal justice system, and vice versa. When it comes to defining maltreatment, it even can become unclear which definition will be used in which system. This is significant in that the lack of consistency is permissible in child welfare law, which could be quite intrusive, yet it is impermissible in criminal law simply because the criminal justice system finds vague standards less permissible and individuals have more robust rights against state actions. These difficulties increase given that the systems often intermix. Thus, legal systems have developed ways to address diversity and vagueness, but the developments in how different systems approach child maltreatment highlight the need to revisit how legal systems respond to definitions of maltreatment.

# Chapter 5
# Removing Children From Maltreating Families

As we have seen in the last chapter, child welfare law deems children who are harmed or at risk of harm as "neglected," "dependent," or "abused." The process by which children receive this label is straightforward. Reports of suspected abuse by mandated reporters and others to state or local hotlines trigger child abuse and neglect investigations. These calls are then screened to determine whether the allegations warrant a fuller investigation. Reports that meet the standard for investigation result in dispatching a child protection worker to examine the child, interview caregivers, and assess the situation's risk of harm to the child. On the basis of those initial conversations and other gathered information, child protection workers determine whether available evidence supports allegations and, if so, then those reports are deemed "substantiated," "indicated," or "founded." This determination leads a caseworker to several options: to close the case, open the case for services, or seek court intervention. It is at this point that the caseworker, often in consultation with others, typically determines whether to remove the child from the home. This process reveals the significance of legal designations of what constitutes abuse. Those definitions allow the state to intervene and, if desired, remove children from their caretakers, typically their parents who either perpetrate abuse themselves or house the abusers. In this chapter, however, we see how those legal designations only initiate states' responses. What states do in response to what they deem as maltreatment is just as important to consider if we are concerned about how child protective systems work in practice and the rights of children and parents in families alleged to be maltreating.

Depending on specific cases, removals can develop in different ways to achieve different ends. Those different ways tend to depend on whether the case develops into one that removes the children temporarily, for an extended period of time, or permanently. Differently abusive situations obviously require different responses. As a result, removals vary greatly in the length of time the child welfare system will separate children from their families. This variation is of significance; it guides the rights family members have against a state's actions. As expected, the legal system sets the broad parameters that guide a state's obligations when state officials separate children from their families. As we will see, however, those broad parameters do

Roger J.R. Levesque, *Child Maltreatment and the Law*
© 2008 Springer Science+Business Media, LLC

allow states considerable flexibility in the manner they will recognize and protect the rights of parents and children. The legal system's tolerance of variations leads us to consider broad principles and the extent to which states should be encouraged to embrace some practices over others. Removals, then, can include a broad diversity of processes used to separate and protect children from their caretakers as well as to rebuild healthier relationships.

For our purposes, removals involve three decision-making processes worth delineating. First, removal necessarily involves an initial "rescue." Rescues occur when the state tentatively takes children from their homes to secure their immediate safety. Important consequences attach to the emergency or temporary component of rescues, for that component legally distinguishes it from extended separations that lead the state to offer family members greater legal protections from state intervention. Second, the removal process necessarily involves the provision of services. Those services can take a variety of forms, but they inevitably deal with the provision of alternative care. This alternative care can be temporary, as when the state places children in foster care while parents remedy their inadequacies, or they can be permanent, such as when the state places children for adoption when parents cannot remedy their inadequacies. Again, we find that children and parents' legal protections often vary depending on the types of services provided to families. Finally, removal can involve the termination of parental rights. If the children will not be returned home, their relationships with their parents must be severed so that the state can secure permanent alternative care. As expected, this dramatic step requires states to provide parents and children with considerable protections from potentially erroneous and unjust decisions. The complexity of removal warrants the legal system's complex mechanisms. No simple rules guide this area of law.

The process of removing children from abusive parents most likely involves many complicated legal rules that, when put into practice, raise even more complex challenges. Rules often only provide broad guidelines and allow for considerable discretion and flexibility to address practical challenges. Although each case brings its own challenges, we concern ourselves here with the broader challenges states must consider when balancing the protections they will offer parents and children from state intrusions and the speed, decisiveness, efficiency, and intrusiveness of their efforts to protect children from harm. Each of the three processes on which we center brings its own set of issues. If removals are an emergency and temporary response, legal issues focus on the types of protections that should be in place to protect families from unwarranted intrusions. These protections typically involve whether caseworkers or even police officers could have unilateral discretion to act when they believe children are in harm's way or whether they should involve others, either supervisors or even judges, to help determine the appropriateness of the government's intervention. When separations are to be extended or permanent, concern again focuses on the type of proof a state should provide and what kinds of procedures adequately protect the rights of parents and their children.

Removals also reach issues regarding what types of rights families have when the state fails to intervene appropriately under law. In addition to the legal system's concern for the sanctity of the parent–child relationship, important legal challenges arise regarding the provision of alternative care, both temporary and permanent, as well as the provision of services to the family. These latter issues become key concerns that must be addressed when a state considers removing children from their homes, and they even influence the extent to which an initial rescue will be deemed appropriate. Although we can best understand the removal process by looking at its component parts, then, we must realize that it is important to keep the entire system in mind, for all processes and possible outcomes ultimately influence each other as families and states act to protect children from harm.

## Rescuing Children From Their Parents

Child welfare law operates on the unquestioned assumption that federal statutes and regulations actually do not dictate when or how a state can rescue children from their parents. To be sure, constitutional protections still apply. Likewise, federal mandates may influence state responses to the extent that they, for example, encourage states to define maltreatment in certain ways and influence, as we will soon see, the services families receive. However, these mandates still largely leave states the power to regulate rescues within quite broad parameters. As a result, state rescue laws differ in their specific language. Despite important differences, state statutes also evince considerable similarities. Most notably, rescue laws tend to require "probable cause" as the proper standard for temporarily removing children from their homes. Following this standard, legal considerations focus on whether the facts and circumstances would lead a reasonable person to conclude that a child has been, is being, or might be abused. Importantly and as with criminal law, probable cause is not equated with certainty, or even likelihood, of child maltreatment. This "reasonableness" standard allows the state to remove the child temporarily, pending a more thorough judicial review when time permits. To gain a sense of a state's obligations, we examine both legislative and constitutional mandates regulating the rescue of children from their homes.

### Legislative Mandates

The state's direct intrusion in relationships and seizure of children obviously involves actions that must be done carefully and with a sense of certainty. Typically and as we will see in this chapter, the need to act reasonably, accurately, and legitimately in the implementation of laws results in requiring judicial oversight, as evidenced by the general preference for judicially approved warrants when law enforcement conduct invasive searches and arrest suspects. All jurisdictions agree that state actions that lead to children's temporary rescue from their families require judicial oversight. States, however, considerably disagree about when they require that supervision. States tend to take either of two approaches. Several states have enacted measures generally demanding prior judicial authorization for rescues and removals. Judicial approval, under these schemes, is only excused by "exigent" or "necessary" circumstances (see Appendix B for citations). For example, New York law authorizes warrantless removals when there is "reasonable cause to believe that the child is in... imminent danger" and "there is not time enough to apply for an order...." Arkansas law states that warrantless removals are permissible only when the child is in "immediate danger," when "removal is necessary to prevent serious harm," and when "there is not time to petition for and to obtain an order of the court prior to taking the juvenile into custody." Similarly, Illinois law authorizes dispensing with prior judicial process when "there is not time to apply for a court order." Iowa and Tennessee statutes also take similar approaches. The central factor that characterizes this group of states is the exigency of the circumstances that vitiate an immediate need for an independent approval. Importantly, these statutes do not eliminate judicial review altogether. When emergencies cease, these statutes require those acting on behalf of the state to obtain a judicial review of their decisions.

A number of jurisdictions pursue a different approach and have dispensed with warrants (and other forms of *ex ante* court orders) altogether in the child abuse arena. Rather than condition initial removal on warrants or what commonly constitutes "exigent circumstances," this group of states requires only probable cause to believe the child has been, or is being, abused. Several illustrative examples highlight how these states approach children's removals. Rhode Island allows removal by law enforcement officers when the child's condition or surroundings reasonably appear to be such as to jeopardize the child's welfare, and by social workers when there exists "reasonable cause to believe that the child or his or her sibling has been abused and/or neglected and that continued care of the child by his or her parent or other person responsible for the child's welfare will result in imminent further harm to the child." In Kansas, children can be removed when officials have reasonable grounds to believe that circumstances are "harmful to the child," even when there is sufficient time to seek a warrant. Oklahoma law authorizes removal "by a peace officer or employee of the court, without a court order if... continuation of the child in the child's home is contrary to the health, safety or welfare of the child...." Oregon allows warrantless removals "when the child's condition or surroundings reasonably appear to be such as to jeopardize the child's welfare...." Similarly, Montana authorizes social workers and police officers who have "reason to believe any youth is in immediate or apparent danger of harm" to "immediately remove the youth and place the youth in a protective facility." Unlike the broad category we examined previously, this group of states emphasizes child protection and trusts more that the state personnel can determine when a child should be removed from one's home.

The emergence of two distinct approaches to protecting the rights of parents and children during rescues exhibits a lack of consensus about the proper balance between both approaches. One approach favors warrants, court orders, and judicial assistance. Under this approach, only true, factually specific emergencies concurred by an independent decision maker justify rescues. Many benefits attach to this approach. Prior judicial review, for example, checks executive license and reduces the risk of errors. This enhanced accuracy, however, is not without costs. Judicial time remains a scarce and expensive commodity. In addition, the demands of the warrant process might dissuade government officials from pursuing abuse complaints in close cases, allowing abuse to continue. The other approach trusts police officers and social workers to make proper rescue decisions, at least in the first instance and for a limited amount of time. This approach tends to view the potential harm of child maltreatment as a categorical emergency that justifies immediate rescue on probable cause. This regime finds irrelevant the time and ability to seek warrants or court orders. The approach also deems exigent circumstances as unnecessary to justify removal. The approach simply requires that a caseworker reasonably believe that a child will, is, or has suffered maltreatment. Importantly, dispensing with the need for prior judicial review may save time (and money) and may facilitate detection, but this approach risks unnecessary invasions of privacy and familial harmony. Further, invasive governmental practices risk alienating parents who need assistance and who would otherwise cooperate with social workers. Invasive policies also, of course, run the risk of creating a more harmful environment for already vulnerable children. Putting fiscal considerations aside, the question comes down to determining the optimal way to uncover child abuse while respecting familial privacy. It is the notion of privacy, and the legal rights that support it, which leads to the potential involvement of constitutional issues.

## *Constitutional Mandates*

As with many areas dealing with child protection, the Supreme Court has left much unaddressed. As we have found, state law governs this area of law and remains only broadly guided by federal statutes that encourage states to define certain harms as maltreating. By largely leaving these matters to state level jurisdictions, this area of law tends to avoid Supreme Court scrutiny. The Court defers to states when disputes involve state matters, and this area broadly remains beyond constitutional scrutiny given the pervasive belief that matters of family law belong in state legislatures and state courts. We can cull from a wide variety of cases, however, to get a sense of the legal system's response to the complex issues raised. Although potentially involving many constitutional issues, two doctrines appear most relevant to determining whether judicial participation must precede, or may follow, a state's rescue of an allegedly abused child. This section examines these two broad doctrines ("Search and Seizure" and "Due Process"), but we remain mindful that the Court has yet to address these matters forthrightly in the context of child protection laws.

### Fourth Amendment Protections

The Fourth Amendment normally bans unreasonable searches and seizures by government officials or agents. The Amendment, made applicable to the states through the Fourteenth Amendment, reads:

> The right of the people to be secure in their persons, houses, papers, and effects, against unreasonable searches and seizures, shall not be violated, and no Warrants shall issue, but upon probable cause, supported by Oath or affirmation, and particularly describing the place to be searched, and the persons or things to be seized.

As currently conceptualized, the need for a Fourth Amendment analysis arises only when the government intrudes into an individual's legitimate expectation of privacy through a search or seizure. The expectation of privacy requires that the person exhibited an actual, subjective expectation of privacy, and that the expectation be one that society recognizes as reasonable (Levesque, 2006). Determining the existence of an expectation of privacy is a threshold question for the court and, if it finds none, then the court will not subject the search to constitutional scrutiny. If the court does find an expectation of privacy and intrusion in it, the court then engages in analyzing the search's "reasonableness." The term "reasonableness" contains a certain level of ambiguity, and courts have struggled to formulate a useful definition. Nevertheless, the Supreme Court has provided a guiding principle: reasonableness requires a balancing of the need for the search against the invasion of personal rights that the search entails. In performing this balancing test, the courts must consider the scope of the particular intrusion, the manner in which it is conducted, the justification for conducting the search, and the place in which it was conducted. What is reasonable depends on the search's context (see, *New Jersey v. T.L.O.*, 1985, p. 337). Because the rescue of a child generally qualifies as a seizure of a person or of something that belongs to a parent, the Fourth Amendment may offer an obvious constitutional barrier against the state's effort to rescue children.

Children's rescues may implicate the Fourth Amendment, but that Amendment is far from absolute in its protections. It matters greatly, for example, whether the search is conducted in pursuit of law enforcement goals or of other state's interests, like public health concerns, that do not involve criminal law enforcement. In the context of criminal law enforcement, the Fourth Amendment requires a warrant, supported by probable cause to believe that a crime has been committed and that evidence of the crime will be found in the place to be searched, to render a full-scale search and seizure reasonable. Despite these mandates, the Supreme Court has enumerated numerous exceptions, the most famous of which includes exigent circumstances and minimally invasive searches to protect officers (see *Terry v. Ohio,* 1968). In these circumstances, the Fourth Amendment protections apply, but the Court allows for flexibility as long as the officer conducts a limited search based on the reasonable suspicion of the suspect's involvement in criminal activity. The Court indicated that reasonable suspicion exists where the officer conducting the search can "point to specific and articulable facts which, taken together with rational inferences from those facts, reasonably warrant that intrusion" (*Terry v. Ohio,* 1968, p. 21). The facts must be judged against an objective standard, not against a subjective standard based on an officer's acting in good faith. The facts available to the officer at the moment of the search must "warrant a man of reasonable caution in the belief that the action taken was appropriate" (p. 22). Under these circumstances, the law justifies a search by the fact that the state holds an important governmental interest, and that the search is minimally intrusive on the individual's privacy and liberty interests. Thus, where the search is less intrusive, it will be reasonable when based at least on some quantum of individualized suspicion. And if the court deems the search reasonable under these circumstances, the court rules the Fourth

Amendment's requirements fulfilled. That finding, in turn, legitimizes the seizures resulting from the search.

Another important departure from the warrant/probable cause requirement involves situations that require no level of individualized suspicion at all. For our purposes, the most relevant aspect involves the regulation of search and seizures outside of the law enforcement context. In such contexts, government officials need neither a warrant nor probable cause to conduct a search and seizure "when special needs, beyond the normal need for law enforcement, make the warrant and probable cause requirement impracticable" (*New Jersey v. T.L.O.*, 1985, p. 351). The existence of a special need, however, does not automatically validate a search conducted without individualized suspicion. A court must conduct a fact-specific balancing of the intrusion on the Fourth Amendment rights against the promotion of legitimate governmental interests. If a court finds the government's need sufficiently compelling and the search minimally intrusive, it will rule that a search and seizure based on less than individualized suspicion sufficiently justifies the invasion of a person's privacy interest. Particularly because the state increasingly involves itself in matters outside of law enforcement contexts, the Court has liberalized the special needs exceptions to searches and seizures and allows states to apply them to administrative searches, such as those by school personnel and child welfare caseworkers. As a result, this extension of exceptions to Fourth Amendment law essentially reduces the need for judicial involvement in child welfare law.

Numerous Supreme Court cases, many of which we will review later, emphasize critical legal distinctions between the civil and criminal justice system as they relate to child welfare law. These differences gain significance to the extent that several state and federal courts unquestionably adopt the view that child welfare systems are civil systems, not criminal justice systems (see Levesque, 2002a). This, in turn, may be prohibitive to the extent that the distinction between civil and criminal justice systems may be clear in theory, but that distinction becomes increasingly complicated and somewhat mythical in practice. One of the most troublesome complications that has arisen most forcefully involves the intertwining of the criminal and civil legal systems' goals. Most notably, law enforcement increasingly takes place in what used to be civil child welfare law. This means that, as the child welfare system increasingly adopts law enforcement goals, it may well need to adopt the protections the criminal justice system provides. Even if the civil child welfare system did not adopt law enforcement goals, the child welfare system, which did not exist at the founding of our nation and ratification of the Constitution, increasingly means that the state involves itself in intrusive ways in family life and personal liberties. We will see in the next chapter that some justices have difficulty accepting these distinctions as relevant, but they are a continued source of litigation. Indeed, the Court has articulated the distinction in *Ferguson v. City of Charleston* (2001) and has noted its potential ramifications.

*Ferguson* addressed a public hospital's use of drug testing to deter pregnant women from harming their unborn children. The hospitals used urine screens on maternity patients who were thought to be using cocaine. Positive tests were used to "leverage" patients into formal treatment programs. Patients who refused, or who failed to live up to the treatment program's terms were referred to law enforcement officials for possible prosecution. Potential charges included child neglect and unlawful delivery of a controlled substance to a child. Because the hospital's urinalysis program was not "divorced from the State's general interest in law enforcement" (*Ferguson v. South Carolina*, 2001, p. 79) but instead used "law enforcement to coerce the patients into substance abuse treatment" (p. 80), the Court concluded that the program did not qualify for treatment under the special-needs exception. "All the available evidence" demonstrated that the hospital's "primary purpose" was "indistinguishable from the general interest in crime control" (p. 81). Local prosecutors and police were extensively involved in the policy's day-to-day administration. Police coordinated arrests with hospital staff. Even though the hospital's motives could have been benign and did address a serious problem, the program's pervasive involvement with law enforcement rendered it unqualified for the special needs exception. As the Court reasoned, "[T]he gravity of the threat alone cannot be dispositive of questions concerning what means law enforcement officers may employ to pursue a given purpose" (p. 86).

As *Ferguson* demonstrates, the Court presumes that searches motivated by law enforcement purposes should be governed by law enforcement standards, and those standards generally require some level of suspicion. Along these same lines, child abuse investigations that further law enforcement aims should be subjected to basic law enforcement standards; at least, they should not be excused outright. The issue then would center on whether child abuse investigations further the objectives of law enforcement. Regrettably for those liking clear distinctions, child abuse investigations (and resulting rescues) proceed along considerably ambiguous and uncertain paths. Rescue is often entwined with law enforcement. Children can be rescued without prosecutors later filing corresponding criminal charges against parents, but the reality is that prosecutors can use evidence culled by caseworkers to mount a prosecution against caretakers. Conclusions drawn from child abuse investigations commonly form the bases for criminal charges. Further entangling law enforcement into abuse investigations is the common practice of enlisting the aid of police to facilitate rescues. This is an understandable practice, given the propensity of parents to forcibly resist turning their children over to strangers. The law, however, currently conceptualizes child abuse investigations as civil matters, a conceptualization that supports policies that subject parents to reduced legal protections. Those reduced protections, coupled by a mixture of law enforcement with child welfare practices, are of concern beyond issues of entanglement with law enforcement. Most notably, they are problematic to the extent that subtle pressures could encourage parents to waive their rights as they are encouraged to cooperate with state officials and voluntarily accept intervention. Constitutional law, then, grants individuals subject to the child welfare system reduced Fourth Amendment protections. The Court, however, now recognizes the need to proceed cautiously in this area and has required states to grant parents more robust rights when state actions take on the character of law enforcement.

**Due Process Protections**

The Fourteenth Amendment's Due Process Clause ordinarily requires state officials to take certain steps to protect individuals from unwarranted state intrusions. These steps are necessary before the state can deprive individuals of life, liberty, and property. As we already have seen, the greater the intrusion on these protected interests, the more likely there will be increased protections and an increased compelling state interest to justify intrusion. Sometimes these steps, which together constitute "due process," may require judicial processes in some instances whereas at other times they will not. At other times, these protections may require judicial processes, but may permit them to occur at different stages of removal.

We already have seen that parents' interests in caring for and controlling their children have long been recognized as "liberty" within the Fourteenth Amendment's terms. Given this highly protected interest, it would seem that due process protections would be quite rigorous if the state wished to remove children from their homes. As we also have seen, however, the interest in child protection also is quite strong. Due process, at first blush, would thus appear to require some sort of process before a state can intrude and remove children from their homes. Because parental rights clearly constitute protected "liberties," the argument is that those liberties can only be interrupted after some sort of hearing. Unfortunately, the rule is not that simple; procedural due process permits exceptions and is marked by considerable flexibility. Procedural due process protections quite often allow postdeprivation processes rather than require legal processes before the state can act. Indeed, the classic case that guides this area of law, *Mathews v. Eldridge* (1976), actually approved of postdeprivation hearings, an approval that reveals how due process can be delayed and even modified in civil cases.

In *Mathews*, a Social Security disability recipient, Eldgridge, challenged the termination of his benefit payments, arguing that the state must afford him an opportunity for an evidentiary hearing before termination. After considering reports from Eldridge and his physician, as well as other information in his file, the agency informed Eldridge by letter that it had made a tentative determination that he no longer had a disability, which meant that the state soon could terminate his benefits. The letter included a statement of reasons for the proposed termination of benefits and advised Eldridge that he might request reasonable time in which to obtain and submit additional information pertaining to his condition. In his written response, Eldridge disputed one characterization of his medical condition and concluded that the agency already possessed enough evidence to establish his disability. The state agency then made its final determination that he had ceased to be disabled; the agency then proceeded to terminate his benefits. The notification also had advised him of his right to seek, within six months, reconsideration by the state agency of this initial determination. Instead of requesting reconsideration, Eldridge took legal action to challenge the constitutional validity of the administrative procedures for assessing whether a continuing disability existed. Eldridge, who suffered from chronic anxiety and back problems, argued that he had a right to an "evidentiary hearing" before the termination of benefits.

The Supreme Court disagreed with Eldridge. In announcing its decision, the Court reemphasized the flexibility of due process that calls for such procedural protections as the particular situation demands. The Court then formulated what has become the standard test for determining whether processes afforded in a governmental adjudication comport with Fifth and Fourteenth Amendment due process protections. *Mathews* held that procedural safeguards are to be evaluated using a three-part test: (a) the nature of the private interest to be affected by the government action; (b) the risk of erroneous deprivation and the effect of additional safeguards; and (c) the governmental interests involved, including the fiscal and administrative burdens of additional or substitute procedural requirements would entail (p. 335). Recognizing the administration of child welfare regulations and policies as constituting a civil system, the Court frequently applies this test throughout child welfare law, as we soon will see below. Lower courts follow suit; the test has become so common that it proceeds unquestioned.

*Mathews* may well apply in rescue situations and most likely does, but the Court has yet to address the matter. Other areas of law that have examined the provision of due process after state intrusion—called post-deprivation cases—are illustrative. Using variations of the *Mathews* test, the Supreme Court has found many instances in which post-deprivation protections can satisfy due process requirements. Most notably, for example, the court has held that the existence of common law remedies (which follow wrongs) can satisfy procedural due process under certain, unusual circumstances. This was so in *Ingraham v. Wright* (1977), in which the Court concluded, in light of common law remedies, that a hearing is not needed before a student can be subjected to corporal punishment in schools. The Court also has found that statutorily created postdeprivation processes can prove sufficient to protect civil liberties. This was the case in *Parratt v. Taylor* (1981, p. 539), in which the Court held that postdeprivation remedies can satisfy procedural due process when the wrong is "random and unauthorized." States can satisfy the requirements of procedural due process when they require either the necessity of quick state action or the impracticality of providing any meaningful predeprivation process, when coupled with the availability of some meaningful means by which to assess the propriety of the state's action at some time after the initial taking. Note, however, that the Court has explicitly stated, for example, in *Medina v. California* (1992), that the *Mathews* test does not apply to criminal cases. These cases are of significance. Given that remedies may exist after the initial rescue and that we are dealing with civil deprivations that may involve exigent circumstances, existing jurisprudence supports the claim that due process protections may be satisfied after a child's initial removal. Although we are left with the need to consider the potential implications of using law enforcement in child protection cases, it appears clear that deprivations in rescues may satisfy due process requirements either before or shortly after rescues.

Whether the deprivations actually can survive the *Mathews* test in practice depends on the test's application. The Court can quite readily find rescues permissible without much process before the rescue as long as adequate protections exist after. We know that parents clearly have important rights at stake. So does the government have an important interest, which, for the purposes of the *Mathews'* balancing test, is less a general interest in protecting children than a more narrow interest in protecting children in the short time before the state can hold a termination or shelter hearing. The state obviously can take more narrow approaches to the initial rescue, such as monitoring, interviewing, and inspecting. But, these alternatives do not negate the appropriateness of rescues. Rescues may well be the most reasonable response in the state's effort to create a system that efficiently responds when children have been removed from their families and homes. The balance of protections reveals the premium placed on child protection. Even if investigations indicate no support for allegations of abuse, rescued children in those situations were not necessarily removed improperly. The state must act to determine the weight to place on allegations.

The practice of foregoing prerescue judicial authorization in favor of contested postrescue process in child abuse cases certainly receives constitutional support. Indeed, the Court, a few years before *Mathews*, summarily ruled that *ex parte* judicial proceedings can be constitutionally used to rescue children from their homes. (*Ex parte* proceedings are those brought by one person in the absence of another.) In that case, *Newton v. Burgin* (1974), a mother had been placed in custody after having been arrested for unlawful possession of narcotics while sitting in the backseat of a car with her 2-year-old daughter. Not knowing what else to do with the daughter, the state placed her in an emergency receiving home maintained by the state. The mother was released a few hours after her arrest but was unable to regain physical custody of her daughter without waiting for a hearing. In her legal challenge to the law, she alleged that the temporary, emergency removal violated her due process rights. The court was asked whether the state had violated the mother's rights by only offering a hearing on the merits at the earliest practicable time within 5 days after assuming custody or the child must be released. Considering the interests of both parties, the court did not find it an unreasonable or arbitrary length of time. The Supreme Court summarily approved of the lower court's rejection of the mother's complaint. Regrettably for us, the Court did so without writing an opinion. The absence of a written Court opinion on the matter leaves the case open to different interpretations, but the case itself reveals that rescues require fewer procedures to protect the rights of those involved, mainly because the law deems it tentative and less of an infringement on the rights of caretakers or the rights of the child to be with those caretakers. In many ways, the Court's position was unsurprising. The Supreme Court remains careful not to limit the concept of due process to a particular set of rules. The Court leaves room for extraordinary situations that can justify postponing hearings until after the state's intervention, even in contexts that reveal a general need for close judicial oversight.

## Providing Services and Alternative Care

When a state fears for the endangerment of a child's health or safety, it can intervene in an otherwise-autonomous family to resolve the threat or remove the child. The state's efforts to resolve the threat before removing the child or to permit the child to return home after the threat is removed are parts of a "reasonable efforts" mandate. When the state retains custody of the child, the court often orders the state to provide certain services for the parents or orders the parents to obtain needed services. Such services may include psychological counseling, substance-abuse treatment, parenting classes, homemaker assistance, and other services to remedy deficiencies that led to the child's removal from the home. Such services serve to facilitate the reunification of the family. However, in certain situations, the court may relieve the state from making reasonable efforts to reunify a family. Once a child has been placed in foster care, the court holds periodic reviews with the parties. Various rationales support the need for reviews, but the major reason for their use rests on the manner the foster care system operates on the assumption that it provides temporary shelters meant either to expedite children's return home or to successful adoptions. The length of time a particular child stays away from the family and the ultimate decision regarding the child's long-term care largely depends on the nature of the state's response, the manner it defines and implements its reasonable efforts mandates.

Although it may seem that children's needs would dictate a state's response, the nature of the state's response generally depends on self-imposed burdens. Individual states design and maintain prevention and foster care programs. The federal government, however, still plays an important role as it uses the power of the purse to guide state policies toward its preferred ways of designing child welfare programs. Congress grants funds to states only when their laws comply with congressional mandates. As a result, understanding the provision of services and alternative care again requires that we closely examine federal, state, and constitutional mandates.

## Federal Mandates

Two major legislative efforts guide the federal government's role in ensuring that maltreated children receive adequate care. The *Adoption and Safe Families Act* (ASFA) (1997) now primarily regulates the implementation of efforts that seek to prevent and, where necessary, provide alternative care. The statute, however, is best understood in light of the groundbreaking legislation it amended, the *Adoption Assistance and Child Welfare Act* (Child Welfare Act) (1980). The Child Welfare Act was Congress's first major effort, through its spending powers, to help states provide services to keep children in their homes and secure adoptions for children who cannot return home after having entered the foster care system. Before 1980, the federal government had reimbursed states for foster care expenses but had not offered comparable financial support for adoption or prevention and reunification services. As passed in 1980, the Child Welfare Act continued to reimburse states for foster care maintenance payments but it also offered additional funding for child protection, family intervention, and adoption services for children with special needs. The federal government conditioned each state's funding, however, on their compliance with federal requirements. ASFA pushed federal mandates into somewhat different directions, most notably toward a more obvious focus on ensuring child safety and hastening stability. Together, these two statutes reveal the remarkable extent to which federal mandates can shape responses to children at risk.

A requirement most relevant to our discussion was Part E of the Child Welfare Act. That part required states to have an approved plan for administering child protective services. Each state's plan must provide, among other things, that "in each case, reasonable efforts will be made (A) prior to placement of a child in foster care, to prevent or eliminate the need for removal of the child from his home, and (B) to make it possible for the child to return to his home." This mandate has become commonly known as the "reasonable efforts" provision. The Child Welfare Act had sought to provide adequate services early to diminish the need for more costly foster care placements. By requiring states to provide adequate services, the reasonable efforts provision narrowed the criteria for entering foster care to those children who could not sufficiently benefit from family preservation services. Once children entered foster care, the reasonable effort provision narrowed the criteria for remaining in foster care to those children who could not sufficiently benefit from reunification services. The reasonable efforts mandate, then, encouraged states to reduce the use, especially the extended use, of the child welfare system. The mandate did so by reducing the need for the foster care system through family preservation efforts and promoting adoption incentives whose primary economic purpose consisted of expediting exits from the foster care system.

The general understanding of reasonable efforts as a service enforcement provision made theoretical sense, but it had and continues to face many practical challenges. The federal requirement to make reasonable efforts was not guided by standards to assess reasonable efforts. This eventually led to criticisms that the focus on reunification inhibited child safety and protection and that too many children were caught in "foster care drift" without a sense of permanency. These criticisms and other similar ones led to a major overhaul of the Child Welfare Act. That overhaul took the form of the Adoption and Safe Families Act. As the title suggests, the focus of the new and still controlling legislative mandates sought to promote permanency and prioritize child safety. Congress did so by modifying the reasonable efforts requirement and by setting strict deadlines for implementing placement plans (the case plans the state must have in place for every child under state supervision).

For our purposes, ASFA urged two important changes especially worth considering. The first change dealt with the act's new timelines regulating the amount of time children can remain in foster care before being placed for adoption. The Child Welfare Act had required that every child in foster care receive a dispositional hearing within the first eighteen months in state custody. ASFA reduced that time frame as it, quite tellingly, relabeled ASFA "dispositional" hearings as "permanency" hearings. ASFA required states to hold those hearings within the child's first 12 months in foster care and at least once every 12 months as long as the child remained in state custody. ASFA also required every child in foster care to receive a permanent plan within 12 months. Significantly, ASFA directed states to petition a court for termination of parental rights once a child had resided in state custody for 15 of the most recent 22 months. Importantly, a state could be excused from this obligation if: (a) the state has placed the child in the care of a relative; (b) the state can provide a compelling reason for maintaining the parental relationship; or (c) the state has failed to provide reasonable efforts to reunite the family. By establishing a new and shortened timeline for termination of parental rights, this amendment would become ASFA's hallmark provision.

The second change involved clarifying what was meant by reasonable efforts. The amended section 671(a)(15) has six subparts. Subpart (A) requires that, in making reasonable efforts and in determining whether reasonable efforts had been made, "the child's health and safety shall be the paramount concern." Subpart (A) explicitly requires reasonable efforts to not compromise children's safety. Unlike prior legislation, this mandate provides that "reasonable efforts shall be made to preserve and reunify families: (i) prior to the placement of a child in foster care, to prevent or eliminate the need for removing the child from the child's home; and (ii) to make it possible for a child to safely return to the child's home." This subpart essentially preserves the reasonable efforts language under the 1980 Child Welfare Act. However, subpart (C) extends the reasonable efforts mandate beyond family preservation and reunification to include permanency. Under this part, the state must make reasonable efforts "to place the child in a timely manner in accordance with the permanency plan, and to complete whatever steps are necessary to finalize the permanent placement of the child." Subpart (D) excuses states from making reasonable efforts based largely on a parent's current and previous conduct. This shift in focus away from preservation permits states to not make reasonable efforts where the parent has performed any of several specific acts: (a) subjected the child to aggravated circumstances (as defined by state law); (b) committed murder or voluntary manslaughter of another child of the parent; (c) aided or abetted, attempted, conspired, or solicited to commit such murder or manslaughter; or (d) committed a felony assault that results in serious bodily injury to the child or another child of the parent. Subpart (E) holds that a state that adopts subpart (D)'s approach must provide a permanency hearing within 30 days rather than the usual 18 months under the Child Welfare Act. Finally, subpart (F) explicitly authorizes concurrent planning, a form of case management that permits states to make, simultaneously, reasonable efforts toward a permanent out-of-home placement and reasonable efforts toward reunification at the same time. The reasonable efforts amendments and the revised timelines significantly redefine and reduce the force of the reasonable efforts standard that had been meant to secure efforts to reunify children with their families. To a large extent, by focusing on child safety, federal legislative mandates tend to encourage out of home care.

## State Legislative Responses

What constitutes reasonable efforts to address a child's circumstances obviously varies from one case to the next. Broad legal rules, however, determine the state's various possible responses. Federal mandates leave state legislatures with the authority to define reasonable efforts, promulgate regulations and policies for implementing reasonable efforts, and set criteria for determining whether the state has complied sufficiently to directives. Understanding the general shape of responses to ASFA provides us with a good understanding of laws regulating the use of alternative care.

A close look at state legislative mandates reveals several general patterns (see Appendix B for citations). One pattern shows that states generally have not availed themselves of the opportunity to define standards by which to assess the provision of child welfare services. States have responded to federal legislative mandates by, for example, making child safety the paramount concern in determining the extent to which reasonable efforts should be made to reunite families. Typically, these statutes simply repeat the reasonable efforts provision as it appears in federal law or add language limiting the state's burden to make reasonable efforts. For example, Alabama, Maryland, Georgia, Texas, and Rhode Island all enacted statutes that essentially mimic ASFA's reasonable efforts provision. These states appear to have done little else legislatively to define reasonable efforts. In a few states, such as Arizona, Kentucky, Louisiana, and Missouri, lawmakers have specified more aspects of the reasonable efforts requirement, but these additions limit those states' obligations to make reasonable efforts. For example, Arkansas law provides that the "agency shall exercise reasonable diligence and care to utilize all available services." The limitation that emerges from this kind of statute rests in the availability of services. Limitations like these could be interpreted as relieving a state from making reasonable efforts even if the unavailable service consists of a basic offering within the child protective services field. By limiting a state's obligation to available services, these statutes run the risk of failing to hold a state adequately accountable for services that families could need to overcome their circumstances.

Another pattern that emerges in states' responses to federal mandates deals with the manner states provide more reasons for not making reasonable efforts to preserve or unify families. All states now provide, for example, several ways to avoid providing rehabilitative services, such as when the parent has subjected the child to aggravated circumstances (torture, sexual abuse, abandonment) or the parent has committed murder or voluntary manslaughter of a sibling. Most notable in this pattern is that many states now have gone beyond mandates and include rather lengthy lists of conditions that no longer require states to provide reunification services. These conditions include, for example, the parent has committed murder or voluntary manslaughter of the other parent (Alaska, Indiana, Maryland, New Hampshire, New Mexico, Oregon, Virginia, Washington, and West Virginia), the parent suffers from chronic abuse of drugs or alcohol and has refused or failed treatment (California, Kentucky, North Dakota, Ohio, Oklahoma, and South Dakota), the parent has allowed the child to be present where a clandestine illegal laboratory is operated (Utah), the parent has been found to be a sexual violent predator (Washington) or a registered sex offender (Oklahoma), the parent has been incarcerated for a long term in relation to the child's age, and there is no suitable relative to care for the child (Alaska, Arizona, California, Kentucky, Maryland, and Utah), the parent has been convicted of a violent felony (California), the child was conceived as a result of a sexual offense (California), or the parental rights of the parents to a sibling have been terminated involuntarily (e.g., Alaska, Arizona, Arkansas, California, Colorado, Connecticut, Florida, Georgia, Hawaii, and Idaho). These provisions reflect states' move toward expediting children's transfer to more stable care, and the recognition that some relationships must be severed so that the state can secure permanent, alternative care.

Yet another pattern involves attempts to delineate more clearly the meaning of reasonable efforts. These statutes range from those that generically describe the kinds of services or actions expected of the state agency to those that delineate the needed services with much more specificity, sometimes enumerating particular services to be provided by families. Many states describe reasonable efforts by providing that the agency must act "diligently" and offer "appropriate services." Florida law, for example, provides that "reasonable effort means the exercise of reasonable diligence and care by the department to provide the services ordered by the court or delineated in the case plan." North Dakota defines reasonable efforts as "the exercise of due diligence, by the agency granted authority over the child...to use appropriate and available services to meet the needs of the child and the child's family." New Hampshire law provides that in deciding "whether the state has made reasonable efforts...the district court shall consider whether services to the family have been accessible, available, and appropriate." Note here that New Hampshire uses the availability of services as a standard for a reasonable efforts judicial determination rather than a limitation on what the state must do. Pursuant to this statute, the question could be whether the state made services available, not whether the state used available services.

Other state statutes require agencies to use "every reasonable opportunity" for reunification (Hawaii) or to "actively offer" reunification services (Alaska). Statutes in other states define reasonable efforts in ways that clearly exceed the more common and somewhat basic requirements to act diligently and provide appropriate services. Colorado law expands the reasonable efforts definition to include the responsibility "to provide, purchase, or develop the supportive and rehabilitative services" required to prevent placement or achieve reunification (Colorado). Under South Dakota law, reasonable efforts "mean provision by the department of any assistance or services that:...are available pursuant to the comprehensive plan of preventive services of the department; [or] could be made available without undue financial burden on the department...." New York law calls for "diligent efforts" defined as "reasonable attempts" by the agency to "assist, develop and encourage a meaningful relationship between the parent and the child." New York law further provides that the court may order diligent efforts to include assistance "in obtaining adequate housing, employment, counseling, medical care or psychiatric treatment."

Other states go even further as they specify that the burden of making reasonable efforts begins not with the parent but with the state, the party intervening in the family. Ohio and other states (Montana and Tennessee) have added language to their statutes explaining that the "agency shall have the burden of proving that it has made those reasonable efforts." Similarly, Alaska law establishes that the "department's duty to make reasonable efforts...includes the duty to: identify family support services...; actively offer the parent or guardian, and refer the parent of guardian to, those services;...and document the department's actions that are taken...." Although parents must be held accountable for failing to participate in the services provided, the obligation to make reasonable efforts begins with the state, not the parent. Together, these states reveal how surprisingly few have taken steps to specify what they would provide families when the state has concluded that it must intervene. This lacunae again reflects more concern for child safety than for delineating the state's responsibility to maintain relationships.

Another important pattern that emerges involves the manner some state statutes provide guidance relating to the provision of reasonable efforts. For example, statutes can guide court determinations of whether state agencies have made reasonable efforts. Several states detail the type of efforts agencies must provide or the quality of services the courts should consider when assessing reunification efforts for reasonableness. Under Iowa law, for example, the court considers the "type, duration, and intensity of services or support offered or provided...." According to Minnesota's statute, courts must consider whether services were relevant, adequate, culturally appropriate, available, accessible, consistent, timely, and realistic. The New Jersey regulations also require an ongoing assessment of agency efforts through consultation and observation of services and through the identification of barriers and formulation of ways to overcome those barriers. Nevada law instructs courts in determining reasonable efforts to "evaluate the evidence and make findings based on whether a reasonable person would conclude that reasonable efforts were made," and to consider "any input from the child." In Wisconsin, a court's consideration of reasonable efforts includes whether "a comprehensive assessment of the family's situation was completed" and whether the family received "financial assistance." These are important developments that highlight the judicial control over state agencies. Another major example of the ways states provide guidance in the implementation of reasonable efforts requirements involves how some statutes instruct courts in how to draft orders regarding reasonable efforts determinations. A few states (e.g., Connecticut, Iowa, Minnesota, South Dakota, and Wisconsin) have expanded the meaning of reasonable efforts in the instructions they have provided to state courts reviewing agency compliance. Another handful of states (e.g., Oregon, Florida, Louisiana, and West Virginia) charge courts with a general duty to detail what reasonable efforts were made and why further efforts are not needed. These states generally ask reviewing courts to enter a brief description of what preventive and reunification efforts were made and why further efforts could or could not have prevented or shortened the separation of the family. These important efforts reveal not only the power of courts to direct the work of agencies but also the power of legislatures to direct the courts.

A last pattern worth highlighting involves the use of concurrent planning to limit reasonable efforts (see Appendix B for citations). All states now either permit or require concurrent planning, which allows states to make both reasonable efforts to place a child for adoption or other permanent care while making reasonable efforts to preserve and reunify the family. This approach is of significance in that it means that states do much more than identify alternative plans; states also make reasonable efforts to implement both plans simultaneously. In the absence of concurrent planning (when it is not mandated but merely permitted), states follow the traditional approach of sequential planning for permanency. The statutes' language relating to concurrent planning varies considerably. For example, the majority of states simply allow for it or note that concurrent planning may be used (Alabama, Alaska, Arizona, Arkansas, Colorado, Florida, Georgia, Iowa, Louisiana, Maine, Maryland, Minnesota, Montana, Nebraska, Nevada, North Carolina, North Dakota, Rhode Island, South Carolina, Tennessee, Washington, West Virginia, and Wisconsin). Others state that concurrent planning shall be used (California, Idaho, Illinois, Massachusetts, Mississippi, New Hampshire, New Jersey, New Mexico, Oregon, Texas, Utah, and Wyoming). Some simply state that guidelines shall be established (Connecticut), whereas others mandate that concurrent planning "shall be considered" as opposed to being required (Oklahoma). Note, however, that there are complexities as to when concurrent planning should occur. Wyoming, for example, finds that efforts to reunify while making alternative plans are to be concurrent with termination of parental rights petition as well as with concurrent with efforts to reunify. Regardless of the diversity, these statutes reflect the trend toward giving less time for families to ameliorate their circumstances and less time for children to be without a more permanent, stable family environment.

Overall and with some differences, a close look at state legislative mandates reveals that nearly all states have enacted legislation requiring state agencies to make reasonable efforts to preserve or reunify families. The extent to which states incorporated ASFA's mandates in their legislation suggests a softening of the significance of reasonable efforts after ASFA. This weakening of the reasonable efforts clause can be seen in the strong emphasis states have placed on making health and safety the paramount concern and the relatively weak emphasis states have given to requiring reasonable efforts to finalize a permanent placement. The vast majority of states have enacted legislation emphasizing the "paramount" nature of the child's health and safety in dependency proceedings. Neither the "health and safety" provision nor the provision permitting states to waive their reasonable efforts obligation impose on states an affirmative duty to provide services. Indeed, both provisions arguably encourage the opposite. In addition, it is important to note that state courts have discretion to waive reasonable efforts to protect a child's health and safety, even if none of the conditions that waive reasonable efforts exists. State courts need such flexibility to respond appropriately to individual cases. Yet, granting such flexibility unintentionally weakens the requirements of the reasonable efforts clause, as further demonstrated by the relatively soft legislative emphasis states have placed on reasonable efforts toward permanency and the comparably heavy emphasis they have placed on the provisions that waive reasonable efforts. This suggests that states view ASFA's clarification of reasonable efforts primarily as legislation diluting the obligation to make reasonable efforts to reunify families. The legislatures thus appear to agree with the primacy ASFA accords to the health and safety of the child.

## Constitutional Mandates

We already have seen that the Court recognizes the importance of family integrity, but the Court has stopped short of requiring states to provide parents with funds that would enable them to raise their own children. Instead, rights associated with family life have been defined negatively—as the right to have the government leave you alone. This approach to respecting rights gains considerable significance when we consider the rights of family members when the state deems it appropriate to interfere to protect children's welfare. To understand the implications of this approach in this context, we return to two cases we have explored briefly before for different reasons and proceed to examine two others that highlight their significance.

The difference between two cases we already have examined, *Wisconsin v. Yoder* (1972) and *Dandridge v. Williams* (1970), highlights well the narrowness of the constitutional right to affirmative assistance, even when the right involved is fundamental, such as the rights of parents to raise their children as they see fit. Recall that *Yoder* remains one of the most powerful cases establishing the fundamental right of parents to direct their children's upbringing. Weighing the state's interest in ensuring that its citizens receive public educations against parents' right to family integrity, the Court fell squarely on the side of families and the need to provide them with opportunities to reach state goals through different means. In that case, the state of Wisconsin had criminally prosecuted a group of Amish parents for failing to send their children to high school. The Court had found the state's application of its compulsory schooling law to this particular group of parents contrary to the Constitutional right of parents to raise their children without unnecessary government intrusion, in accordance with their religion. A strong majority opinion had hinted that the Court was willing to enforce such a right only within certain limits. Explaining its reasoning, the Court had noted that the Amish are financially independent and do not take advantage of public assistance programs. This observation suggests that the Court would have been less enthusiastic about reaffirming the "primary role of the parents in the upbringing of their children . . . now established . . . as an enduring American tradition" if the plaintiffs had been poor families who depended on the state for financial assistance (*Wisconsin v. Yoder,* 1972, p. 232). When the Court had addressed a poor family's right to financial assistance, it clearly had noted the limits of the state's largesse on behalf of parental rights to control their children's upbringing. Given the status of family integrity as a fundamental right protected by the Constitution, one might expect the federal courts to require the government to ensure poor families a subsistence-level income to preserve the integrity of their families. Yet the Supreme Court has declined to treat financial assistance as a constitutionally protected right, viewing it instead as an economic issue, an area in which the government enjoys wide discretion to support or ignore. The leading case in this area, *Dandridge v. Williams* (1970), involved Maryland's public assistance scheme. That scheme capped benefits at a fixed maximum once families had reached a certain size. Additional children born after families had reached that size would not receive the benefits to which additional children in smaller families were entitled.

The Court found nothing unconstitutional about the state's limitations on what it financially offered parents to raise their children. It held that this differential treatment of children based on the size of their families did not violate the Equal Protection Clause of the Fourteenth Amendment. Finding that the benefit cap did not impact the families' constitutionally protected fundamental rights, the Court declined to apply a heightened standard of equal protection review and concluded that the state should be allowed great discretion in deciding how to allocate its limited funding for social services. Thus, the self-sufficient Amish plaintiffs in *Yoder* were free to keep to themselves and offer their children community supported opportunities, whereas the families in *Dandridge* were rebuffed when they asked the Court to protect them from a threat—poverty—considered not of the state's creation.

The difference between the above two cases gains significance in light of the constitutional obligations states have to individuals when a state takes them under its care. The Court already has examined the extent to which individuals who are in state care have a right to services in furtherance of their rehabilitation. The leading case in this area is *Youngberg v. Romeo* (1982). In that case, the Supreme Court considered whether and to what extent civilly committed individuals have rights to state-provided rehabilitation and training. In this instance, a mother had become unable to care for her developmentally disabled child and had relinquished his care to the state. The Court concluded that such persons have a limited positive right to receive such rehabilitative training services as are required by minimum standards of professional judgment, in order to reduce the risk of endangering themselves or others and to reduce or eliminate the institution's need to use bodily restraints. Failure to provide such training—resulting in deterioration and the need for restraints—would amount to an additional and impermissible intrusion on their liberty interests, beyond that justified by the state's interest in maintaining their confinement. In rendering its ruling, the *Youngberg* Court identified circumstances under which the Constitution does require the state to take affirmative steps to protect its citizens. When the government takes individuals into protective custody against their will, removing them from other sources of assistance, it undertakes a positive obligation to provide them with basic necessities, a safe environment, and treatment designed according to minimum standards of professional judgment to maximize their liberty.

*Youngberg* clearly reveals the state's obligations, but those obligations arise when individuals are directly in the state's care. If the state intervenes to protect children, but the child's formal custody remains with a parent, children who are harmed in these situations do not have a constitutional claim against the state. This was the result of *DeShaney v. Winnebago* (1989). That case involved a claim that the state had failed to fulfill sufficiently its obligations to protect children. In *DeShaney*, a case manager, acting as an agent of the state, observed a pattern of child abuse that ultimately resulted in irreversible brain damage. Despite knowing virtually every significant step in the escalation of abuse, the case manager took no concrete action to rescue or otherwise protect the child. Joshua DeShaney's father had severely beaten him over a period of more than 2 years, during which time Joshua had made at least four abuse-related hospital or emergency room visits. After the second emergency room visit, Joshua remained in the temporary custody of the hospital, but the state released him back to his father's custody when the father agreed to comply with certain goals. The father never fully complied. During the next year, Joshua's case manager observed injuries to the child's head and eventually realized that his father had failed to comply with the earlier agreements about how he would address Joshua's needs. On two attempts to visit Joshua, his case manager was told that the child was too ill to see her. On his final trip to an emergency room, Joshua lapsed into a coma. He suffered a series of hemorrhages that left him severely brain damaged, causing him to spend the remainder of his life in an institution for the profoundly retarded. The majority framed the issue before the Court as determining when, if ever, the failure of a state or local government entity or its agents to provide an individual with adequate protective services constitutes a violation of the individual's due process rights. More specifically, the Court asked whether the state had a constitutional duty to protect DeShaney where the Child Protective Services case manager knew or should have known that the child was a victim of abuse. The Court concluded that the state does not assume a constitutional duty to protect despite its knowledge that a child suffered from abuse. Only by acting in a way that restrains freedom, such as by bringing a child into state custody, does the state assume a reciprocal duty to protect the child. The Court held that because the government has no original obligation to extend any kind of assistance to children who are abused or neglected, the Constitution cannot hold states for failing to protect all children from harm caused by private actors. The majority decision distinguished *Youngberg* on the grounds that the state in that case had acted affirmatively to take the plaintiff into custody and effectively had cut him off from other sources of aid and support. Thus, the state did not owe the same obligation of reasonable care and safety to the child who was injured by his father while in his father's custody. The majority opinion rested this area of constitutional jurisprudence on a view of the world in which we can neatly divide harms into two categories: those that are directly caused by some overt act of the state, for which the due process clause provides redress, and those that happen in a separate, private realm, outside of the direct reach of the government and therefore beyond constitutional scrutiny. In the end, *DeShaney* would stand for the simple rule that a state owes no constitutional, affirmative duties to those not in its custody.

The *DeShaney* majority left open the question of whether *Youngberg* might have applied if the plaintiff had been injured while in the state's custody. Given that children placed in care tend to have been placed in that care voluntarily by their parents, it remains quite unclear if constitutional issues would arise given that parents retain control over their children and the state, at least in theory, has not acted in a way that disturbed parents' private actions. When children are placed in foster care against their parents' wishes, *Youngberg* may well support the claim that such children have a right to be free from harm. It still is unclear, however, what would constitute protected rights. *Youngberg* held that those in state custody are entitled to some amount of government assistance to preserve their liberty. It is unclear whether protecting those liberties would also include services designed to preserve their relationships with their families. By taking children away from their parents, the state takes on all the responsibilities of a parent to act in their best interests. The state could therefore be held responsible for taking affirmative steps to fulfill not only their physical needs for safety, food, clothing, and shelter, but also their emotional need to preserve family bonds. The state could be required to mitigate the harm of removing children from their parents, by providing concrete assistance that will help the families overcome the barriers to reunification. Although reasonable, it would be unwise to interpret *Youngberg* so broadly.

The dissenting opinions in *DeShaney* reveal *Youngberg*'s limits. One dissent argued that, by creating a child protective system intended to prevent the type of harm suffered by the plaintiff, and by intervening to protect him, the state had created a legitimate expectation of protection on the part of the plaintiff and any other private parties who might otherwise have acted to help him. Thus, the state harmed the child by failing to assist him while at the same time preventing him from obtaining other forms of assistance, in violation of the holding in *Youngberg*. Another dissent pointed out that *Youngberg* placed an affirmative obligation on the state to remedy not merely the limitations on individual liberty imposed by the custodial arrangement, but also, to some extent, those caused by the condition that led to the state's involvement. This approach viewed *Youngberg* as requiring affirmative steps to protect individuals from harm and that a state must do so in a way that does not cause additional harm and that helps individuals overcome whatever problem they needed protection from, even if that problem was not directly caused by the state. These dissenting views, which highlight what the law does not require, reveal well the limits of the state's constitutional obligations.

The extent to which poorly served children can gain redress in federal courts also finds reflection in cases that have reached the Supreme Court on statutory rather than constitutional grounds. *Suter v. Artist M.* (1992) is illustrative. In *Suter*, the Court more specifically addressed the question of whether an individual child taken into state custody has a federal right to enforce the reasonable efforts mandate directly under the Child Welfare Act, or through an action under 42 U.S.C. 1983 as a beneficiary of the Child Welfare Act. The facts and arguments proposed in *Suter* were straightforward and quite compelling. Section 1983 actions provide individuals with access to federal courts to litigate claims that officials acting under state law deprived them of a constitutional right. As a condition of receiving federal funds under the Child Welfare Act, the state of Illinois had agreed to make reasonable efforts to prevent the removal of children from their homes and to reunify those children with their families should removal become necessary. Artist M., representing a class of plaintiffs including all children who resided or would reside in the custody of Illinois' child protective services agency, argued that the state had failed to make reasonable efforts by failing to promptly appoint case managers to children entering the Child Protective Services system and to reassign children promptly to new case managers when necessary. The *Suter* Court, however, did not even reach the issue of whether the state had satisfied its agreement to make reasonable efforts. The Court instead held that individual private plaintiffs did not have a federally enforceable right to reasonable efforts. Rather than private enforcement by individuals, the Court believed that Congress had intended to have only the Secretary of Health and Human Services enforce the reasonable efforts provision because the Child Welfare

Act granted the Secretary authority to approve each state's plan, and the reasonable efforts provision was part of that plan. The practical impact of the Court's rationale was to soften significantly the enforcement of the Child Welfare Act. *Suter* reveals the immense legal obstacles in the way of efforts to ensure that states enforce their own legal mandates.

## Severing Children's Ties From Their Parents

The termination of parental rights involves the most dramatic legal interference in family life. Termination of parental rights permanently ends the legal parent–child relationship. Parents may voluntarily end their right to their children. To do so, parents can petition the court that has jurisdiction to act in termination and adoption cases. Voluntary termination may be had if a parent's decision is based on their informed consent. Although these cases often result from allegations of maltreatment, we concern ourselves more with involuntary terminations. In these instances, the state, through a child-welfare agency, brings an action for involuntary termination of parental rights when the agency believes it in the children's best interests to free them for adoption. In those instances, the state must prove the parent to be unfit. If the agency is successful, the parents' rights are terminated and a caregiver approved by the state may adopt the children. After parental rights have been terminated, children may be adopted without parental consent. The issue that arises for us to consider is the nature of court proceedings needed to protect the deference paid to the natural rights of parents in their children. Unlike rescues, legal processes that relate to the termination of parental rights have been guided by federal legislative mandates. This section reviews these mandates, the states' responses to them and the constitutional foundations of these requirements.

### *Constitutional Protections*

We already have seen important cases in which the Supreme Court articulated its position that raising one's children involves a basic, fundamental right. The Court did so many times, but its most direct observation derives from *Stanley v. Illinois* (1972), where the Court clearly stated that neither fathers nor mothers can have their children taken from them absent a particularized showing that they are "unfit" as parents. The *Stanley* Court emphatically stated that a parent's right to his or her children is fundamental—"It is plain that the interest of a parent in the companionship, care, custody, and management of his or her children 'come(s) to this Court with a momentum for respect lacking when appeal is made to liberties which derive merely from shifting economic arrangements'" (*Stanley v. Illinois*, 1972, p. 651). The Court continued and recognized that governments that sought to terminate parent–child relationships needed to secure procedural protections for parents. The Court "conclude[d] that, as a matter of due process of law, Stanley was entitled to a hearing on his fitness as a parent before his children were taken from him...." (*Stanley v. Illinois*, 1972, p, 649). The Court was speaking to procedural protections that must accompany permanent deprivations (unlike those involving, for example, rescues). *Stanley* certainly stands for the proposition that the termination of parental rights implicate due process, and that protections must precede permanent separations. Importantly, however, *Stanley* did not involve allegations of maltreatment; it involved a presumption of unfitness; the Court required states to treat unwed fathers more like natural fathers and, to terminate parental rights, the state would need to support its claim of unfitness.

Requiring states to support claims of unfitness raises the complex issue of how much evidence is needed to support such claims. The Court squarely answered this question in *Santosky v. Kramer* (1982). The *Santosky* case began with a determination by a New York state social agency that the Santosky parents, for years, had been neglecting and abusing their children. After determining that the children were in danger of irreparable harm, the sate ordered proceedings to determine whether to legally and permanently terminate the Santosky's parental rights so that their children could be placed for permanent adoption. As with most states, New York made use of bifurcated termination hearings. The first hearing, the fact-finding stage, ensured the due process rights of the parents whereas the second, the dispositional stage, sought to determine the best interests of the child. In *Santosky*, the state had met its threshold burden at the first, fact-finding, stage and had shown by a preponderance of the evidence both that it had (a) provided the parents ample opportunity and assistance in rehabilitating their parental relationship with their children, but that, despite doing so, (b) the parents still had failed to improve their familial situation adequately enough to care for their children. Thus, the Santoskys' case was headed to the second, dispositional, stage where the court would make a final decision as to whether the termination of parental rights would, in fact, be in the children's best interests. Before the dispositional hearing, the Santosky parents challenged the constitutionality of the preponderance of the evidence standard at the fact-finding stage. Although most civil cases use this evidentiary standard, the Santoskys argued that the critical and fundamental interests of parents required greater safeguards, especially in the context of termination. Because the taking of one's children is so traumatic and damaging to a parent, it was argued that the law must take extraordinary steps to ensure the justness of such a decision. The State of New York countered that: (a) its State legislature had already determined that there were vast procedural measures in place that more than adequately protected the due process rights of parents, and (b) the state legislature had already lowered the standard because previously there had been too many children unnecessarily being left to severe abuse and neglect. The state also argued that, in this case, the Santosky parents had benefitted from four-and-a-half years of hearings and appeals that specifically had provided them with opportunities to improve their situation. The state also argued that the only effect of raising the evidentiary burden to the clear and convincing standard would be to make more difficult the removal of children from abusive parents, which would result in leaving more children in troubled homes and overload the already overburdened foster care system. The New York courts affirmed the "preponderance" standard, and the Santosky parents appealed to the U.S. Supreme Court.

Relying on *Meyer v. Nebraska* (1923), *Pierce v. Society of Sisters* (1925) and their progeny, the Supreme Court rejected the use of the preponderance of the evidence standard in parental rights termination proceedings. First, the Court viewed the parents' interests as greater than the interests of their children. It reasoned that the parental interest from termination was grievous and permanent and that society evinced a strong preference to err on the side of keeping families united. The majority thus held that the "only" way to ensure that the greater status of parents—and thus to reflect properly "the value society places on individual liberty" (meaning the liberty of the Santosky parents)—was the clear and convincing evidentiary standard (*Santosky v. Kramer,* 1982, p. 756). In contrast, the "preponderance" standard was said to afford parents only an equal status with children and, therefore, it was declared to be "constitutionally intolerable" (p. 768).

The majority specifically identified how the higher evidentiary standard serves to protect both the substantive and the procedural components of a parent's Due Process rights under the Fourteenth Amendment. The majority found the higher standard necessary to ensure the substantive interests of parents. The Court reasoned that the state would be failing to meet its burden at the fact-finding stage if it used the clear and convincing standard. As the second hearing will thus not be occurring as often, there again will be less intrusion, more families left intact, and more parents with the interests protected. The majority did acknowledge the obvious in that both children (as well as foster parents) are "deeply interested" in the outcome of that fact-finding hearing (*Santosky v. Kramer,* 1982, p. 759). Yet, the Court further decided that at the initial stage "the focus is emphatically not on them," but only on the due process rights of the parents (Id.). In terms of procedural due process rights, the *Santosky* majority noted that there is a particularly high risk that a procedural error committed by a social worker, psychologist, lawyer, or judge, could lead to the undue termination of parent's rights. However, because termination is so devastating to a parent, the Court found a need to increase accordingly the procedural safeguards in these cases. Although the risk of error can never be eliminated altogether, the clear and convincing standard was enlisted to ensure that the analysis favors the more valued interest: those of parents. Thus, the law intends to have any potential procedural error in these cases less likely to harm a parent; and it intends to increase the likelihood that the state will leave the family intact and follow the parents' wishes.

The Court has expanded parents' protections beyond the state's need to reach a high burden of proof. Among the most important provisions have been those involving whether parents are entitled to the appointment of counsel in termination proceedings. The Court directly addressed this issue in *Lassiter v. Department of Social Services* (1981). In this case, a North Carolina state court had found Lassiter's son neglected and transferred his custody to the Department of Social Services. A year later, Lassiter was found guilty of second-degree murder and began serving a sentence of 25–40 years. Two years later, the state petitioned the court to terminate Lassiter's parental rights, alleging that she had failed to have any contact with her son for more than 2 years and had not made efforts to see him. Lassiter was served with the petition and given notice of the termination hearing. Although she appeared at the hearing, she had not retained counsel. The court allowed her to act as her own counsel and, after hearing testimony, it terminated Lassiter's parental rights on the grounds that she had not expressed any concern for the welfare of her child and had willfully failed to maintain responsibility for the child's welfare. Lassiter eventually retained counsel and appealed. Apparently wishing to have her mother raise her child, she argued that indigent parents facing termination of parental rights proceedings have a constitutional right to counsel. The Court disagreed. It held that the Fourteenth Amendment Due Process Clause creates a presumption for the appointment of counsel for indigents only when they will be deprived of their physical liberty. The Court apparently limited full due process rights to cases that would involve criminal proceedings that limit physical freedoms. The Court, however, did recognize that due process rights were involved. It noted that under a case-by-case analysis parents may be able to rebut the presumption and demonstrate that the risk to their First Amendment Right of Association with their child requires appointment of counsel. The Court returned to the *Mathews* approach to determine whether a state must provide certain due process protections. The Court held that the Due Process Clause of the Fourteenth Amendment requires that parents receive representation when "the parents' interest [is] at [its] strongest, the State's interests [are] at their weakest, and the risks of error [are] at their peak" (Lassiter v. Department of Social Sciences Services, 1981, p. 31). The Court observed, for example, that in complicated cases, such as those relying on expert opinions, counsel might be demanded as a matter of due process. It also reasoned that counsel should be appointed when an indigent respondent-parent can show the Court that fundamental fairness presumptively requires appointment of counsel due to the threat of a loss of a child. The majority opinion noted that due process may be violated under certain circumstances if counsel is denied in dependency cases. The Court emphasized that most states recognize the importance of court-appointed counsel for indigent parents are entitled to representation in neglect proceedings as well as in termination proceedings. It even noted that public policy and statutory law prudently recognize the need for these protections, but it still concluded that the Constitution did not.

More recently, in *M.L.B. v. S.L.J.* (1996, p. 128), the Court held that the Constitution entitles indigent parents to a "record of sufficient completeness" to enable an appellate court to thoroughly review a termination order. In that case, M.L.B. sued the father of her two children. The children had been in his custody, as agreed to in the divorce. The father had remarried, and the stepmother wanted to adopt the children; they even sought to have the stepmother declared the birth mother on the children's birth certificates. The father and stepmother claimed that M.L.B. had been remiss in both visitation and child support payments; M.L.B. contended that the father did not allow her reasonable visitation. The mother, however, was unable to appeal because she could not afford to pay for the court records that she would need to challenge the termination of her parental rights. Unable to appeal the decision itself, she appealed to the Supreme Court on the grounds that the state had an obligation to provide her with copies of the records. The Court recognized the state's involvement in severing her rights to her children, the seriousness of terminating parental rights, and the importance of the rights at stake. In holding that the state could not condition M.L.B.'s right to an appeal on her ability to pay, the Court stated, "We place decrees forever terminating parental rights in the category of cases in which the State may not 'bolt the door to equal justice'" (*M.L.B. v. S.L.J.*, 1996, p. 124). The Court viewed termination proceedings as "quasi-criminal" (p. 124) and differentiated these cases "even from other domestic relations matters such as divorce, paternity, and child custody" (p. 127). By equating the liberties to those that could be lost in criminal cases, the Court elevated the rights to a level that would require more protection.

Several holdings, including *Stanley*, *Lassiter*, *Santosky*, and *M.L.B*, demonstrate that families are exceptional in the constitutional scheme of things. Although familial rights are not absolute, they enjoy more constitutional protection than most other rights and interests. This does not mean that states do not have a compelling interest in protecting children. Rather, it simply suggests that parental rights must be constitutionally accommodated. This accommodation comes in many forms, but legislative responses to child maltreatment reveal the extent to which the state takes on the role of parents when parents are deemed to have failed. Indeed, a close look to the statutes to which we now turn reveals that states have become quite aggressive and have given themselves considerable power and discretion to interfere and terminate the rights of parents.

## Federal Statutes

The termination of parental rights may be governed directly by state statutes, but those statutes continue to be guided by federal mandates. On the federal level and as noted earlier, the primary law is the *Adoption and Safe Families Act* of 1997 (ASFA). We already have reviewed previously ASFA's basic components. We noted, for example, that the federal mandates require state agencies to seek termination of the parent–child relationship under a series of specific circumstances that include the parents' behaviors, the child's placement, and the state's resources. The federal mandates also decreased the time all parties have to remedy situations that led to children's removal in the first instance. In addition to those tightly delineated requirements, ASFA provides further guidance to states even when circumstances do not fall within the already delineated circumstances. Most notably, the federal mandates reveal a shift to efforts that make the child's health and safety "paramount." The law places priority on a child's health and safety and on a child's need to have a secure, permanent home as soon as possible. Permanency planning, especially concurrent planning, can influence state's efforts in seeking to terminate parental rights. Together, these mandates encourage states to shift their child welfare programs toward similar priorities and directions.

**State Statutes**

Each state has enacted laws that implement ASFA's requirements for the termination of parental rights, but these laws still differ greatly. For our purposes, we must consider three components of laws. The first aspect of laws to consider involves the standards that states provide courts and child welfare systems to guide the termination of parental rights. The second factor deals with the state standards that describe children's best interests. These considerations are of significance given that what constitutes the best interests of the child is taken into consideration when deciding matters involving the termination of parental rights. As we have seen, ASFA affected both of these standards: petitions for termination are more readily sought and the safety and health of the child are now paramount when considering children's best interests. The third factor, however, has not been guided much by federal statutes, as it involves the types of due process rights parents have to legal representation when states seek to terminate their parental rights.

States vary considerably in the extent to which they elaborate what constitutes grounds for the termination of parental rights. See Appendix B for citations. Generally, state statutes allow the termination of parental rights for harmful conduct directed toward the child and personally destructive behavior that indirectly results in harm to the child, including: failure to correct circumstances that initially brought the child before the court, abuse or neglect of the child, abandonment of the child, failure to treat a substance abuse problem, or a severe mental illness or deficiency that prevents the parent from properly caring for the child. The best interests of the child are taken into consideration when deciding matters involving the termination of parental rights. Some statutes do seem to provide limited grounds for revocation of parental rights, but their key terms are quite vague and permit considerable judicial discretion.

Georgia's approach is illustrative. Georgia law provides numerous grounds for termination based on parental misconduct or inability by finding that, for example, the child has been deprived, lacks proper parental care or control, the deprivation is not likely to be remedied, and the deprivation will cause or is likely to cause serious physical, mental, emotional, or moral harm to the child. In determining whether the child is without proper parental care and control, the court shall consider (without being limited to) the following: a medically verifiable deficiency of the parent's physical, mental, or emotional health of such duration or nature as to render the parent unable to provide adequately for the physical, mental, emotional, or moral condition and needs of the child; excessive use of or history of chronic unrehabilitated abuse of intoxicating liquors or narcotic or dangerous drugs or controlled substances with the effect of rendering the parent incapable of providing adequately for the physical, mental, emotional, or moral condition and needs of the child; conviction of the parent of a felony and imprisonment therefore that has a demonstrable negative effect on the quality of the parent–child relationship; egregious conduct or evidence of past egregious conduct of the parent toward the child or toward another child of a physically, emotionally, or sexually cruel or abusive nature; physical, mental, or emotional neglect of the child or evidence of past physical, mental, or emotional neglect of the child or of another child by the parent; and injury or death of a sibling under circumstances which constitute substantial evidence that such injury or death resulted from parental neglect or abuse. When the child is not in custody, the court will consider whether the child is without proper parental care and control, without being limited to, whether the parent without justifiable cause has failed significantly for a period of 1 year or longer prior to the filing of the petition for termination of parental rights: (a) to develop and maintain a parental bond with the child in a meaningful, supportive manner; (b) to provide for the care and support of the child as required by law or judicial decree; and (c) to comply with a court ordered plan designed to reunite the child with the parent or parents, or the parent has been convicted of the murder of the child's other parent. The statute continues and notes that the standard for review shall be clear and convincing evidence. If there is clear and convincing evidence of such parental misconduct or inability, the court shall then consider whether termination of parental rights is in the best interest of the child, after considering the physical, mental, emotional, and moral condition and needs of the child who is the subject of the proceeding, including the need for a secure and stable home. If the court finds clear and convincing evidence of the circumstance alleged, the court shall presume that termination of parental rights is in the child's best interest. As the statute illustrates, the legislation provides considerable discretion to the court. That discretion, however, may be somewhat limited by two factors. The first limiting factor is the consideration courts use to determine what is in the best interests of children and the second factor involves procedures that courts must respect, such as those involving the right to counsel.

In terms of the best-interests standard, most states provide lists of factors for courts to consider. This approach generally leaves considerable discretion to courts (see Appendix B for citations to statutory mandates). Some statutes are quite detailed, whereas others are quite narrow. For example, Nevada states that "[T]he legislature finds that the continuing needs of a child for proper physical, mental, and emotional growth and development are the decisive consideration in proceedings for termination of parental rights." On the other side of the spectrum, Florida's approach is illustrative as it enumerates many factors. The Florida statute lists numerous factors the court "shall consider" but notes that the evaluation of relevant factors are not limited to the list. For example, the court examines the ability and disposition of the parents to provide for the child; the capacity of the parents to care for the child's child's safety, well-being, and physical, mental, and emotional health; the present and future needs of the child; the love, affection, and other emotional ties existing between the child and the child's parent or parents, siblings, and other relatives, and the degree of harm to the child that would arise from the termination of parental rights and duties; the likelihood of an older child remaining in long-term foster care upon termination of parental rights, due to emotional or behavioral problems or any special needs of the child; the depth of the relationship existing between the child and the present custodian; the reasonable preferences and wishes of the child, if the court deems the child to be of sufficient intelligence, understanding, and experience to express a preference; and the recommendations for the child provided by the child's guardian ad litem or legal representative.

The second approach to determining the child's best interests appears much more narrow and follows directly from federal mandates that place a premium on child safety. For example, although some courts are required to consider the best interests of the child, statutes now explicitly require courts to keep the health and safety of the child as its paramount concern (Alaska, Arizona, Idaho, Illinois, Iowa, Louisiana, Massachusetts, Montana, New Jersey, New York, North Carolina, Washington, and Wyoming). Importantly, the other statutes are so vague that they allow for this focus over, for example, family preservation. This focus is revealed by, for example, by statutes that center on preserving the unit of the family whenever possible or receive care, preferably in the child's own home (Alabama, Colorado, Indiana, Pennsylvania, and South Carolina). Whether the factors to be considered in determining the best interests of the child are provided by statute or determined by the judge, courts make decisions on an individual case by case basis. As we can tell from the typical statutory language, this approach leaves much discretion to courts.

Several states provide a statutory right to counsel for indigent parents involved in termination proceedings (see Appendix B for citations). The procedural safeguards provided by such laws differ widely. Most states explicitly provide for counsel at all proceedings involving states' responses to abuse and neglect allegations and require appointment of counsel in instances of indigence. Iowa's statute is illustrative. It provides that, upon the filing of a petition that the child is in need of services, the parent, guardian, or custodian identified in the petition "shall have the right to counsel in connection with all subsequent hearings and proceedings;" it further provides that, "if that person desires but is financially unable to employ counsel, the court shall appoint counsel." Several states tend to take a similar approach, including Alaska, Arkansas, Connecticut, Florida, Kansas, Louisiana, Maryland, Massachusetts, Missouri, Montana, New Mexico, North Carolina, North Dakota, Oregon, South Carolina, South Dakota, Utah, Virginia, Washington, and West Virginia. Some states, like Arizona, have provisions that simply state that individuals are entitled to counsel in such proceedings, without stating how secure that right is if, for example, they cannot afford to retain their own counsel. Others, however, explicitly provide for counsel at termination proceedings. This means that the scope of representation may not include the dependency hearings that precede the adjudication of parental rights; see Colorado, Idaho, Indiana, Wisconsin, Nebraska, New Jersey, New York, Pennsylvania, Rhode Island, and Texas. In yet other states, Alabama and Maine, parents may not be entitled to court-appointed representation (such as in case of indigence) unless it is requested. Other states, such as Georgia, make is less clear and provide only if parents desire counsel. Other states simply leave matters to the court and condition the right on the court's discretion, such as Wyoming and Nevada. Yet others limit it to whether it "appears reasonably necessary in the interests of justice" (Kentucky) or in cases in which the court "feels that such an appointment is appropriate" (Minnesota). Importantly, some states more explicitly provide for the procedural rights possessed by parents. Illinois and Washington, for example, require that when a parent, guardian, legal custodian or responsible relative are parties to dependency proceedings, they have the right to be present, to be heard, to present evidence material to the proceedings, to cross-examine witnesses, to examine pertinent court files and records and also the right to be represented by counsel. At the request of any party financially unable to employ counsel, the state will provide counsel. These more specific statutes, however, still remain a rarity.

## Representing Children's Independent Interests

We just have found that parents' rights in child protection proceedings, especially proceedings that seek to terminate parental rights, involve the type of rights that deserves considerable protection. This is not necessarily the case for children's own rights to relationships. It is not always clear what rights children control when they become involved in child protection efforts. This ambiguity derives from children's peculiar legal status. Children in child protective proceedings generally lack a clear legal status, even though the proceedings are about them. This ambivalent status is of significance given that an individual's legal status determines the nature of their rights, their entitlement to legal representation in legal proceedings, and, if entitled, the representative's relative authority and obligations. This section examines this lack of clear consensus about children's status and their rights and details important implications these uncertainties have for the legal representation of children in child protection proceedings.

### *Constitutional Mandates*

As with many other areas of child welfare law, no firm legal precedent guides our analysis of children's right to representation relating to child welfare proceedings. As with the rights of parents, however, we can identify two constitutional bases to support the need for representation. Entitlement to legal representation could result from either the constitutional right to counsel under the 6th Amendment or the more general constitutional due process protections under the 14th Amendment. Although it may well be that the Court would not recognize children's own independent rights, understanding the potential contours of this area of law requires us to understand the nature of these rights that would support the right to legal representation.

Individuals involved in legal proceedings against the state tend to believe that they have a right to counsel. Yet, the legal rule providing for legal proceedings is not that absolute. For example, the 6th Amendment to the United States Constitution, the only one that directly speaks to these issues, only provides that "in all criminal proceedings, the accused shall enjoy the right . . . to have the assistance of counsel for his defense." Unlike the broader reach of many Constitutional protections, this clause is directed, not to all persons, but to those accused of a crime. Early interpretations of the 6th Amendment right were actually quite narrow and uncontroversial, as the clause was interpreted as providing for the right to be represented by retained counsel. *Gideon v. Wainwright* (1963) changed this view as it expanded the right to counsel under due process grounds, not the 6th Amendment itself. In *Gideon*, the defendant was charged with breaking and entering into a poolroom with the intent to commit a misdemeanor—a charge that constituted a felony under Florida state law. Unable to afford an attorney, Gideon formally requested that the court provide him with a court-appointed counsel. The trial judge rejected the request on the grounds that, under Florida law at the time, courts could only appoint counsel to indigent defendants in capital cases.

In a sweeping opinion overturning clear precedents to the contrary, the Court viewed the Florida procedures as violating the Fourteenth Amendment. In so doing, the Court found that every person accused of committing a felony must be afforded legal representation, regardless of their financial ability. This right has come to stand for the recognition that, in the interests of fairness, the complexity of the American criminal justice system demands the assistance of counsel. The Court's analysis emphasized its earlier reasoning that it would be unfair to require a layperson to defend himself against a trained prosecutor; it extended that reasoning to the reality that some defendants cannot afford to retain their own counsel. The Court found the lack of equal access to legal counsel fundamentally unfair. Allowing some defendants to retain their own defense attorney whereas others must face the prosecutors alone because of their financial situation undermined the ideal that all are equal under the law, one of the foundational ideas supporting the existence of due process rights. This fundamental fairness, due process approach would be the framework that would guide subsequent decisions involving the right to legal representation.

Just 4 years after *Gideon*, in *In re Gault* (1967), the Court extended its fundamental fairness approach to cases involving juvenile delinquency, which are proceedings designed to determine appropriate responses to minors accused of committing crimes or status offenses. This landmark case, as we already have described and presented for different reasons, involved a fifteen year old boy who had been committed for several years to a state institution for making indecent phone calls to a neighbor. Given that 6th Amendment rights must involve the criminal justice system, the issue before the Court was whether the Due Process Clause could sustain the need to provide representation and related rights (notice of charges, need for a written factual record, ability to appeal decisions) in the delinquency proceedings. The Court held that juvenile proceedings must follow due process principles. The scope of those due process rights included the right for juveniles to have timely, written, and adequate notice of the charges against them, the right to counsel if they are in danger of losing their liberty, the right against self-incrimination, and the right to confront and cross-examine opposing witnesses. Given that delinquency proceedings are not criminal proceedings, the expansion of these due process protections to this context was quite remarkable, the impact of which has yet to be fully felt today.

*Gault's* significance derives from the Court's reasoning. The Court stated that "neither the Fourteenth Amendment nor the Bill of Rights is for adults alone" and took the opportunity to recognize children as "persons" under the Fourteenth

Amendment deserving of due process rights (*In re Gault*, 1967, p. 13). In so doing, the Court criticized the *parens patriae* doctrine. The Court explained that the right of the state, as *parens patriae*, to refuse to accord juveniles constitutional procedural rights was justified by the belief that a child has a right to custody, but not to liberty. Under this approach to children's legal status, when the parents of the child default in effectively performing their custodial functions, the state has the right to intervene, and in so doing does not deprive the child of any rights because he had none. The state only provided the child that to which children are entitled, i.e., custody. In delinquency proceedings, this was deemed permissible because they were described as "civil" not "criminal" and therefore not subject to the requirements that restrict the state when it seeks to deprive a person of his liberty. The Court found debatable the constitutional and theoretical basis for what it deemed a peculiar system of justice. It reasoned that departures from the principles of due process had led to arbitrariness rather than the hoped for enlightened procedures. The Court recognized the risks to the benign mission of the juvenile justice system, and it saw those risks as deriving from the system's focus on providing decision makers with immense discretion in the name of rehabilitation. Not wanting to rid delinquency proceedings of their rehabilitative mandates, the Court focused on what it deemed necessary to rendering juvenile adjudications fairer but, at the same time, did not accord juveniles all those rights enjoyed by adult criminal defendants. This circumscribed approach to the fundamental fairness doctrine, the Court argued, guaranteed that the rehabilitative principles of the juvenile system would be preserved and that the essential protections of the adult criminal process would be observed in juvenile adjudications.

Although the right to counsel in criminal and juvenile justice cases remains secure, its extension to other contexts remains to be determined. The ethos of *Gault*, with its sweeping dicta about the applicability of the Fourteenth Amendment to juveniles, certainly argued for broad procedural protection for children. The Court, however, carefully circumscribed its holding: "We do not in this opinion consider the impact of these constitutional provisions upon the totality of the relationship of the juvenile and the state. We do not even consider the entire process relating to juvenile 'delinquents'" (*In re Gault*, 1967, p. 13). To this day, the Court has yet to extend similar rights to children in child protective proceedings that necessarily also involve children's liberties. As a result, *Gault* produces a strange result: children in the juvenile-justice system have more constitutional guarantees of procedure than children in the child-welfare system, despite the grave liberty interests at stake in both systems. Importantly and as we already have seen, the Court has held that indigent parents are not automatically entitled to assigned counsel, at least in termination of parental rights actions (*Lassiter v. Department of Social Services*, 1981). The refusal to recognize the constitutional basis of indigent parents' need for counsel in proceedings for termination of parental status certainly diminishes the probability that the Court will recognize that children themselves possess a constitutional right to independent representation by counsel. This is especially true given the strong precedent recognizing the rights of parents to raise their children as they see fit (e.g., *Meyer v. Nebraska*, 1923;

*Wisconsin v. Yoder*, 1927). This is not to say that the Court fails to recognize that children may have significant interests at stake. The Court seems to focus on the rights of parents to address children's concerns by waiting for parents to fail and then interfering to protect children's rights. This approach reflects the historic resistance to the idea that children have liberty interests. Thus, just as when children had no independent rights in delinquency proceedings before *Gault*, children now essentially have no independent, constitutional rights in child protective proceedings. The Court has yet to recognize the need for independent rights in this context.

## Federal Statutes

Congress has created statutory rights that address children's own independent rights in child protective proceedings. Congress initially did so in the *Child Abuse Prevention and Treatment Act* (CAPTA) of 1974. Under this statute, in order to receive federal funds to support their child welfare programs, states must provide every abused or neglected child a guardian ad litem (GAL) in a judicial proceeding. In 1996, Congress amended CAPTA to provide that the appointed GAL may be an attorney or a court appointed special advocate (or both). CAPTA also defined GALs' roles. The statute promulgated that GALs are to obtain, first-hand, a clear understanding of the situation and needs of the child and to make recommendations to the court concerning the best interests of the child. By using the power of the purse, then, Congress has sought to achieve much of what appears to have been missing in constitutional jurisprudence.

The significance of these legislative developments cannot be overstated. The legislation certainly indicates a move away from the belief that children should play virtually no role in judicial proceedings affecting them. Before CAPTA, no federal, comprehensive mandates prevented states from considering children as incompetent, dependent beings incapable of having a voice in determining what should be in their interest when they were alleged to have been maltreated. Historically, child protective proceedings were deemed parent-state contests. Although a child could have had a cognizable interest in the case's outcome, children were not recognized as independent parties. In a real sense, either their rights were controlled by parents or they were controlled by the state. The legal system generally adopted a paternalistic, informal approach that focused on the "best interests" and welfare of the child. This was the case even though the Court had ruled in *Gault* that such presumptions were problematic, regardless of the minors' legal status. Yet, child protection proceedings, until CAPTA, were able to proceed without providing children with a voice in judicial decisions that would affect them.

Despite CAPTA's important recognition, significant ambiguities and shortcomings remain. CAPTA was enacted during the emerging recognition of the need to provide children with representation and reflects the dilemmas and conflicts that continue to plague efforts to design effective ways to represent children in legal proceedings affecting them. CAPTA's prescriptive language incorporates several ambiguities and inconsistencies. CAPTA does mandate that every child be "represented" in some manner when their cases involve judicial proceedings. That representation, however, can vary considerably. The initial response to CAPTA was the establishment of the Court Appointed Special Advocate program (CASA), involving the appointment of "citizen" or lay volunteers to represent the interests of children. The use of volunteers meant that children had gained a guardian ad litem representative (a CASA representative, an attorney, or both) who might advocate for their interests or who simply might make recommendations to the court regarding the child's best interests.

The federal statute also required that children's representatives receive appropriate training for satisfactorily fulfilling their role's obligations. That representative, however, did not need to have formal legal training. As a result, the legislation abrogated the most important traditional purpose of a guardian ad litem, the guidance of legal counsel. Although groundbreaking, then, the legislation left much unclear. In addition and yet to be determined, for example, was whether children would have a voice in determining the appointment of their court appointed advocate or attorney. To complicate matters, when courts did appoint legal counsel, their roles often remained unclear in terms of their fundamental obligation to either further their client's wishes or act in the child's best interests. Not surprisingly, these ambiguities permitted a variety of ways to address children's needs, and states' mandates reveal a wide variety of ways to approach children's legal representation in child protective proceedings.

## State Statutory Mandates

Over the course of the three decades since the initial CAPTA legislation, the majority of states have responded to its mandates by enacting statutes that require states to provide children with their own, independent representatives in child welfare proceedings. These statutes either mandate the assignment of an attorney or other representative to represent the child or grant courts discretion to assign representatives. As yet another result, no national consensus exists in terms of the nature of the child's representation. Consequently, we find a mixture of legal and lay representation, with states permitting children's attorneys to act as guardians ad litem or as counsel to children (with or without the assistance of a CASA volunteer) or with states simply blending the two potentially inconsistent roles. We also find a failure to develop a consistent approach to addressing children's own interests: a broad mandate reveals a focus on children's best interests, but variations exist in terms of whether those who speak for children advocate for the child's wishes or for the representative's own views of what would be in the child's best interest. Despite a wide plethora of approaches to providing representatives to children in abuse or neglect proceedings, however, state statutes do evince a few commonalities and trends worth highlighting.

States do provide for a representative that can be filled by either an attorney, a guardian ad litem who may be an attorney, or court-appointed special advocate (see

Appendix B for citations). At least 41 states mandate or permit the appointment of a guardian ad litem. Nationally, more than half of the states require or permit the assignment of an attorney. Some states make appointment mandatory and require courts in dependency proceedings to appoint counsel. We still, however, end up with a wide variety of approaches within the states that either require or permit the appointment of guardian ad litems. For example, some states, like Texas and Nevada, do not require assignment in every case of neglect or abuse but do mandate appointment in cases in which termination of parental rights is at issue. Other states (e.g., Washington) require the appointment of an attorney if an older child requests one. Other states require the appointment of attorneys if the guardian ad litem's recommendations conflict with the child's wishes (New Hampshire and Wisconsin). Rather than guide courts, however, some states (approximately fifteen) render appointment discretionary; they leave it to individual judges' determination on a case by case basis. Together, these statutes point to the recognition that at least some children in dependency proceedings deserve representation.

In addition to specifying the permissible types of representation, state statutes also address the extent to which children are actually a "party" to the litigation involving them. Although CAPTA required either the assignment of counsel or a guardian ad litem, there exists no discernable national rule regarding the extent to which states grant children "party" status. Some states, such as Indiana, Minnesota, and Maryland, statutorily grant the child party status. The more prevalent approach simply avoids the issue by statutorily providing specific party rights to the child, while refraining from explicitly conferring party status itself. Thus, Illinois grants the child the right to be present, to be heard, to present evidence, examine records, and cross-examine witnesses. In New York, the child, acting through counsel, has the statutory right to file certain motions. However, in other states, the child possesses less than the full array of "party" rights, or the issue has yet to be addressed. The outcome of this approach means that most, but not all, jurisdictions view the child as a "virtual" or de facto party with many, if not all, rights of an "actual" party. Specific rights, however, vary from state to state. The focus on the term "party" permits courts and legislatures to confer many party rights on a piecemeal basis and grant children less than full party rights.

There may be inconsistencies in children's party status, but several states have enacted statutes granting children the right to choose their counsel. Thus, in California, the relevant statute states that a minor has the right to be represented by counsel of his or her own choice. New York law provides that the minors "should be represented by counsel of their own choosing or by law guardians." Several other states that follow the prevalent guardian ad litem model provide either that the child may request the appointment of independent counsel or that the court may assign counsel when the child and guardian ad litem disagree. Note that the focus here is on "may" assign. Thus, in Hawaii, when a child and guardian ad litem disagree, the court may appoint counsel for the child. Wisconsin allows the court to appoint counsel for the child if the best interests and the child's wishes are substantially inconsistent; and in New Hampshire, when the child's expressed interests conflict with the guardian ad litem's assessment of best interests, the court may appoint counsel for the child. In other states, like Maine, a child simply may request the appointment of "legal counsel." Although stopping short of an absolute right to counsel, these statutes recognize the need for the child's position to be represented independently and for the competent child's right to be represented though the normal attorney–client relationship. The child who requests representation always intends that counsel will advocate his position, or at least that the attorney will develop a position with the close collaboration of the child. Several statutes provide for the appointment of counsel when conflict exists between the child's position and that of the guardian ad litem. For example, in New Hampshire "where the child's expressed interests conflict with the recommendation for dispositional orders of the guardian ad litem, the court may appoint an attorney to represent the interests of the child." In Ohio and other states (e.g., Mississippi, Minnesota, and Rhode Island), an attorney guardian ad litem serves as both guardian and counsel, but if a conflict exists the court may substitute the guardian ad litem, leaving the original assigned attorney as counsel. These provisions provide a strong statement in favor of the child's need and right to be considered as an equal party to the proceedings, as capable, in many cases, of entering into a normal attorney–client relationship.

The provision of legal representation, however, does not end all ambiguities. Even the fundamental matter of what an attorney should advocate remains unsettled. It is unclear, for example, whether the attorney should advocate the child's "best interests" or the "child's wishes." Regardless of who acts as the child's representative, most states require representatives to act in the child's best interests. Thirty-five states explicitly stipulate that the child's representative, attorney or lay, shall advocate the child's "best interests" (see, e.g., Colorado). Recall that CAPTA requires states to appoint a guardian ad litem or an individual who fulfills the guardian ad litem role, language that which strongly promoted the "best interests" aspect of child representation. State legislators have continued to embrace this concept. Some states even require attorneys to act on the child's best interests (see California and Wyoming). Despite this trend, state statutes are not always consistent. A few states stipulate that the attorney shall not consider or be bound by the child's wishes (e.g., Wisconsin). Other statutes provide that counsel may consider the child's wishes when determining the child's "best interests" (e.g., Maine and South Carolina). Others require the attorney to apprise the court of the "child's wishes" (California). Other states essentially require the representatives to work for the court, such as some states that include the provision of independent factual information to the judge (Delaware and Louisiana) or assurance to the court that it has before it all relevant information (Oregon) or, even more daunting, that the court fulfill its obligations to the child (Oregon and Louisiana). These states foster a "hybrid" model of inherent inconsistencies. Other states simply remain silent regarding the extent representatives are to respect children's wishes. No simple rule seems to address the place of children's wishes in decisions affecting them.

The lack of specificity in rules guiding the representation of children's interests also finds reflection in the extent to which state statutes tend not to provide standards that limit the discretion of courts trying to determine the child's best interests. As we have seen already in this chapter, several states do provide broad guidelines. Other states leave the determination of which factors are material to the discretion of the court. Whether the factors to be considered in determining the best interests of the child are provided by statute or determined by the judge, courts make decisions on an individual case-by-case basis, and statutes do not establish the weight to be accorded to any particular factor. This discretion becomes rather consequential if we consider that the court typically retains the power to decide whether to appoint counsel for children. The power of this discretion becomes even more obvious when we consider the lack of consensus about what representatives should present courts. We are left with the conclusion that children increasingly have rights to representation, although it is unclear what constitutes those rights.

## Conclusions: The Law's Attachment to Diverse Responses and Discretion

The Supreme Court has long recognized that family integrity is a fundamental liberty interest protected by the Constitution. As a result, laws infringing on families' self-determination must be tailored narrowly to serve a compelling state interest—in this case, the prevention of harm to children—without unnecessarily restricting the right of parents to manage their children's upbringing. This rule firmly applies to child welfare law. The state may deny parents the right to raise their children and may remove their children from their custody only on a showing of the parents' unfitness. That removal, however, is quite complex. Our legal system does remain strikingly consistent in the manner it frames much of the discussion in terms of the rights of parents against the state. However, this broad approach leaves much undetermined. As a result, what governments must do to protect the rights of parents varies considerably depending on federal, state, and constitutional mandates.

No one contests the government's compelling concern about child maltreatment; nor does anyone question the fundamental rights of parents to care for and protect their children. Given the weighty interests on both sides of these matters, it is questionable whether any meaningful insight can be garnered through simple, straight-up balancing of parental and state interests. No matter how compelling the state interest, states' interventions still must be necessary and narrowly tailored. These two requirements lead us to focus on the interventions themselves. As we have seen, understanding this area of law requires examining the character of child abuse investigations, effectiveness of rescues, ability to assist families to remedy inadequacies, and the effectiveness of efforts to provide children with secure and permanent homes. This wide variety of possible steps to addressing children's harms do not lend themselves well to simple rules. As a result, recognized constitutional protections do not lead to predetermined outcomes.

The failure to predict outcomes need not mean that discretion should proceed without broadly accepted guidelines. Our current system, however, generally remains resistant to narrowing discretion and variation. This resistance derives from two sources. The first source involves the federal government's recognition that responses to child maltreatment must embrace diverse ways to address children's circumstances. Federal law strongly encourages states to respond to child maltreatment by enacting laws and making policy choices. Federal law does so by using the power of the purse: only complying states receive federal funding for their child welfare services. Although the federal government can be quite forceful, it often provides only broad guidelines and often vaguely defined terms that leave states considerable freedom. The second major source of resistance derives from the manner the Supreme Court also has left much unaddressed. By largely leaving child welfare law matters to state level jurisdiction, this area of law tends to avoid Supreme Court scrutiny. The Court defers to states when disputes involve state matters. As a result and given the pervasive belief that matters of family law belong in state legislatures and state courts, this area broadly remains beyond constitutional scrutiny. These two sources center on the need to focus on local, state-level responses. This focus may be appropriate, but it at least results in one significant consequence: the failure to develop broader standards that would guide a more standardized development of child welfare law.

Despite enormous diversity, we still can cull from a wide variety of cases and principles to gain a sense of the legal system's response to the complex issues raised by efforts to respond to child maltreatment. Although we remain mindful that the Court has yet to address these matters forthrightly in the context of child welfare laws, this very lack of jurisprudential development provides us with important opportunities to consider and it allows us to chart directions for future development. Before doing so, however, we must turn to examine how the criminal justice system has responded to the societal recognition that we must address harms against children.

# Chapter 6
# Enlisting Criminal Justice Systems in Child Protection

The criminal justice system retains overlapping jurisdiction with legal authority to intervene along with the civil, child welfare system. We already have seen that such an approach creates increasing peculiarities as it shapes legal responses to child maltreatment. Understanding those peculiarities, however, requires a firm understanding of the nature of the criminal justice system and the way it has sought to adjust itself to addressing children's harms. Issues raised by this adjustment may parallel many of those addressed in civil responses, that is, the need to protect individuals from unfair state intervention and need to protect individuals as well as society from harm. However, the system adopts a fundamentally different orientation.

Well-recognized characteristics mark the criminal justice system and render it different from the civil justice system we have examined. The government does initiate criminal litigation that responds to victimization: The victimization formally constitutes a harm against the state rather than, as we have seen, harm against a particular individual. The victimization provides a reason to intervene, but the focus is not on the child. Alleged offenders also must defend themselves against the state. However, the intervention no longer assumes that the state acts benevolently and in the alleged offenders' interests. When the state initiates its responses, it still uses its own investigative army—technical experts, attorneys, judges, and correctional personnel. However, the state holds the power to incapacitate defendants pending the outcome of litigation and, if it prevails, it can temporarily or permanently deprive individuals of their liberties. When the state wins, it gains the right to assign moral blame to offenders. These powers, however, are not absolute. In fact, much of the Constitution relating to these issues devotes itself to placing limits against the state's power. These constitutional protections seek to restrain the government's power and prevent abuses as it seeks to respond to harms. Unlike what we have seen in cases involving child welfare systems, these protections have attracted considerable Supreme Court attention and have contributed to well-established jurisprudence.

Our legal system has developed at least two broad kinds of restraints that limit the state's power to identify, adjudicate, punish, and control those deemed offenders. The first type of restraint is substantive. For example, the law seeks to impose criminal penalties only for conduct, not for status (e.g., one can be arrested for drunk driving but not for being an alcoholic). The conduct must be blameworthy. The legal system must also declare that conduct illegal, and that declaration must be done in a way that provides potential offenders with notice that their actions and penalties for those actions are subject to the law's control. In considering harms, our criminal laws presuppose that most individuals have the capacity to choose; our legal system rests on the belief that people are autonomous, that they have a choice whether to cause harm and to violate the law. That choice provides the moral foundation of a wide variety of possible punishments. These restraints are quite muted in civil, child welfare systems. Recall that those systems do not focus much on assigning blame, do not formally seek to punish, and do not presuppose that parents choose to harm. Rather, they focus on whether harm does or can exist and how to protect children in ways that foster their healthy development, which may or may not include protecting their relationships with those who have or could harm them.

The second type of restraints is procedural. Among other reasons, our legal system enacts procedural limitations to protect against the government's condemnation of those factually innocent. The limitations also are meant to protect against forms of government abuse in the processes it uses to decide whether and how to deprive individuals of their liberties. Thus, the criminal justice system requires the government to prove beyond a reasonable doubt that individuals are responsible for alleged actions. Finding responsibility based on this high level of certainty requires special procedural protections. These protections include familiar procedural rights, such as the right to confrontation and cross-examination as well as the right to counsel. The protections also include prohibitions against requiring individuals to be witnesses against themselves. These procedural protections are supplemented by other equally important prohibitions, such as the requirement that the state may punish only once and that it cannot retroactively increase penalties. In addition to basic fundamental rights that support these procedural mechanisms, courts and legislatures have enacted rules of evidence that regulate the admission of evidence, such as the numerous rules of evidence that limit the testimony of experts to ensure that parties present reliable facts to juries rather than, for example, junk science. Together, these substantive and procedural rules constitute barriers that limit inappropriate state action. As we have seen, however, these protections are very much reduced when states use their civil, child welfare system to address children's harms. Civil responses, for example, reduce the burdens of proof, relax evidentiary standards, limit the right to counsel, and remove rights against self-incrimination.

The differences in the above powers and restraints are part of the common understanding of our legal system and our sense of what constitutes a just society. Those principles, however, have been the subject of considerable change. In this chapter, we focus on these trends as they relate to the criminal justice system's responses to child maltreatment. Given the vastness and complexity of the criminal justice system's responses, we select exemplars of trends, challenges, and assumptions rather than attempt to provide a broad overview. we focus on changes relating to trial procedures for admitting children's testimony and reforms that aim to incapacitate and control offenders. My analysis focuses on Supreme Court cases that reveal national trends and also examines the diversity of state's responses to the Court's broad parameters. These responses highlight the need for the civil child protective system to address the harms the criminal justice system, for a variety of reasons, cannot address. By doing so, however, my analysis also highlights the inadequacies of the civil, child welfare system. We return to these issues in our concluding chapter.

## Crafting Procedural and Evidentiary Modifications

The Confrontation Clause of the Constitution's Sixth Amendment provides, in part, that "in all criminal prosecutions, the accused shall enjoy the right...to be confronted with the witnesses against him...." Read literally, the clause forbids the use of any statements made by declarants that are not actually called as witnesses at trials. This right means that individuals providing testimony should be available at trials and that trials should allow those accused to "confront" testifying individuals face to face. Many rationales support the need for confrontations, among the most persuasive being the assumption that confrontations provide defendants with an effective means of responding to false allegations. In considering allegations, however, it is important to recognize that the legal system entrusts judges and juries, the "triers of fact," with the task of evaluating the perception, memory, narration, and sincerity of witnesses. Removing witnesses from the presence of those who decide the outcomes of cases, then, does more than deprive defendants of opportunities to confront; removals challenge the abilities of triers of fact to evaluate witnesses' demeanor, credibility, and reliability in the effort to determine guilt or innocence. Even this brief understanding of the clause—its specific constitutional language and its centrality to adversarial systems—would lead one to conclude that the Court would seek to protect vigorously the right to confrontation. The Court actually does, but it also struggles to determine the parameters of the clause's dictates.

The Supreme Court has long rejected the need for a literal interpretation of the Confrontation Clause, even despite the clause's apparent clarity and utility in the adjudication of disputes. The Court announced this position in its first major examination of the right to confrontation, *Mattox v. United States* (1895). *Mattox* provided the Court with a somewhat-simple case. The case asked the Court to determine the permissibility of admitting, at trial, official transcripts containing the testimony of two deceased witnesses. The two witnesses had testified in the defendant's initial first-degree murder trial. Those two witnesses, however, had died before the defendant had successfully appealed and earned a new trial. The Court ruled that admission of the transcripts at the new trial did not violate the defendant's rights under the Confrontation Clause because "the substance of the constitutional protection is preserved to the prisoner in the advantage he has once had of seeing the witness face to face, and of subjecting him to the ordeal of a cross-examination" (p. 244). By relying on the defendant's prior opportunity to confront and cross-examine the witnesses fully, the *Mattox* Court found that the trial court had not impermissibly infringed on the defendant's rights when it had ruled the evidence admissible at the new trial. Although the ruling did seem to be but a slight move away from a strict adherence to the clause's mandates, the Court had reached this conclusion by arguing that "general rules of law of this kind, however beneficent in their operation and valuable to the accused, must occasionally give way to considerations of public policy and the necessities of the case" (p. 243). This reasoning left open the possibility that there could be ways around a narrow interpretation of the clause's strictures. Allowing for flexibility, *Mattox* launched an area of jurisprudence that seeks to articulate the appropriate circumstances under which the Confrontation right should give way to policy considerations.

Cases dealing with children would provide some of the most compelling cases supporting the need to accommodate overriding policy concerns and to relax the requirement of actual face-to-face confrontation. As one would expect, testifying in court, although it could be a difficult experience for anyone, would seem particularly difficult for children, especially child victims whose vulnerability inextricably relates to their victimization. Legal systems recognize these differences and have embarked on widespread reforms to facilitate the prosecution of cases involving children. For example, many states statutorily permit attorneys questioning children to ask leading questions during direct examination. Some allow children to testify without swearing an oath or to testify without understanding the obligation to testify truthfully. Other states permit support persons to accompany children during questioning; others permit trials to be closed to the press and public. Although these developments allow for admitting evidence in ways that generally would be objectionable, they remain much less controversial than efforts that directly implicate defendants' rights to "confront" child witnesses in open court.

States now use procedural modifications in the presentation of children's testimony and use hearsay exceptions to facilitate the introduction and admission of children's statements. The reason for these accommodations has been that crimes against children require special consideration. When dealing with cases involving child maltreatment, children's vulnerability, age, and the nature of their trauma render inherently difficult their presentation of testimony. For example, child maltreatment allegations tend to lack physical evidence and thus rely on victims' statements as the primary source of evidence. Yet, obtaining child victims' direct testimony may traumatize alleged victims. If accommodations were not secured, prosecutors would have much more difficult cases to support. Although it could be argued that a state simply should forego prosecutions in these cases, society increasingly has been unwilling to do so. Commitment to prosecuting these cases has led to accommodations that contradict the literal interpretation of the right to confrontation. *Mattox* provides some support for these special accommodations, but it remains controversial how far the legal system can accommodate policy concerns. In this section, we examine these more controversial accommodations.

## *Procedural Modifications*

The most illustrative example of the legal system's effort to accommodate prosecutions to children's special needs involves the use of alternative procedures in the provision of testimony. The most typical alterations involve the use of videotapes rather than (and sometimes in addition to) live testimony and the use of closed-circuit television. The central rationale for these alterations was the perceived need to separate some alleged victims from defendants so that they could provide their testimony without suffering the additional trauma that would come from being confronted by defendants. Many states recognized the benefits of these approaches and, by the mid-1980s, the majority of states had enacted statutes allowing their use. These statutes were not, however, without controversy; and issues involving special accommodations quickly reached the Supreme Court. The Court's responses to these early statutes provide a good starting point to understand the nature of these statutes.

The Supreme Court first addressed the use of alternative forms of providing testimony in *Coy v. Iowa* (1988). In *Coy*, the state had charged the defendant with sexually assaulting two 13-year-old girls while they were camping in their backyard next to his house. The trial court had permitted the girls to testify with a screen placed between them and the defendant. The Supreme Court reversed the conviction on the grounds that the procedure violated the defendant's right to confrontation. In its reasoning supporting the decision, the majority emphasized the truth-telling effects of face-to-face confrontation, stating that "it is always more difficult to tell a lie about a person 'to his face' than 'behind his back.' In the former context, even if the lie is told, it will often be told less convincingly" (*Coy v. Iowa,* 1988, p. 1022). Despite the preference for face-to-face confrontations, however, the Court acknowledged that it did not find absolute the rights preserved in the Confrontation Clause. Although the Court declined to identify specific exceptions, it conceded that exceptions might be justified "when necessary to further an important public policy" (p.1021). This language allowed for confrontation rights to give way, in more appropriate cases, to other competing interests so as to permit, for example, the use of certain procedural devices designed to shield a child witness from the trauma of courtroom testimony. The Court's apparent flexibility was tested in the next leading case in this area, *Maryland v. Craig* (1990).

Decided shortly after *Coy*, *Craig* provided the Court with another opportunity to evaluate the Confrontation Clause's limits in the context of children's testimony. This time, a different set of facts led the Court to decide the issue quite differently. *Craig* involved a defendant's conviction for sexually abusing a 6-year-old child. At a pretrial hearing, the state's expert witness had testified that the victim would have great difficulty testifying in the presence of the accused. The court had determined that the child would suffer such emotional distress that she would be unable to communicate reasonably if she were forced to testify in front of the accused. The trial court allowed the child to testify outside the presence of the defendant by way of one-way closed circuit television. This approach let her testify outside the presence of the jury, judge, and defendant. Although the defendant remained in the courtroom, she still could communicate with her counsel electronically. To permit these special procedures, the trial judge was required to make a determination that the child witness would be traumatized by testifying and that this trauma would prevent the child from communicating reasonably well. Resting on the reasoning of cases like *Mattox*, the Supreme Court reaffirmed the importance of face-to-face confrontation. However, it also held that the Confrontation Clause right is not absolute and that this right could be satisfied without the accused's face-to-face confrontation of the witness. The Court held that a face-to-face confrontation would be unnecessary if an alternative procedure advanced a compelling public policy interest, and if the testimony was reliable and trustworthy. The Court reiterated:

> If the State makes an adequate showing of necessity, the state interest in protecting child witnesses from the trauma of testifying in a child abuse case is sufficiently important to justify the use of a special procedure that permits a child witness in such cases to testify at trial against a defendant in the absence of face-to-face confrontation with the defendant. (p. 855)

Because the trial judge determined the necessity of the protective measure for the particular child, the state's interest in avoiding emotional trauma to the child outweighed the accused's right to confront witnesses against him.

The *Craig* Court found it significant that the statute guiding the option to use closed-circuit television preserved all of the other essential elements of the right to confront witnesses. The child had been deemed by the trial court to be competent, had taken and understood the significance of the oath to testify truthfully, and had been subjected to cross-examination. In addition, the jury had been able to observe the child's demeanor while testifying. The majority found that the only difference between the kind of protection available under the statute in *Craig* and live, in-court testimony was that the court proceedings did not force child witnesses to see defendants. The Court found safeguards provided by the use of one-way closed circuit television testimony to be more protective of the essential elements of the confrontation right of the accused than those required for the admission of hearsay testimony, which is the other major exception to the right of confrontation. In its reasoning, the majority stated that "the central concern of the Confrontation Clause is to ensure the reliability of the evidence against a criminal defendant by subjecting it to rigorous testing in the context of an adversary proceeding before the trier of fact" (*Maryland v. Craig* (1990, p. 845). The Court emphasized that the Confrontation Clause protects not only defendants' right to look upon their accusers, but also the right to have their accusers (a) give their statement under oath, (b) submit to cross-examination, and (c) be visible to the jury so that they may observe the witnesses' demeanor and evaluate their credibility. The Court concluded that "our precedents confirm that a defendant's right to confront accusatory witnesses may be satisfied absent a physical, face-to-face confrontation at trial only where denial of such confrontation is necessary to further an important public policy and only where the reliability of the testimony is otherwise assured" (p. 850). The Court reasoned that Maryland had an important state interest in preserving the physical and psychological well-being of the child witness and held that the use of one-way closed circuit testimony did not impinge on neither the truth-seeking nor the symbolic purposes of the Confrontation Clause.

The *Craig* Court carefully emphasized that the need for protective measures for child witnesses should be determined on a case-by-case basis and that states must present an "adequate showing of necessity" to justify an alternative form of testimony (p. 855). This necessity should mean that the child must be traumatized by the very presence of the accused in the courtroom and the prospect of testifying in front of him. The Court found a child's general anxiety about the courtroom atmosphere or testifying in general insufficient to outweigh an accused's right of confrontation. Generalized anxiety also was insufficient to invoke the requisite finding that the child would be better protected by testifying outside the accused's presence. "The determinative inquiry required to preclude face-to-face confrontation is the effect of the presence of the defendant on the witness or the witness's testimony" (*Maryland v. Craig,* 1990, p. 858). Thus, the trial court must find that the child witness would be traumatized, not by the courtroom generally, but specifically by the defendant. Finally, the trial court must determine that the emotional disturbance to the child witness resulting from testifying in front of the accused will be more than *de minimis*. "Mere nervousness or excitement or some reluctance to testify" will not suffice (p. 856). The *Craig* Court, then, stipulated quite well what courts must find to use special procedural accommodations in specific cases. Despite these stipulations, we soon will see that even clear language and principles lend themselves to different interpretations and that states' efforts to accommodate them necessarily vary and vary form the court's recommendations.

## Federal Statutes

The federal government took *Craig* as an invitation to develop a statute that would accommodate children's specific needs while, at the same time, protect the rights of defendants. Late the same year that *Craig* was decided, Congress enacted the *Child Victims' and Child Witnesses' Rights Act* (1990) as a part of the Comprehensive Crime Control Act of 1990. Although Congress acknowledged that most cases of this nature would proceed through state courts and involve state statutes, Congress deemed it necessary to keep pace with the states' enactment of procedural innovations dealing with problems child abuse prosecutions encounter and sought to provide federal courts with guidelines for determining whether public policy interests are strong enough in a particular case to justify allowing remote testimony.

The new statute applies the public policy exception to face-to-face confrontation articulated by the *Craig* majority. The new statute provides two alternatives to live, in-court testimony where the defendant is represented by counsel: live testimony by two-way closed-circuit television and videotaped depositions. The statute permits the use of these alternatives when the trial court finds that the child is unable to testify in open court because (a) of the child's fear, (b) there is substantial likelihood that the child will suffer emotional trauma, evidenced by expert testimony, (c) the child suffers a mental or other infirmity, or (d) conduct by the defendant or defense counsel causes the child to be unable to continue testifying.

In addition to these special accommodations, the statute permits courts to support witnesses in many ways, such as by appointing a guardian ad litem and permitting an adult to accompany the child while testifying. The statute further accommodates the legal system to the special circumstances of cases by extending the statute of limitations for child physical or sexual abuse. The statute, however, does deviate from the holding in *Craig* in several important respects. It specifies that federal courts must use a two-way closed circuit system rather than a one-way system. It also expands the grounds for allowing a child witness to testify remotely to include, in addition to fear, a substantial likelihood of trauma, mental or other infirmity, or conduct by the defendant or defense counsel that causes the child to be unable to continue testifying. Unlike *Craig*, then, the statute does not require the presence of the defendant to be the specific and exclusive source of the victim's fear. The statute seeks to protect more than child victims of physical or sexual abuse or exploitation; it included protections for witnesses to a crime committed against others. Whether these extensions are problematic remains to be seen; but, for now, they do seem to comport with efforts to accommodate the prosecution of these cases to children's needs while still preserving, as much as practicable, the right of defendants to confront witnesses and juries to hear them.

## State Statutes

As we noted previously, states had embarked on statutory reforms long before cases came to the Supreme Court, and long before the federal legislature adopted a statute guiding federal courts. See Appendix C for citations. A look at state statutes reveals that only eight states (Maine, Michigan, Montana, North Carolina, Oklahoma, Oregon, South Carolina, and Wyoming) do not have specific statutes that would guide trial courts in criminal proceedings involving child witnesses. A look at when the statutes were adopted and the statutes themselves reveals that a few states, such as Idaho and Nevada, simply adopted parts of the federal mandates. The vast majority of states already had statutes in place that addressed the use of alternative methods of providing testimony. These statutes focus on the use of videotapes or closed circuit television as the dominant means of admitting the testimony of children without requiring them to testify in the presence of defendants and juries.

States have adopted quite similar statutes, but they vary in the extent to which they permit the use of alternative methods. Most states tend to focus directly on the potential negative effects of the testimony on the child witnesses. The most common approach requires courts to find that child witnesses would suffer serious emotional distress or trauma that would render them unable to reasonably communicate if they were required to testify in court; states that adopt language similar to this include Colorado, Delaware, Georgia, Hawaii, Idaho, Illinois, Indiana, Iowa, Kentucky, Louisiana, Maryland, Tennessee, Washington, and Wisconsin. Some states note the need to show a compelling need (Montana), traumatic emotional or mental distress (Mississippi), moderate emotional or mental harm (Florida), significant emotional or psychological trauma (Missouri), severe emotional distress (Vermont and New Jersey), emotional or mental strain (New Hampshire), unreasonable and unnecessary harm (New Mexico and Rhode Island), severe mental or emotional harm (New York, Virginia), serious emotional trauma (North Dakota and Ohio), more than *de minimus* emotional distress and necessary to protect the welfare of the child (South Dakota), undue psychological or physical harm (Texas), serious emotional or mental strain (Utah) or simply a "harmful or detrimental effect" (Arkansas). A few states, Arkansas and Idaho, explicitly provide judges with discretion to consider any other matter the court considers relevant. Given the short history of allowing the use of alternative methods, that so many could permit their use is quite remarkable.

Although the above statutes may seem to permit courts to infringe on defendants' confrontational rights, states limit the circumstances that can call for their use. In addition to requiring specific findings regarding the need for the alternative method, the states have limited when the methods could be used. Many states limit the procedural accommodations to children of a certain age. The following states, for example, show the wide range of ages that statutes permit the use of alternative methods of providing testimony: ages 10 (Georgia and Washington), 11 (Delaware and Montana), 12 (Arkansas, Colorado, Kentucky, South Dakota, and Vermont), 13 (California, Kansas, and Tennessee), 14 (New York and Utah), 15 (North Dakota), 16 (Alaska, Florida, Mississippi, New Mexico, and Wisconsin), 17 (Rhode Island) and 18 (Illinois). Several states simply point to the relevant statutes that define victims and, as we have seen, states very considerably in terms of their definitions of what constitutes child victimization. In this regard, note that states also limit the use of these statutes to child witnesses who have been victims of certain crimes, mainly sex crimes; see, as examples, Hawaii, Illinois, Kentucky, Mississippi, New Jersey, Tennessee, Vermont, and Wisconsin. A few states explicitly permit the use of these alternatives to witnesses of crimes against others: Alabama, South Dakota, Virginia, and Washington. As these examples reveal, courts place a focus on the need to protect child victims, but the accommodations vary considerably from state to state.

In addition to delineating when the use of alternative methods would be permissible, state statutes also tend to delineate the procedures courts must follow when considering whether the testimony is to be televised or otherwise reported. This guidance includes, for example, the presence of attorneys, persons necessary to operate the equipment and any person whose presence would contribute to the welfare and well-being of the minor may be present in the room with the minor during his testimony. Most states explicitly note that, if courts order the testimony of a child to be taken in this manner, the child shall not be required to testify in court at the proceeding for which the testimony was taken (see, for example, Arizona, Colorado, Rhode Island, Tennessee, Utah, and Vermont). Several states also note that the provisions of this section do not apply if the defendant is an attorney *pro se*; see, for example, Arkansas, Delaware, Georgia, Illinois, Maryland, and Washington. Several explicitly provide that the statutes may not be interpreted to preclude, for purposes of identification of a defendant, the presence of both the child victim and the defendant in the courtroom at the same time; Arkansas, Delaware, Georgia, Illinois, and Maryland. Thus, although children can be removed from courtrooms when providing testimony, they still may be required to appear in court and face juries and defendants.

## *Hearsay Exceptions*

Although fraught with technicalities and exceptions that guide whether they will be admitted as evidence, hearsay statements are declarations made outside of court that are introduced in court as valid declarations. Generally, such statements are excluded from trial. The reason for the exclusion is that our Anglo-American legal tradition disfavors hearsay because the declarant does not testify under oath in the presence of the fact finder. By not testifying under oath in court, declarants are unburdened by the solemnity of trials and the factors typically used to determine witnesses' veracity and reliability of their evidence. Traditionally, the courts have identified four dangers associated with reliance on hearsay. Hearsay testimony may be mistaken because it is based on: (a) an inaccurate impression of reality, (b) a false belief that develops from events because of memory deficiencies or fantasies, (c) an imperfect communication or interpretation between the recipient and declarant of statements, or (d) an intentional falsification by either the recipient or declarant. Given these possibilities, our legal system has designed hearsay rules to ensure that convictions rest on reliable and trustworthy evidence.

Children's out-of-court statements, admitted as hearsay, may be particularly susceptible to problems of untrustworthiness. This is not to say that the legal system should automatically reject children's reports and those who report children's statements. However, as with adults' statements, the legal system must vet evidence to avoid problems associated with false and exaggerated allegations. These problems typically are addressed through excluding hearsay, especially hearsay not subject to cross-examination, and only allowing hearsay in a very narrow set of circumstances that evince trustworthiness. When it comes to declarations involving children, difficulties arise because traditional hearsay rules and exceptions were designed for adult's testimony, not those of children. By treating these two sources of testimony identically, valuable evidence may be excluded by hearsay rules designed to counter problems that may not be relevant to child witnesses. Recognizing potential differences, the legal system has sought ways to adapt. It has done so by building on established cases that permit the admission of hearsay statements under a very narrow set of conditions.

In one of the Supreme Court's most significant Confrontation Clause decisions, the Court provided a two-part test to determine the admissibility of evidence from individuals unavailable at trial. That case was *Ohio v. Roberts* (1980). At issue in *Roberts* was the admissibility at trial of testimony given by an unavailable witness against the defendant at a preliminary hearing. The Court began by succinctly summarizing its Confrontation Clause philosophy by stating:

> When a hearsay declarant is not present for cross-examination at trial, the Confrontation Clause normally requires a showing that he is unavailable. Even then, his statement is admissible only if it bears adequate 'indicia of reliability.' Reliability can be inferred without more in a case where the evidence falls within a firmly rooted hearsay exception. In other cases, the evidence must be excluded, at least absent a showing of particularized guarantees of trustworthiness. (p. 66)

This short paragraph revealed much. Under *Roberts*, the Supreme Court rejected the notion that the Constitution requires cross-examination of every statement introduced at trial since that would eliminate every exception to the rule against hearsay. The Court noted, instead, that the Confrontation Clause operates to restrict the range of admissible hearsay in two distinct ways. First, the Sixth Amendment establishes a rule of necessity: "[T]he prosecution must either produce, or demonstrate the unavailability of, the declarant whose statement it wishes to use against the defendant" (p. 65). Second, once the witness is deemed unavailable, his statements are admissible only if they bear adequate "indicia of reliability" (p. 66). Reliability can be automatically inferred if the hearsay falls within one of the firmly rooted hearsay exceptions. In all other cases, courts should exclude hearsay testimony unless there is a showing of "particularized guarantees of trustworthiness" (p. 66). The phrases "firmly rooted hearsay exception" and "particularized guarantees of trustworthiness" essentially comprise what would become the two-part test for admissibility of statements by unavailable declarants. The Court found guarantees of trustworthiness in the accouterments of the preliminary hearing itself because the defendant was represented by counsel and had already received an adequate opportunity to cross-examine the witness. Given a "firmly rooted hearsay exception" or "particularized guarantees of trustworthiness," the Court allowed for the admissibility of statements by "unavailable" declarants without cross-examination (p. 66). These phrases, however, still left much unclear; and two of the leading cases that clarified these phrases dealt with children's hearsay testimony.

In *Idaho v. Wright* (1990), a pediatrician asked a two- and one-half year old girl a series of questions about alleged acts of molestation against her. After determining that the girl could not communicate with the jury and, therefore, was unavailable, the trial court allowed the pediatrician to testify as to the girl's statements via Idaho's residual hearsay exception. The rules of evidence provide this category of exceptions to capture those that do not fall in other established categories; this exception permits hearsay that would otherwise be excluded from trial. Pointing to the very reason for the residual hearsay exception, the Court necessarily could not consider it "firmly rooted." However, that did not mean that it should be excluded. The Court clarified that a "firmly rooted hearsay exception" was an exception "so trustworthy that adversarial testing [can be expected to] add little to its reliability" (p. 821). Thus, under the *Roberts* doctrine, statements not falling clearly in already recognized categories still would be admissible if they bore "particularized guarantees of trustworthiness." The Court further indicated that these guarantees are "shown from the totality of the circumstances, but . . . the relevant circumstances include only those that surround the making of the statement and that render the declarant particularly worthy of belief" (p. 818). The Court carefully noted, however, that in order to avoid "bootstrapping" on other evidence at trial, corroborating evidence plays no role in determining "particularized guarantees of trustworthiness" (p. 823). Although it ruled that trial courts must not use corroborative evidence of the acts to determine a statement's trustworthiness, the Court listed five factors for future trial courts to consider when evaluating whether children's out-of-court statements exhibit particularized guarantees of trustworthiness: spontaneity, consistency, the declarant's mental state, the use of terminology unexpected of a child of similar age, and the existence of any motive to fabricate (p. 821–22). *Wright's* holding provided support to efforts that sought to admit children's hearsay testimony. Having settled that declarations would be admitted if they could be found trustworthy, the Court would turn to clarify what constituted "unavailability" to support the admission of hearsay.

The Court directly addressed the issue of "unavailability" in the next case dealing with child victims' hearsay testimony—*White v. Illinois* (1992). Addressing the issue of unavailability was of significance given that, for the hearsay exception to apply, the declarant would have to be unavailable to testify in court. This simple rule was a fundamental aspect of confrontation rights: if declarants are available, then they should testify in court. When dealing with children, however, there are many ways by which they could be deemed unavailable: they may be unavailable, for example, due to lack of competency or the fear of testifying in court. As we have seen previously, this was not even an issue in prior cases that presumably assumed, for example, that children incompetent to testify are, in fact, unavailable. The issue that arises is whether such reasons could suffice to support a claim of unavailability or whether, when dealing with these cases, unavailability needed to be shown at all.

*White* involved a trial court's admission of a 4-year-old child's out-of-court statements regarding sexual assault, choking, and threatening by her mother's friend in the child's bedroom. At trial, the child was brought to the witness stand several times, but she was too upset to testify. The court made no showing that she would have been competent to testify. The court admitted the testimony of five witnesses who reported what the victim had told them. The first group consisted of the child's babysitter, the child's mother, and a police officer; the second group was an emergency room nurse and a physician. The Court considered the child's out-of-court statements to the first group under the spontaneous declaration hearsay exception and those spoken to the second group under the medical examination hearsay exception. The Supreme Court unanimously found the defendant's conviction constitutional. The Court held the out-of-court statements to be sufficiently reliable, that the defendant's confrontation right had not been violated. The Court explained that the unavailability of the declarant to testify at trial did not have to be shown, nor did the declarant have to be produced at trial. The Court refused to apply an "unavailability rule" to the hearsay exceptions for spontaneous declarations and statements made in the course of receiving medical care. It reasoned that "such out-of-court declarations are made in contexts that provide substantial guarantees of their trustworthiness [and that] ... the statements' reliability cannot be recaptured even by later in-court testimony" (*White v. Illinois*, 1992, pp. 355–356). The Court continued:

> We therefore think it clear that the out-of-court statements admitted in this case had substantial probative value, value that could not be duplicated simply by the declarant later testifying in court. To exclude such probative statements under the strictures of the Confrontation Clause would be the height of wrong-headedness, given that the Confrontation Clause has as a basic purpose the promotion of the 'integrity of the fact finding process.' (pp. 356–357)

The Court also provided some guidance as to whether the two hearsay exceptions in question were "firmly rooted," referring to their respective age, enumeration in the Federal Rules of Evidence, and acceptance among the states. Under *White*, if out-of-court statements fall within a firmly rooted exception to the hearsay prohibition, they are admissible in child abuse cases without cross-examination regardless of whether the prosecution can prove that the hearsay is necessary because the declarant is unavailable. This was a remarkable development that permits prosecutors to forgo live testimony entirely for statements within firmly rooted exceptions without proving unavailability. A strongly worded concurring opinion disagreed with this approach. It argued that the "federal constitutional right of confrontation extends to any witness who actually testifies at trial" (p. 365). As for the admissibility of statements "the made by those who do not testify, the argument was that Athe Confrontation Clause is implicated by extrajudicial statements only insofar as they are contained in formalized testimonial materials, such as affidavits, depositions, prior testimony, or confessions" (p. 365). Under this approach, statements not made in more formalized testimonials would not be admitted at trial. This line of reasoning essentially would limit exceptions to those supported in *Mattox*. Nevertheless, through *White*, the Court held to *Roberts'* "firmly rooted hearsay exception" and "particularized guarantees of trustworthiness" two-part test. As we will soon see, this test has now been challenged; the place for exemptions has been narrowed considerably; and how this new case will influence this area of law remains to be seen.

## Federal Statutes

Despite recent challenges to the Court's constitutional analyses supporting exceptions to hearsay rules, it is important to note that the Federal Rules of Evidence codified many hearsay exceptions and that those rules, until specifically found deficient, remain good law. The federal rules reflect common law developments that allowed certain out-of-court statements to be admissible when the hearsay was made under specific conditions that insure a degree of reliability similar to that provided by the safeguards of cross-examination. These traditional, or "firmly rooted," exceptions include, for example, the excited utterance (or spontaneous declaration), the medical diagnosis or treatment, and the dying declaration exceptions. For instance, a hearsay statement is admissible under the excited utterance exception as long as it was spontaneous and made under circumstances of shock or nervous excitement. The rationale for the exception is that the declarant was so startled by an event that all normal thought processes stopped functioning and that the statement was made as a spontaneous result of that event, without time, for example, to fabricate. The same could be said of dying declarations, when it could be assumed that declarants had no motivation to fabricate. Statements also may be admissible under the medical diagnosis or treatment exception to the extent that they describe medical history, symptoms, or pains, and are reasonably pertinent to diagnosis or treatment. This exception's underlying rationale is that doctors will seek, and patients will give, truthful information because both the doctor and the patient want the patient to get better. Following this rationale, the legal system deems reliable statements reasonably pertinent to diagnosis or treatment. These exceptions have now been commonly recognized and accepted. Thus, even though children may make statements out of court, those statements may be admitted at trials against defendants if they fall within these well recognized exceptions.

The two most commonly used exceptions in child abuse prosecutions are the excited utterance and the medical diagnosis or treatment exceptions. These exceptions, however, are quite narrow. Accordingly, many states have chosen to make it easier for prosecutors to admit children's out-of-court statements by applying the traditional hearsay exceptions in a more lax manner when the case involves child sexual abuse. The expansion of the hearsay exceptions for child declarants, however, creates special problems. The exceptions do not necessarily work well in cases involving child maltreatment. For example, children in maltreatment cases rarely make statements that normally would qualify as excited utterances because fear, loyalty, or a lack of comprehension cause children to delay reporting abuse, especially if the abuse was perpetrated by a parent or close relative. The child's having had time for reflective thought removes the reason to find these nonspontaneous statements trustworthy. Likewise, statements made in the course of diagnosis typically are done in contexts in which children are suspected of having been maltreated; statements made in preparation of the case would thus fall outside of hearsay exceptions and not be allowed in court. Finding that the traditional exceptions to the hearsay rule were not always sufficient, many states have developed additional ways to admit hearsay by child declarants in prosecutions for child maltreatment. Courts have turned to residual exceptions since these allow considerably more flexibility.

The residual exceptions are easily understandable from a look at the Federal Rules of Evidence. The rules include residual or catch-all exceptions that are to be applied in new and presently unanticipated situations that demonstrate a trustworthiness within the spirit of the specifically stated exceptions. Rules of evidence 803(24) and 804(b)(5) find statements not specifically covered by another rule admissible if (a) it must have circumstantial guarantees of trustworthiness equivalent to those possessed by the specific hearsay exceptions, (b) it must concern a material fact, (c) it must be more probative than any other evidence that the proponent can reasonably procure, (d) admission of the statement must best serve the general purposes of the evidence rules and the interest of justice, and (e) the opponent must have appropriate notice that the statement will be offered. Rule 804(b)(5) is used when the declarant is unavailable; Rule 803(24) is used regardless of whether the declarant is available. The first requirement is the only one that concerns trustworthiness, and the indeterminacy of the other criteria, such as best serve the interest of justice, provide no real guidance in deciding whether a statement is reliable. Not surprisingly, the grant of discretion to trial judges leaves this rule the subject of considerable scrutiny since one of the primary purposes for evidence rules is to reduce unpredictability and arbitrariness. These exemptions, however, have become important ways to admit children's declarations into evidence.

## State Statutes

Since the promulgation of the federal rules, the vast majority of states have enacted evidence codes that substantially mimic them. Indeed, several states simply have adopted the federal hearsay rules. Unlike the federal legislature, however, states have recognized that traditional hearsay exceptions were not designed, and hence do not work well, for child witnesses. As a result, most states have enacted "tender years" hearsay exception statutes to govern child hearsay, and most of these statutes focus on child sexual abuse cases. See Appendix C for citations. Through these specialized statutes, most states have developed a formally recognized way under which child hearsay—not otherwise admissible under the state's other hearsay exceptions—would be admissible.

Statutes may be placed into different categories based on how they deal with the issues of unavailability and corroborative evidence. The largest group of statutes makes hearsay of a child under a specific age admissible if (a) the court finds the statement reliable, (b) the adverse party has notice, and (c) the child either (i) testifies or (ii) is unavailable and there is corroborative evidence of the act. The states in this group include Alabama, Arizona, Colorado, Florida, Idaho, Illinois, Maryland, Minnesota, Mississippi, New Jersey, Oklahoma, Oregon, Pennsylvania, South Dakota, Utah, and Washington. Note, though, that these statutes have met considerable judicial scrutiny. Indeed, some statutes, those of Arizona, Idaho, and Mississippi, have been declared invalid by their state courts.

A few other groups of states are worth noting for how they approach child hearsay rules. Nine states—Georgia, Indiana, Kentucky, Maine, Massachusetts, Michigan, Rhode Island, Texas, and Vermont—permit hearsay by children if the statements are reliable and the child either was cross-examined when the statement was made or is available to testify about the statement. Four other states—Arkansas, California, Hawaii, and Kansas—admit children's hearsay if the court determines (a) the statements are trustworthy and (b) the child is unavailable. These states do not require corroborative evidence of the act. Other states—Delaware, Missouri, and Nevada—permit children's trustworthy statements when the child is unavailable but require corroborative evidence of the act, even if the child is never cross-examined about the statement. Those three states also are different from the Arkansas-like approaches in that they do not require that a child be available to testify to admit that child's hearsay under the Tender Years Statute.

A few other states take approaches different from others. Ohio, for example, only admits child hearsay if (a) the statement is as reliable as statements admitted under other hearsay exceptions, (b) the child's testimony is not reasonably obtainable by the proponent of the statement, and (b) there is "independent proof" of sexual or physical violence. Ohio takes a different approach that, like several states, requires corroboration but, unlike those states, only allows child hearsay if the child is unavailable to testify. Alaska also currently stands on its own. In Alaska, the child must testify in front of the grand jury or be available to testify at the trial and there must be additional evidence that corroborates the statement. Like other states, Alaska requires corroboration, but that only applies when the child testifies.

As our brief overview suggests, states have taken somewhat different approaches to dealing with children's hearsay testimony. What is important to keep in mind is that the majority of states have loosened their evidentiary exclusionary rules regarding the admission of hearsay evidence of child declarants. Much of the legislation has been controversial; many state cases address these statutes, and some have been overturned. Together, these statutes reveal how states aim to determine the admission of trustworthy hearsay and encourage children to testify.

## Recent Challenges

An important Supreme Court case recently has challenged key aspects of the jurisprudential foundations for many rules of evidence, including the new procedural accommodations and hearsay exceptions. It is unclear how the case will be interpreted and how it will influence the statutes and cases we have discussed previously. That case, however, is worth close consideration not just for what it tells us about potential future directions but also for what it reveals about the nature of legal responses to child maltreatment.

The Court recently overruled *Roberts* and its progeny with it. This development questions the extent to which many hearsay exceptions remain good law. The case that initiated this shift was *Crawford v. Washington* (2004). *Crawford* involved a challenge to the use of hearsay exceptions to admit into evidence statements that otherwise would be inadmissible because of a statute prohibiting the declarant's testimony. The defendant, Crawford was charged with assault and attempted murder for the alleged stabbing of Lee. In her tape-recorded interview with a police officer, the defendant's wife and witness to the incident indicated that the incident was not in self-defense. Despite that statement, however, she could not testify at trial. She could not do so because of the state's marital privilege, a statute that prohibits admission of a spouse's testimony if certain conditions are met. The state, quite reasonably, interpreted her inability to testify as rendering her unavailable. Given the reliability of her statement, the state introduced it at trial. Crawford objected on the grounds that its admission would violate his Sixth Amendment Confrontation Clause rights. The state appellate court disagreed with Crawford, it found that the statement bore particularized guarantees of trustworthiness and should be admitted under *Roberts*. Crawford appealed to the Supreme Court.

In a far-reaching opinion, the Court took the opportunity to revisit *Ohio v. Roberts* (1980). The Court found *Roberts* too subjective in that its rule allowed evidence to be admitted "untested by the adversary process" and "based on a mere judicial determination of reliability" (*Crawford v. Washington,* 2004, p. 61). In adjusting its approach to the Confrontation Clause, the Court indicated a preference that jurors rather than judges determine the reliability of testimonial statements. Specifically, the Court stated that the Confrontation Clause is a "procedural rather than a substantive guarantee," requiring that "reliability be assessed in a particular manner: by cross examination" (p. 61). Under *Roberts*, because a judge rather than a jury determined the reliability of statements, *Roberts* "replaced the constitutionally prescribed method of assessing reliability with a wholly foreign one" (p. 62). The majority summarized its position with the following:

> Where nontestimonial hearsay is at issue, it is wholly consistent with the Framers' design to afford the States flexibility in their development of hearsay law—as does Roberts, and as would an approach that exempted such statements from Confrontation Clause scrutiny altogether. Where testimonial evidence is at issue, however, the Sixth Amendment demands what the common law required: unavailability and a prior opportunity for cross-examination. (p. 68)

The Court, however, explicitly qualified its *Roberts* holding by finding that, when involving testimony, confrontation was the only indicium of reliability sufficient to satisfy constitutional demands. This qualification implied that analyses initially required a determination of whether the statement seeking to be admitted is testimonial or non-testimonial. Unfortunately for legal analyses, the Court explicitly left "for another day" the task of determining the definition of "testimonial" (p. 68). Although the Court failed to define "testimonial," it did state that, at a minimum, the term covers "prior testimony at a preliminary hearing, before a grand jury, or at a former trial; and to police interrogations" (p. 68). Whether it is to include more remains to be determined. However, at least for now, it does appear that testimonial declarations require confrontation.

*Crawford's* precise implications are not yet known and will be apparent only as lower courts work to interpret and apply its ruling. On its face, *Crawford* strikes a sweeping blow at the use of hearsay exceptions to admit prior statements by child complainants. In cases involving children, these issues have arisen in two forms that illustrate well the legal system's attempts to address the peculiar needs of prosecutions involving child maltreatment. First, *Crawford* raises important concerns for *Craig*. Most notably, the *Craig* Court had found that a defendant's "right to confront accusatory witnesses may be satisfied absent a physical, face-to-face confrontation at trial only where denial of such confrontation is necessary to further an important public policy and only where the reliability of the testimony is otherwise assured" (p. 850). That language, cited to *Ohio v. Roberts* (1980, p. 64), now has been limited, if nor completely overruled, by *Crawford*.

The majority appears to have overruled *Roberts* only with respect to testimonial statements. In that regard, *Crawford* held that there is a constitutionally guaranteed right to confront witnesses, and that out of court statements intended for use as evidence require the witness to be available for cross-examination. Even though the element of cross-examination is preserved by two-way testimony, actual face-to-face confrontation is not, which raises the question of whether *Craig* would survive a Confrontation Clause challenge under *Crawford*. Second, *Crawford* potentially raises concerns in the realm of nontestimonial evidence, such as exceptions that involve children deemed incompetent because of an inability to discern truth from falsity, or because they cannot communicate with the jury. So far, there has been no direct judicial attack on *Craig* even though *Crawford* clearly has a vision of the Confrontation Clause that rejects the type of balancing approach that *Craig* applied. Regardless of these developments, however, *Craig* retains its status as the Court's most recent opinion on the issue of child witness shielding procedures. Subsequent statutes, both federal and state provisions, that follow *Craig* remain good law given that the Supreme Court has not ruled on the constitutionality of any shielding statute since the specific Maryland provision at issue in *Craig*.

*Crawford* reveals that the Court appears ready to limit the exceptions that have marked this area of law. Given that the developed rules have been meant to respond to changing social demands (prosecutions and public policy), it is not surprising that they continue to change. These rules reveal that the Supreme Court rejected this literal interpretation and sought to balance the values of the Confrontation Clause with public policy considerations, especially the necessities of criminal prosecutions. For example and following *Mattox*, the language of the Sixth Amendment has been widely interpreted to require an actual face-to-face confrontation between defendants and their accusers, which renders allowing a witness to testify outside the presence of the defendant, for any reason, a technical violation of this constitutional guarantee. These developments, then, are of considerable significance. The state statutes we have reviewed reveal a wide range of possibilities. In considering these statutes, however, it is important to keep two points in mind. First, we are looking at specialized statutes. It may well be that a particular state's rules of evidence and criminal procedure permit other methods to present children's testimony and it also may well be that some provisions have been (or soon will be) struck down by state courts. Second, given that evidentiary errors are reviewed under an abuse of discretion standard, these developments mean that lower court determinations of the key legal issue—admissibility under a hearsay rule—are largely immune from careful appellate scrutiny, even when effectively deciding the constitutional issue as well. Together, then, the exceptions that allow for accommodating children's needs appear quite wide and deep.

# Incapacitating Offenders

Statutes seeking to incapacitate sexually violent predators constitute the most recent manifestation of an enduring effort to combat the problems of sexual violence and crime. These innovative statutes borrow a mix of rationales to support the civil commitment of offenders. Understanding these complex laws requires understanding these rationales that legitimize the incapacitation of individuals by committing them to mental health institutions against their will. Traditionally, the power of the state to use civil statutes to incapacitate the mentally ill by committing them to institutions has been predicated on two different state power rationales: the *parens patriae* power and the police power.

The *parens patriae* power grants states the power to care for citizens who are unable to care for themselves. Under this theory, the state acts as a parent and may restrain the individual, but such restraint must be for the individual's own good. The classic formulation of commitments under the doctrine of *parens patriae* requires at least three predicates. First, the individual must be mentally ill. Second, the mental illness must be such that it renders the individual unable to make competent decisions about his need for medical treatment. The state does not proceed legitimately when it acts as parent and mandates the treatment (and incarceration) for a mentally competent individual who does not desire it. Third, the state may commit the individual if the commitment is "therapeutically appropriate" for the individual. In most cases, there must be some form of treatment that accompanies incarceration.

The state's police power also provides states with the authority to use civil systems to commit the mentally ill. Under this theory, the state is permitted to detain individuals who are mentally ill and who, as a consequence of their mental illness, pose a danger to the community. Unlike the *parens patriae* rationale, this rationale holds that commitment serves the interests of the state, not those of the detainee. In its most robust form, police power commitments require only two bases. First, the individual must be mentally ill. Second, the mental illness must cause the individual to be imminently dangerous to the community. Strictly speaking, police power commitments need not turn on whether the detainee has the capacity to determine what is best for him. Because society's safety is at stake, if the danger is sufficient, the police power should support the detention of even a mentally competent individual. Given that it is the state's interest that is paramount, valid commitment need not rest on the individual's treatment. If the mentally ill individual is an imminent danger, the police power theory would support commitment even if no effective treatment were available for the individual.

Although the above two theories rely on separate powers, traditional civil commitment law tends to blend them together, which suggests that they may be jointly necessary for civil commitment. Until quite recently, the Supreme Court was arguably ambiguous about the bases underlying civil commitment. For example, in *Addington v. Texas* (1979 p. 426), a case dealing with the burden of proof in civil commitment cases, the Court identified both a *parens patriae* power of the State to provide care to citizens "unable because of emotional disorders to care for themselves," and a "police power to protect the community from the dangerous tendencies of some who are mentally ill". In subsequent cases dealing with what were clearly police power commitments, the Court continued to offer *parens patriae* justifications for the incarcerations. *Kansas v. Hendricks* (1997) resolved this issue. *Hendricks*, and the cases relying on it, provides good examples of the legal system's efforts to accommodate societal needs.

## Supreme Court Jurisprudence

Supreme Court jurisprudence dealing with efforts to incapacitate offenders by civilly committing them begins with *Kansas v. Hendricks* (1997), the watershed case in this area of law. Leroy Hendricks was convicted for taking "indecent liberties" with two teenaged boys, and he had been sentenced to 5 to 20 years in a state prison. Shortly before his scheduled release from prison, the state invoked a new statute to have Hendricks civilly committed as a sexually violent predator. The statute at issue was enacted in 1994, 10 years after his 1984 conviction. The statute, the *Kansas Sexually Violent Predators Act* (SVP), provided for the civil commitment of sexually violent predators. The statute defined a sexually violent predator as "any person who has been convicted of or charged with a sexually violent offense and who suffers from a mental abnormality or personality disorder which makes the person likely to engage in predatory acts of sexual violence." At a hearing, Hendricks testified as to his past history of sexual offenses and his self-described inability to refrain from committing such offenses, stating that he could not control his urge to offend. Hendricks' diagnosis, as put forward by expert witnesses, was personality trait disturbance, passive–aggressive personality, and pedophilia. The jury unanimously found beyond a reasonable doubt that Hendricks was a sexually violent predator. In reviewing the case, the trial judge concluded, as a matter of law, that pedophilia was a "mental abnormality" within the meaning of the Kansas statute. Hendricks was committed under the civil statute and challenged his commitment. The Kansas Supreme Court struck down the SVP statute because it was found to violate the Due Process Clause of the U.S. Constitution. The court held that the "mental abnormality" threshold violated substantive due process requirements for failing to require "mental illness" as a precondition for detention. Hendricks and the state of Kansas were both unsatisfied and appealed to the Supreme Court.

Hendricks challenged the Kansas statute under the Due Process Clause, the Double Jeopardy Clause, and Ex Post Facto Clause. The due process challenge concerned the "mental abnormality" requirement in the Kansas SVP Act and whether it satisfied substantive due process. The majority conceded that freedom from physical restraint was a core interest protected by the Due Process Clause and concluded that this liberty interest could be outweighed by the state's interest in maintaining order and safety. The Court reasoned that it had consistently upheld civil commitment statutes as long as the confinement takes place pursuant to proper procedures and evidentiary standards and does not offend the sense of ordered liberty. The Court held that the Kansas statute's "mental abnormality" or "personality disorder" requirement was consistent with commitment statutes that the Court previously had upheld. The Court avoided a discussion of what these terms meant and posited that their differences were simply semantics. Once the Court found that terms relating to mental conditions are essentially indistinguishable and courts have used them interchangeably, the Court easily dismissed the due process claim on separation-of-powers grounds. The Court reasoned that it had to defer to the state legislature with regard to the nomenclature adopted in civil commitment statutes, that state legislatures had the discretion to define terms of a medical nature that had legal significance. As a result, the "mental abnormality" or "personality disorder" requirement was held not to violate substantive due process. This move was of significance given that the mental abnormality standard is broader than the traditional characterization of mental illness. Indeed, mental abnormality is not even a medically recognized diagnostic term and prior precedent had concluded that if disorders (even recognized personality disorders) do not amount to mental illness, they could not be used to support civil commitments. Rather than engage that issue, the Court simply noted that the term mental illness was "devoid of any talismanic significance" (p. 359). The sate was free to define the type of mental illness that would serve as the basis for commitment.

Addressing the double jeopardy and *ex post facto* claims required the Court to determine whether the sexual predator law was civil or criminal in nature. This was significant in that, if no treatment was provided, then and as argued by Hendricks, the law could be construed as punitive. If the lack of treatment renders such commitment punitive in nature, then it poses a challenge to the characterization of such commitment as "civil." The Kansas Supreme Court had held that, absent a treatable mental illness, Hendricks could not be detained (because such detention would then amount to punishment and would be in violation of the Double Jeopardy and Ex Post Facto clauses). The U.S. Supreme Court, however, held that incapacitation may be a legitimate end of civil law. Regardless of treatment, the law could be considered civil. In determining that the Act was civil, the Court relied most heavily on the legislative designation of the Act as civil and the Court's required deference to such state judgments. The *Hendricks* majority also offered an alternate interpretation of the Kansas Supreme Court opinion, in which it interpreted the lower court's decision as having held that while the statute does provide for treatment as an ancillary goal, treatment was not provided in this particular case. The U.S. Supreme Court essentially was willing to overlook this delay in providing treatment, especially in this case because *Hendricks* was the first case under the statute and the state could claim that it would need some time to organize treatment facilities and programs.

To summarize, the *Hendricks* majority effectively allows the state to commit those who do not suffer from a mental illness, who are not amenable to treatment (or to whom treatment is not given), and who already have been punished for their wrongdoing. The opinion clearly validates police power commitments. The commitment in *Hendricks* was not made for his own benefit. Hendricks did not decide to commit himself and his commitment was not made on his behalf due to his level of competency. The state never argued that he was incompetent to make decisions about whether he could benefit from treatment. The Court, nevertheless upheld the state's power to commit him to protect public safety. The Court also was not persuaded by the argument that the possible lack of treatment for Hendricks' condition invalidated his confinement. The Court declared that confinement of a mentally ill person might be permissible where no treatment were provided if, in fact, no treatment were possible. The decision, however, only ambiguously addressed whether due process required a finding that a person is unable to control his behavior. Hendricks was a pedophile who had admitted that he was unable to control his behavior. Whether a finding that the offender was unable to control his behavior is required in cases where there was no such admission was less clear. *Kansas v. Crane* (2002) squarely addressed that issue.

In January 1993, Michael Crane entered a Kansas tanning salon and exposed himself to a 19-year-old female attendant. Half an hour later, he entered a nearby video store, exposed his genitals to the 20-year-old female clerk, demanded that she perform oral sex on him, threatened to rape her, and then suddenly ran out of the store. Crane was convicted of lewd and lascivious conduct for the former incident and for attempted aggravated criminal sodomy, attempted rape, and kidnapping for the latter. He was sentenced to 35 years to life in prison. The Supreme Court of Kansas reversed the convictions for attempted aggravated criminal sodomy, attempted rape, and kidnapping (in part because the state had not charged the necessary elements). Crane subsequently pled guilty to one count of aggravated sexual battery. He was released from prison after 5 years. The state sought to have Crane committed under the Kansas SVP Act. At his commitment proceeding, Crane requested that the jury be instructed that it could not commit him unless it found that he was unable to "control his dangerous behavior." The trial court rejected this request, and concluded that the jury need only find that Crane was suffering from a personality disorder that made him likely to engage in future predatory acts of sexual violence. The Kansas Supreme Court reversed Crane's commitment, holding that a constitutionally valid commitment required a showing that Crane was "unable to control" his behavior. On appeal to the Supreme Court, the state argued that requiring an inmate to be "completely unable" to control his behavior was unnecessary and unworkable. Crane argued that *Hendricks* required the state to show that a person was completely unable to control his behavior. Crane had been diagnosed as suffering from antisocial personality disorder and exhibitionism. Even the state's witnesses agreed that Crane had significant control over his actions; therefore, had Crane's argument been accepted, his commitment would have to be invalid. The state, on the other hand, argued that *Hendricks* did not require any separate showing of inability to control behavior. The state interpreted *Hendricks* as setting forth the causal link standard—that the person engaged in harmful conduct because of the mental abnormality or personality disorder (the lack-of-control aspect was subsumed by the causal link between the mental abnormality/personality disorder and the harmful conduct). The Supreme Court rejected both of these positions and adopted a middle ground. The Court accepted the state's view that it need not show that an inmate is "completely unable" to control his behavior, but it nevertheless held that a valid commitment required some showing of lack of control.

The Court held that a separate finding of lack of control was required in order to satisfy due process, but it was less than clear when it described how much control an offender needed to have in order to lack control.

The Court easily rejected the argument that *Hendricks* required a showing of complete lack of control. The Court relied on *Hendricks'* reference to the Kansas SVP Act as requiring a mental abnormality or personality disorder that made it difficult, if not impossible, for the dangerous person to control his dangerous behavior. According to the majority, the use of the word "difficult" suggested that *Hendricks* did not envisage absolute lack of control. The Court reasoned that most severely ill people retained some ability to control their behavior, including those commonly labeled "psychopaths." Thus, the insistence on an absolute standard of lack of control would not allow for the confinement of extremely dangerous individuals with a mental abnormality/personality disorder. It is important to note what *Crane* does not address. The opinion does not quantify the lack of control necessary to justify civil commitments. The majority in *Crane* deliberately left the issue of the quantum of lack of control vague, and justified doing so by stating that the "Constitution's safeguards of human liberty in the area of mental illness and the law are not always best enforced by precise bright-line rules" (*Kansas v. Crane,* 2002, p. 413). The very fact that the Court did not know where to draw the line (and left this task to state legislatures) suggests that the standard is difficult to apply in the legal context. It is difficult to determine what constitutes sufficient lack-of-control.

*Crane* also is of interest to us for what also was happening during its litigation. After the Kansas Supreme Court decided *Crane,* but before the United States Supreme Court issued an opinion in *Crane,* the Court decided *Seling v. Young* (2001). That case involved a challenge to Washington State's *Community Protection Act,* which also was a civil commitment statute for sexual predators. In that case, Andre Young appealed from a unanimous jury determination that he was a sexually violent predator, subject to confinement under the Act. Young argued that the Act was unconstitutional because it was punitive in application to him. His argument was that, as applied, the civil statute was actually a criminal statute given that he was being punished; if the civil statute was punitive, then it was unconstitutional because he already was punished when he was sentenced and served time for his crimes.

As with the other cases in this area, Young's record was not one that kindled much sympathy for the offender. Young had been convicted of six rapes over the course three decades. It was upon his latest release from incarceration that the state of Washington sought to commit him as a sexually violent predator. An expert testified that Young suffered from a severe personality disorder with primarily paranoid and antisocial features. Young also was diagnosed with severe paraphilia, classified as either paraphilia sexual sadism or paraphilia not otherwise specified (rape). The Washington Supreme Court concluded that the statute was "concerned with treating committed persons for a current mental abnormality, and protecting society from the sexually violent acts associated with that abnormality, rather than being concerned with criminal culpability" (*Seling v. Young,* 2001, p. 257). The United States Supreme Court agreed with this finding. As it had done in prior cases, the

Court found the statute civil on its face. This was not surprising given that a "facial challenge" is the most difficult to mount successfully, because the challenge must establish that no set of circumstances exists under which the statute would be valid. Even though the Court agreed that he was not receiving treatment, the Court ruled that, because the Act was determined to be facially civil, Young's "as applied" challenge had to fail. The Court concluded that the statute would be unworkable if it allowed such challenges when the statute was civil. "The civil nature of a confinement scheme cannot be altered based merely on vagaries in the implementation of the authorizing statute" (p. 263). Only one sole dissenter urged that Young should have been allowed to prove that the statute was criminal in nature as applied to him. Despite this dissent, Young's constitutional challenge failed; the Court rejected the "as-applied" *ex post facto* challenge to Washington state's civil commitment statute.

The above cases reveal that the Supreme Court's jurisprudence supports distinctions between civil and criminal systems. The move is of significance. Despite being upheld by the courts, the sexual predator statutes produce a contradiction in light of retribution and deterrence concerns and the civil-criminal distinction. Upon a criminal charge, the state argues that sexual offenders are criminally responsible for a sexually violent offense. To do so, the state relies on the assumption that these individuals are rational actors with free will, that they choose to commit crimes. If convicted, the sexual offender faces an indefinite civil commitment upon release. The state then reverses its rationale, arguing that the offender has a mental abnormality, is unable to control himself, and is dangerous to society. The lack of control requirement suggests that sexual predators do not have free will to choose to commit a crime. The sexual predator is then nondeterrable, despite a previous criminal conviction suggesting that the sexual offender had free will and, thus, was deterrable. This area of law exemplifies the challenges facing efforts to develop a principled jurisprudence when we deal with different systems bottomed on different state powers and missions.

## State Statutes

As the Supreme Court cases reveal, states have enacted "sexually violent predator" laws (see Appendix C for statutes). These laws mainly were sought to commit sexually dangerous criminals to mental health facilities for treatment and rehabilitation and to protect society from the dangers posed by these individuals. Washington was the first state to enact a sexually violent predator law, and many other states soon followed. Kansas' statute, the *Kansas Sexually Violent Predator Act* (Kansas Act), was closely patterned after Washington's and has been the one that has gained the most attention since it was involved in the leading cases in this area. New Jersey's statute also has received attention, given that it too ended up scrutinized by the Supreme Court. We focus on these two statutes here to note similarities and key differences among these types of statutes.

Under the Kansas Act, a trial must be held to determine whether a person is a sexually violent predator; that is, whether that person "has been convicted of or charged with a sexually violent offense and who suffers from a mental abnormality or personality disorder which makes the person likely to engage in repeat acts of sexual violence." These trials afford individuals many of the rights associated with a criminal proceeding. These rights seek to ensure the presence of as many safeguards as possible during a proceeding that has far-reaching consequences. The procedures for the use of the statutes are straightforward. When the state wishes to have a person determined a sexually violent predator, several procedural hurdles must be cleared before a court can order a commitment. A petition first must be filed with the court. A judge then determines whether there exists probable cause to believe that the named person is a sexually violent predator. If probable cause exists, the court will order that the state take the person into custody. Within 72 hours, the person in custody will be notified of a hearing where he or she may contest the finding of probable cause. If probable cause is confirmed, the person will be subjected to a professional evaluation prior to trial. A trial follows, and if the fact-finder determines the person to be a sexually violent predator beyond a reasonable doubt, the person will be taken into custody by the Secretary of Social and Rehabilitative Services for "control, care and treatment until such time as the person's mental abnormality or personality disorder has so changed that the person is safe to be at large."

New Jersey enacted its *Sexually Violent Predator Act* (SVPA) to detain sex offenders who otherwise could not be detained because they were not necessarily mentally ill. When it enacted the statute, the state noted that persons with mental illnesses can be involuntarily committed under present New Jersey laws, but that sexually violent persons may have only a mental abnormality that does not necessarily constitute a mental illness. Because of this distinction, the legislature determined that it was necessary to enact a law to apply specifically to the civil commitment of sexually violent predators. The New Jersey SVPA defines a "sexually violent predator" in a manner similar to that of other sexually violent predator laws. Like the Kansas SVPA, the New Jersey version requires notice to the state of the imminent expiration of an individual's prison term, as well as the release of information related to those individuals. After the notice and receipt of information, the State may institute involuntary commitment proceedings. Once the proceedings are initiated, the New Jersey SVPA provides those accused with the right to legal counsel and a full hearing, as well as most of the procedures and rights that would normally be associated with a trial. Among others, the procedures include service of notice upon the accused, provisions for court reporters and transcriptions, expert witnesses, and limited discovery. Unlike a criminal trial, however, the statute calls for a ruling based on "clear and convincing" evidence. Among other rights, the act specifically provides the accused with the right to legal counsel, the right to appear, the right to call witnesses, and the right to present evidence. Unlike Kansas, New Jersey's SVPA does not provide persons with the right to a jury trial. The Act does provide for annual court reviews of individuals' mental condition and for full or conditional discharge based on those reviews and the recommendations of psychiatrists.

Individuals deemed sexually violent predators are committed to the custody of the New Jersey Department of Corrections and their treatment is under the direction of the Division of Mental Health Services in the Department of Human Services. If treatment is successful, they can be recommended for release, subject to judicial review. Individuals need not wait for this recommendation; they may petition for discharge from commitment at any time. No set time frame is made given that the period of confinement is indefinite, as the progress of treatment cannot be determined with specificity. In this petition, individuals must demonstrate that circumstances currently exist that would preclude them from committing violent sexual offenses in the future or that an expert has concluded that they are unlikely to commit violent sexual offenses again. If the petition does not contain either of these provisions, the court can dismiss the petition without a hearing.

The Kansas and New Jersey statutes are illustrative of recent state statutes. The statutes reveal a commitment to incapacitating offenders by using civil laws, an approach that permits states to avoid the typical limitations inherent in criminal justice systems. Many Constitutional protections simply have been determined to not apply in civil settings. As a result, states essentially can achieve the same ends through the civil system that the law does not allow it to do in the criminal justice system. Although issues involving the use of the civil system to achieve criminal justice ends becomes an increasing concern throughout many legal responses to social problems, its use in this area helps to reveal the strong commitment to child protection and the mechanisms available for incapacitating offenders.

## Containing Offenders

Sex offender registration and community notification laws have developed in ways both similar and dissimilar to other recent laws relating to sex offenders. Unlike many other developments in this area, the registration and notification laws have been guided by federal legislative mandates based on fiscal incentives. These mandates have led every state to enact laws and have contributed to a sense of increasing consistency. As with the predator laws, these laws are quite recent, essentially dating to the early 1990s. They were enacted after several high profile cases dealing with kidnapping, child molestation, and murder that captured the interests of politicians, legislatures, and the media. Further similar to other laws, the Supreme Court already has evaluated them and broadly granted them legitimacy. Together, these laws provide us again with valuable insight into how our legal system approaches child maltreatment.

### *Federal Legislation*

Three major federal legislative reforms guide this area of law. In 1994, Congress enacted the *Jacob Wetterling Crimes Against Children and Sexually Violent Offender*

*Registration Act* ("Jacob Wetterling Act") (2004). This federal law requires all states to establish a registration system mandating that certain offenders register with that state. If a state fails to comply with the federal law, it loses ten percent of its federal anti-crime funding. The Act, however, only allows for release of this information to the public if it is "necessary to protect the public concerning a specific person required to register." Soon after the law took effect, public concern arose over the lack of information being released to members of the community concerning the status of registered sex offenders. Continued public concern let to more amendments, known as the federal equivalent to "Megan's Law" that had been adopted by New Jersey. The federal Megan's Law allows the release of registry information to the public in compliance with state law. The statute provides that law enforcement agencies do not have discretion in determining the release of the information and must release the information if it is necessary to protect public safety. Congress also enacted the *Pam Lyncher Sexual Offender Tracking and Identification Act of 1996* (2004) to help law enforcement agencies distribute information about registered sex offenders. This Act allows the Federal Bureau of Investigation and local law enforcement agencies to use a federal database to provide for community notification. Provisions mandate persons convicted of sexual offenses in states that do not have a "minimally sufficient" registration program to register with the FBI a current address, fingerprints, and current photograph. Additionally, the legislation amends the *Jacob Wetterling Act* by changing the duration of state registration requirement, depending on the number of prior convictions and the type of crime committed. The Act also allows authorities to track the movement of sex offenders when they move from state to state, which was difficult before because registration laws were separately created and maintained by each state.

The above federal laws set forth guidelines that require each state to amend its laws. All sates have responded. As we have seen, the federal guidelines provide states with a minimum baseline. As a result, for example, states are free to impose, and indeed have imposed, more rigorous provisions when enacting their own sex offender registries. The *Jacob Wetterling Act* provides that "a determination of whether a person is a sexually violent predator... shall be made by a court after considering the recommendation of a board composed of experts in the behavior and treatment of sex offenders, victims' rights advocates and representatives of law enforcement agencies." States, however, may waive this requirement if they have established equally or more rigorous alternate procedures or legal standards for designating an individual as a sexually violent predator. At a minimum, a state registration program must require each registrant to (a) provide local law enforcement officials with the registrant's name, address, a photograph, and fingerprints; (b) report any change in address and notify proper authorities of any intention to move to another state; and (c) register in the state where he is employed or attending school. Finally, each registrant must read and sign a document informing him of his duty to register as either a sexually violent offender or an offender convicted of crimes against children. Registration is required for ten years. Lifetime registration, however, is mandated for any individual either classified as a sexually violent predator or convicted of an aggravated offense.

More recently and pursuant to the *Commerce, Justice, and State, the Judiciary, and Related Agencies Appropriations Act* (1998), Congress prescribed heightened registration and notification requirements for offenders deemed SVPs, which federal law now requires jurisdictions to take steps to identify. Such an offender is one who has "been convicted of a sexually violent offense and who suffers from a mental abnormality or personality disorder that makes the person likely to engage in predatory sexually violent offenses." Jurisdictions are free to decide the timing of the determination of whether an offender is an SVP (at prerelease or time of sentencing) and how to initiate the determination (either by prosecutorial discretion or routinely after conviction for a sexually violent offense). Federal law is more particular with respect to the procedures used to identify SVPs. A court must make the determination after considering the recommendation of a board composed of experts in the behavior and treatment of sex offenders, victims' rights advocates, and representatives of law enforcement agencies. The Department of Justice, however, can (a) waive these requirements if a state has established alternative procedures or legal standards for designating a person as a sexually violent predator, or (b) approve alternative measures of comparable or greater effectiveness in protecting the public from unusually dangerous or recidivistic sexual offenders. Once categorized as SVPs, individuals must, at a minimum, provide the following information: their name, identifying factors, anticipated future residence, offense history, and documentation of any treatment received for their mental abnormality or personality disorder. Federal law also requires that SVPs verify their address information on a quarterly basis and remain subject to registration and notification requirements throughout their lifetimes.

## State Legislation

Federal guidelines have produced varying state approaches to registration (see Appendix C for citations). Each state's registration law varies in what it requires from the offender, how long an offender is subject to the law, whether an offender is afforded a right to notice of the registration requirements, and who can view the contents of the registration. This area of law again highlights the wide variety of state responses to addressing children's victimizations.

States differ as to the extent to which the public can access information contained in the registry. For example, Florida, New York, and California have created hotlines where callers can obtain information regarding registered sex offenders. Most states disseminate information concerning registrants via the Internet. Others allow individuals to obtain such information through local law enforcement agencies. For example, Colorado authorizes local law enforcement agencies to release to any person residing within the agency's jurisdiction information regarding any person registered with the local law enforcement agency; and South Carolina makes information collected for the registry open to public inspection, upon request to the county sheriff. Other states restrict access. Hawaii does not provide for automatic release of registration information. The state must first petition for release of information in a civil proceeding. At this hearing, offenders have the opportunity to present evidence to show that they are not a threat to the community and that the public release of their information is not necessary to the safety of the community. Like Hawaii, Minnesota does not provide for automatic dissemination of information contained in the registry; the law provides that registration information is considered "private data" and only may be used for law enforcement purposes.

State registration statutes also vary as to whether registration is compulsory or discretionary. In Massachusetts, a state that employs discretionary classification, anyone convicted of a sex crime is entitled to a hearing before a Sex Offender Registry Board, where the offender can argue against inclusion on the registration list. In determining whether to relieve the registrant of the duty to register, the Sex Offender Registry Board must consider whether the offender's criminal history indicates a risk of re-offense or a danger to the public as well as whether any physical harm was caused by the offense and whether the offense involved consensual conduct between adults. In contrast, 19 states use compulsory classification, whereby a court must classify a defendant as a sexual predator if they satisfy the specified criteria in the statute. Alabama, Alaska, California, Connecticut, Delaware, Illinois, Kansas, Michigan, Mississippi, Missouri, Montana, New Hampshire, New Mexico, Oklahoma, South Carolina, South Dakota, Tennessee, Utah, and Virginia all use compulsory classification schemes when adjudicating sex offenders. In states requiring compulsory classification, the court does not have the ability to modify the person's duty to register. For example, Minnesota law states that the Court may not modify the person's duty to register in the pronounced sentence or deposition order. Some states apply these requirements to juveniles. For example, Alabama provides that certain juveniles and all adults convicted of a criminal sex offense are subject to compulsory registration and community notification by means of a notification flyer, which police distribute by hand or regular mail. Importantly, the states that use the compulsory method require registration and notification without regard for recidivism risks of individual offenders.

States that do not have compulsory notification and rely on varying degrees of discretion for registering and classifying offenders for notifying communities approach these decisions in a wide variety of ways. First, several states (Colorado, Georgia, Florida, Idaho, Louisiana, North Carolina, and West Virginia) direct the judiciary to make such determinations. These states tend to have statutory procedures that guide judicial SVP determinations. Other states leave more discretion to various officials. Maryland and Ohio, for example, single out broader categories of particular offenders for discretionary risk classification. These states permit courts to decide whether to classify a statutorily eligible person as an SVP; if not, then they are subject to less-onerous registration requirements and less-extensive notification. Other states grant local law enforcement officials discretion in the decision whether to release notification information. Arizona, Hawaii, Nebraska, Maine, North Dakota, Washington, and Wisconsin direct local law enforcement to make offender classification decisions, which determine the extent and scope of community notification that ultimately occurs. Importantly, law enforcement authorities in this group make decisions informally and outside the presence of offenders, and no right of appeal is afforded with respect to risk classification decisions. Other jurisdictions require that risk evaluations be made of all registration-eligible sex offenders, based on risk-level determinations rendered by persons or entities other than police. Jurisdictions in this group employ a variety of evaluative methods. Several states (Arkansas, Iowa, Massachusetts, Minnesota, Nevada, Oregon, Rhode Island, and Texas) vest primary discretionary authority in an executive agency, such as a parole board, the state department of corrections, or a specially convened board, to conduct risk assessments and categorize statutorily eligible offenders. Although the initial assessment proceeds *ex parte*, upon receiving notice of being designated a class II or III offender, an individual can request reconsideration of the designation, whereupon the offender is permitted to appear personally to present evidence in favor of re-designation, and the state can offer rebuttal evidence. Once the designation is set, local law enforcement then carries out notification in a scope and method consistent with the designated tier.

In New Jersey, prosecutors evaluate each eligible sex offender for notification purposes in terms of "risk of re-offense," by means of a three-tier risk assessment scoring system that accords points to different risk factors identified by mental health and law enforcement professionals. The registrant can appeal to the local county court and is entitled an *in camera* judicial hearing, with counsel provided but not in public, in which the court makes a "case-by-case" determination of the propriety of the prosecutor's determination. Wyoming allocates classification authority entirely to judges; upon application by the district attorney, the court provides notice to the offender and conducts an *in-camera* hearing. The court uses statutory criteria to designate the offender's risk of re-offense as "low," "moderate," or "high." Three other states (Kentucky, Montana, and New York) entrust courts with rendering final classification judgments on all statutorily eligible sex offenders, with varying degrees of deference paid to initial assessments made by experts, on the basis of risk-related criteria and guidelines. These jurisdictions place premium importance on due process concerns, typically affording offenders a right to counsel and requiring that offenders receive notice of and have the opportunity to be heard at the judicial proceeding. At such hearings, standard rules of evidence typically do not apply, and the reviewing court enjoys broad discretion in the amount and type of evidence allowed, including expert testimony proffered on behalf of offenders.

States also differ with respect to the range of offenses that will trigger registration. For example, Alabama law mandates registration for the following offenses: sexual perversion involving a member of the same or opposite sex, sexual abuse involving any member of the same or opposite sex, rape, sodomy, sexual misconduct, indecent exposure, promoting prostitution in the first or second degree, obscenity, incest, or an attempt to commit any of these crimes. Iowa mandates registration for any individual who has been convicted of a criminal offense against a minor, an aggravated offense, sexual exploitation or a sexually violent offense. Pennsylvania requires 10-year registration for the following offenses: kidnapping a minor, indecent assault, incest where the victim is between the ages of twelve and eighteen, promoting prostitution of a minor, obscenity where the victim is a minor, sexual abuse of children, unlawful contact with a minor, and sexual exploitation of children or any attempt to commit these offenses. Lifetime registration is required for rape, involuntary deviate sexual intercourse, sexual assault, aggravated indecent assault, incest where the victim is younger than 12 years of age, and sexually violent predators.

Note that the *Jacob Wetterling Act* specifies that states may impose registration for sexually violent offenses that include or exceed aggravated sexual abuse or any offense that involves engaging in physical contact with another with the intent to commit aggravated sexual abuse or sexual abuse. Consequently, states have developed varying lists of enumerated offenses that require registration. A minority of states demand registration if the defendant's offense was "sexually motivated" or committed for a sexual purpose. California mandates registration if the crime is committed for "purposes of sexual gratification." Kansas requires registration for "any act which at the time of sentencing for the offense has been determined beyond a reasonable doubt to have been sexually motivated," whereas West Virginia demands registration if the offense was "sexually motivated." State laws also vary as to the length of registration. For example, Florida requires lifetime registration for all "sexual predators," whereas Arizona requires lifetime registration after a conviction for sexual conduct with a minor. Hawaii simply requires compliance with registration requirements for the lifetime of the offender. Maine and Minnesota provide for a ten-year registration period.

The penalties for noncompliance also vary among states. New York treats failure to comply as a first offense as class A misdemeanor. North Carolina treats any violation for non-compliance as a Class F felony. South Carolina treats a first offense as a misdemeanor with a mandatory sentence of ninety days incarceration. These variations again reveal significant variation in states' legal responses to child maltreatment, despite the similar recognition of the need to enact these laws.

## Supreme Court Jurisprudence

Soon after federal mandates encouraged the development of state statutes addressing the registration of offenders, the Supreme Court agreed to review two cases directly addressing this area of law. The first case involved Connecticut's Megan's Law, *Connecticut v. Doe* (2003). That statute provides that all convicted sex offenders must register with the Department of Public Safety (DPS) by providing personal information, including their name, address, photograph, and a DNA sample for a period of 10 years or, for life in the case of a sexually violent offense. "John Doe" challenged the statute. Doe was a convicted sex offender who was subject to the Connecticut registration requirements. Doe was subject to the requirement even though his conviction was based on conduct that occurred before the law had gone into effect. Doe represented a class of individuals who were subjected to the registration laws. He claimed that the registration law violated his due process rights because it deprived him of a liberty interest—his reputation combined with the alteration of his status under state law—without notice or a meaningful opportunity to be heard. Doe's basis for the *ex post facto* claim was that the law subjected him to punishment for conduct committed before the law took effect. Doe sought declaratory and injunctive relief prohibiting Connecticut from enforcing the registration law and prohibiting public disclosure of information contained within the registry.

The District Court granted summary judgment on Doe's due process claim, certified a class of persons similarly situated to Doe, and permanently enjoined Connecticut's public disclosure provisions, which resulted in the shutdown of the DPS website regarding sex offenders. The Second Circuit affirmed the decision, finding that the due process clause of the United States Constitution entitled class members to a hearing before the state disseminates information. Despite a disclaimer on the website indicating that DPS had made no determinations as to whether individuals were currently dangerous, the Court of Appeals also found that because the law implied that the offender was dangerous, a "liberty interest" was implicated. Furthermore, the court expressed the opinion that the registration requirements were "extensive and onerous" (*Connecticut v. Doe*, 2003, p. 6).

In a very short opinion, the Supreme Court found for the state. The majority noted that "mere injury to reputation, even if defamatory, does not constitute the deprivation of a liberty interest" (pp. 6–7). The Court continued and stated that the fact that the plaintiff was seeking to prove that he currently does not present a danger to society was inconsequential. The Court stressed the fact that all sex offenders must be publicly disclosed and, barring demonstration by the plaintiff that the substantive rule of law is defective due to a constitutional conflict, a hearing would be useless. Given that issues regarding procedural due process were not before the Court, it refused to address whether the statutes violated substantive due process. In a concurring opinion, it was stated that even if Connecticut's law implicated a liberty interest, the plaintiff still was not entitled to a hearing under a substantive due process argument. Using the requirement that a licensed driver must be 16 years of age as an analogy, the concurrence stated that "a convicted sex offender has no more right to additional 'process' enabling him to establish that he is not dangerous than ... a 15-year-old has a right to 'process' enabling him to establish that he is a safe driver" (*Connecticut v. Doe*, 2003, pp. 8–9).

*Connecticut v. Doe* (2003) had a companion case: *Smith v. Doe* (2003). That case addressed the question of whether Alaska's version of Megan's Law was a retroactive punishment prohibited by the *ex post facto* clause of the United States Constitution. The statute being challenged was similar to many other states' versions of Megan's Law. In this case, Alaska's law was comprised of two retroactive components: a registration requirement and a notification provision. In addition to providing name, aliases, identifying features, address, place of employment, date of birth, conviction information, driver's license number, information about vehicles to which they have access, and postconviction treatment history, under Alaska's version of Megan's Law, a convicted sex offender must also submit to fingerprinting and photographing. Although some information was kept confidential, Alaska, like Connecticut, used the Internet to publish information not held confidential.

To evaluate the statute at issue, the Court began by noting the need to determine whether the intention of the legislature was to impose punishment. If such an intent was found, the inquiry would necessarily end. However, even if the statute was found to be "civil and nonpunitive," the Court still would need to determine whether the statutory scheme was "so punitive either in purpose or effect as to negate [the state's] intention to deem it civil" (*Smith v. Doe,* 2003, p. 92). Even though Alaska's statute was partially codified in the state's criminal procedure code, the Court determined, as did the District Court and the Court of Appeals before it, that the Alaska legislature intended "to create a civil, nonpunitive regime" (pp. 93–95).

The opinion then evaluated the effects of the Alaska statute and, in doing so, sought guidance from the 1963 case of *Kennedy v. Mendoza-Martinez* (1963). In *Mendoza-Martinez,* the Court had set forth seven factors that provided the current Court with useful guideposts for evaluating *ex post facto* claims, despite their being neither exhaustive nor dispositive. Among the factors identified by the Court as potentially relevant to their analysis were questions as to whether the regulatory scheme "has been regarded in our history and traditions as a punishment; imposes an affirmative disability or restraint; promotes the traditional aims of punishment; has a rational connection to a nonpunitive purpose; or is excessive with respect to this purpose" (*Kennedy v. Mendoza-Martinez,* 1963, p. 97).

Using this framework to assess the nature of the Act with regard to punishment, the Court began its analysis by looking at whether the Act had been regarded historically as punishment. The Court rejected the argument that the Act, particularly the notification requirement, resembled shaming punishments of the colonial period. It found that the "stigma" that results from Alaska's Megan's Law "results not from public display for ridicule and shaming but from the dissemination of accurate information about a criminal record, most of which is already public" (p. 98). The Court then noted that the global reach of the Internet does not render the notification procedure punitive where the purpose and effect of notification is public safety. It further found that widespread access was necessary and that the "attendant humiliation is but a collateral consequence of a valid regulation" (p. 99).

The Court also rejected the claim that the Act imposed an affirmative disability or restraint on the respondents. In its view, the Act imposed no physical restraints on sex offenders that would resemble actual imprisonment, nor did it restrain registrants from freely changing jobs or residences. The Court also rejected the argument that requiring offenders to update their information constituted an affirmative disability; it noted that these individuals were still free to move, live and work as they wished, without supervision. The Court also rejected the argument that the registration requirements were retributive because the Act was applied to all convicted sex offenders, without regard to future danger, and also because it failed to limit the number of persons with access to the information. The Court found persuasive findings indicating that sex offenders have high rates of recidivism and that most do not reoffend within the first few years. The Court also rejected the claim that access to information was unlimited; the Court found it important that the notification system at issue was a "passive" one that required interested parties to seek access to the information. Given this line of reasoning, the Court concluded that the act was nonpunitive, and that its retroactive application to the respondents, and others similarly situated, did not violate the *ex post facto* clause of the United States Constitution.

This last line of cases provides us with another example of the Court's permitting the use of the civil justice system to achieve ends unattainable by the criminal justice system. In these cases, the Court does so by defining certain state actions (most notably, punishment) as primarily the concern of our criminal justice system and then limiting certain constitutional protections to that system. These analyses may make considerable jurisprudential sense. They do not, however, mean that other constitutional protections do not apply. In these cases, we noticed that there had been considerable due process protections, not the least of which involved a finding of guilt leading to the initial intervention and a finding that there was a need for continued intervention. It is these other protections, those that are broader and apply to more state actions, that remain the most important source of potential legal developments.

## Conclusions: The Loosening of Protections From State Controls

The legal system's responses to child maltreatment increasingly use the criminal justice system. The system, as we have seen, is increasingly child friendly. In addition, the system now invokes more control over offenders, especially upon their release. These developments reveal important changes in key principles that revealed our common understanding of our legal system and our sense of what constitutes a just society. The Constitution has been read to enumerate important protections from certain state actions, especially in the form of the criminal justice system. Recently, however, these protections have been somewhat loosened, especially in two ways. The first way is quite direct; it involves interpretations of traditional protections that, at least arguably, circumvent procedures historically deemed effective in protecting individuals from erroneous accusations. The second way involves a rethinking of what constitutes criminal proceedings. The state's power, and the restraints on it, implies at least some exclusivity in the use of criminal sanctions. There is some historical precedent for avoiding these restraints by simply approaching the state's actions as "civil" rather than "criminal." This approach has gained increasing use in recent years, especially in response to offenders who abuse children. The approach involves the government's recasting of its criminal proceedings as civil and, in a real sense, seeking to accomplish the goals it might otherwise achieve only through punishment by a change in nomenclature. This area of law, as we have seen, necessarily deals with efforts to switch and cast off many limitations and restraints. The casting off of protections from the state, however, is uneven and varies from one area of law to another. In some areas, restraints seem to disappear while, in others, they seem to be increasing and allow for a more aggressive use of sanctions and controls. We are left with considerable diversity, especially in the flexibility needed to protect children when states need their testimony to prosecute cases and the permissible responses to those identified as having maltreated children.

We may draw several conclusions from these recent developments, three of which are particularly important to highlight. The developments reveal the increasing need for the civil child protective system to address harms that the criminal justice system, for a variety of reasons, cannot address, such as providing protection from offenders who are released to communities. Protections provided by the criminal justice system also highlight important inadequacies of the civil, child welfare system, most notably protections from unreliable testimony and problematic evidence. Finally, even the criminal justice system, which should provide the most stringent protections, reveals considerable diversity in its laws and approaches to dealing with children and those who offend against them. We will turn to these issues in our concluding chapter.

# Chapter 7
# Shifting Rules Regulating the Role of Expertise

Expertise, including testimony by experts who have scientific or technical knowledge as well as the scientific or technological evidence itself, often plays a determinative role in legal responses to child maltreatment. For example, experts can review and explain complex evidence to those involved in the legal system, ranging from caseworkers, attorneys, law enforcement personnel, and judges. Experts also can, for example, help draw inferences from the existing body of medical, psychological, and other scientific literature. These inferences can then serve as the foundation of cases or lead to their dismissals. Experts also can assess how well available evidence supports cases and offer opinions about the strengths and weaknesses of evidence. In addition to assisting law enforcement and caseworkers, experts can assist attorneys in preparation for litigation. If cases are litigated, expert witnesses can testify to their theories, opinions, and conclusions at hearings and trials. Just as the expert's roles have helped shape cases before trials, they can help determine the outcomes of cases. A judge's decision to admit, exclude, or limit evidence offered by either side can have a significant influence on the outcomes of trials. As we have seen, experts also can play important roles in the disposition of cases, ranging from influencing actual penalties to assisting the state to control released offenders. Without doubt, expertise shapes legal responses.

Although evidentiary concerns may attract more controversy in cases that involve punitive sanctions, they also inevitably play a critical role regardless of whether we are dealing with criminal or civil justice system responses to maltreatment. Psychological evaluations, for example, can be used during many stages of civil, child welfare responses. Evaluations may be ordered before determining whether supervised or unsupervised visits should occur, and how they should be supervised or even unsupervised. They also play into ultimate determinations of cases, such as permanency goals. Caseworkers also, of course, rely on scientific knowledge, including their own technical training, when they intervene in families. The place of evidence is of significance, then, given that all cases necessarily deal with the use of specialized information, with determining whether and how best to use specialized information, as the legal system seeks to respond to child maltreatment.

Roger J.R. Levesque, *Child Maltreatment and the Law*                                                    155
© 2008 Springer Science+Business Media, LLC

This chapter examines how the legal system typically addresses expertise. Although we now know that expertise plays an important role throughout all phases of responses to child maltreatment, issues relating to expertise and the appropriateness of evidence typically arise when cases are adjudicated, especially in criminal courts. We thus explore the general rules regulating evidence dealing with expertise: the use of scientific and technical evidence, including testimony proffered by experts. Like many issues we have addressed, this area of law offers exceedingly complex rules, and those rules can vary considerably across jurisdictions. Because of enormous complexities and variations, we mainly focus on three leading Supreme Court cases. These cases help us understand influential themes and trends, because states increasingly are guided by the federal rules of evidence. Although states may eventually follow federal rules; they typically need not do so. As a result, important variations still will likely remain in states' responses. After examining the nature of the federal rules as they relate to scientific and expert evidence, then, we briefly examine state statutes to highlight a few key points. Overall, our analysis reveals that the rules are shifting and that this shift most likely will influence the law's responses to child maltreatment. Our conclusion examines the significance of these rules for shaping legal responses to child maltreatment.

## The Supreme Court and the Federal Rules of Evidence

Three recent Supreme Court cases have emerged as the leading cases that reveal a sea of change in the rules of evidence relating to the nature and use of expert knowledge in both civil and criminal court systems. These cases interpret and apply the federal rules of evidence relating to the admission of expert testimony and scientific evidence. As previously noted, the rules governing this area of law are quite complex, and they are best understood by an examination of their application as well as judicial rationales for adopting particular rules. As a result, we examine these cases in considerable depth.

In many ways, the Federal Rules of Evidence are quite clear when they guide judges in their decisions to permit expert testimony and testimony regarding scientific evidence. The standard requirement of admissibility is "relevance." That requirement is not particularly demanding; Rule 401 expansively defines the relevancy rule as "evidence having any tendency to make the existence of any fact that is of consequence to the determination of the action more probable or less probable than it would be without the evidence." Rule 402 declares that all relevant evidence shall be admitted unless excluded by other rules. Rule 403, however, limits this broad approach as it provides that "although relevant, evidence may be excluded if its probative value is substantially outweighed by the danger of unfair prejudice, confusion of the issues, or misleading the jury, or by considerations of undue delay, waste of time, or needless." For our purposes, it is important to understand that the Rules also highlight the key factor that distinguishes an expert from a nonexpert: experts have specialized knowledge, skill, experience, training, and education. Rule

702 limits testimony to those that stem from this expert background. It merits noting that an expert witness' opinion may not be used as a substitute for a juror's opinion. In effect experts adopt an advisory role. These statutes restrict expert testimony to assisting the trier of fact in understanding the evidence. In fact and if feasible, the expert, might well refrain from offering an opinion if the trier of fact is capable of drawing the requisite inference.

The above apparently simple rules actually are quite deceptive to the extent that they are not that simple. Significant complexity emerges when we seek to apply these rules to real cases. Indeed, their applications often contribute to considerable controversy. It is this complexity and potential for controversy that leads us to focus on leading cases that have become known as the *"Daubert* trilogy" after the case that heralded a new approach to the admissibility of scientific evidence: *Daubert v. Merrell Dow Pharmaceuticals, Inc.* (1993). The trilogy helps us understand how rules are applied, their supporting rationales, and what the legal system seeks to achieve in its use of evidence.

*Daubert* was the first leading case to address modern issues relating to the admission of scientific testimony at trials. *Daubert* involved the drug Bendectin, a popular antinausea medicine that physicians had prescribed to pregnant women for morning sickness. The plaintiffs claimed that Bendectin administered to their mothers during pregnancy caused their birth defects. The defendant moved for summary judgment, arguing that no causal link existed between Bendectin and birth defects. In affidavits from its expert scientists, the defendant correctly noted that none of the published 38 epidemiological studies of Bendectin had identified a causal connection between birth defects and the drug. In response, the plaintiffs offered affidavits from experts who had concluded—on the basis of chemical structure analysis, in vitro (test tube) studies of animal cells, in vivo (live) animal studies, and a "reanalysis" of the previous epidemiological studies—that Bendectin, in fact, could cause birth defects. Concluding that the plaintiffs' proffered expert evidence did not meet the "general acceptance" standard of admissibility, the district court granted the defendant's summary judgment motion, and the appeals court affirmed the finding that the plaintiffs could not win a case on the type of evidence they could present at trial.

On appeal to the Supreme Court, the plaintiffs argued that the lower courts had used the wrong standard to evaluate the admissibility of evidence. They argued that the Federal Rules of Evidence had superseded the *Frye* "general acceptance" standard. It was in *Frye v. United States* (1923) that the federal courts had first recognized a special rule governing the admissibility of scientific evidence. In *Frye*, a federal appeals court had upheld a lower court decision to refuse to admit the results of a systolic blood pressure detection test (a precursor to the polygraph) on the basis that the test had not gained "general acceptance" as a method of assessing truth-telling. Many state and federal courts had embraced this "general acceptance" standard, and its use even had persisted despite the federal government's enactment of the Federal Rules of Evidence that related directly to scientific evidence. At the time of the *Daubert* decision, the relevant federal rule, Rule 702, had provided: "If scientific, technical, or other specialized knowledge will assist the trier of fact to understand the evidence or determine a fact in issue, a witness qualified as an expert by knowledge, skill, experience, training, or education, may testify thereto in the form of an opinion or otherwise." The *Daubert* majority easily concluded that the *Frye* test had not survived the later adoption of the Federal Rules of Evidence. It was not surprising that properly enacted and legitimate legislative mandates superseded a judicial decision to the contrary. The Court overturned the appeals court as it concluded that the Federal Rules do not allow a court to use the degree of acceptance of a subject of scientific testimony as the sole determinant of admissibility. This part of the *Daubert* case was not very controversial.

More controversial, or at least less expected, was the Court's effort to guide lower courts in their determinations of what qualifies as scientific evidence. The Court did so by creating a new gate-keeping role for the judge through a two-step test designed to govern the admissibility inquiry. As a first step, judges must decide whether evidence is scientific knowledge. Because Rule 702 allows qualified experts to testify about "scientific . . . knowledge," the Court reasoned that a trial judge must determine that proposed expert testimony is both "scientific" and "knowledge"—that the subject of the testimony is "grounded in the methods and procedures of science," that it is derived by the scientific method" (*Daubert v. Merrell Dow Pharmaceuticals, Inc.,* 1993, pp. 589–590). To complete this step, judges must critique scientific evidence and exclude from consideration evidence derived from scientific methodology rather than from chicanery. Specifically, the Court stated that a trial court must undertake a "preliminary assessment of whether the reasoning or methodology underlying the [scientific expert] testimony was scientifically valid" (pp. 592–593). The *Daubert* Court explained that it equated "evidentiary reliability" with "scientific validity" (p. 590). This equation meant that the heart of the new test, therefore, was the trial court's screening of scientific evidence to determine whether proffered evidence was reliable or "scientifically valid" (p. 590). An expert's proposed testimony must be "supported by appropriate validation - i.e., 'good grounds.' " (p. 590). From this perspective, expert testimony must be reliable. In efforts to rid legal decisions of reliance on junk science, the Court instructs judges to rely "solely on principles and methodology, not on the conclusions that they generate" (p. 595). After defining the test and the trial court's new gatekeeper responsibilities under *Daubert*, the Court outlined how a trial court could make a determination that the scientific principles and reasoning underlying an expert's opinion were reliable. The guiding factors mentioned by the *Daubert* Court included (a) whether the theory or technique can be or has been tested, (b) whether the theory or technique has been exposed to peer review and publication, (c) the known or potential error rate associated with a particular technique, (d) whether there were standards that controlled a particular technique's operation, and (e) *Frye*'s general acceptance test. The *Daubert* Court emphasized that the five factors it listed were not to be viewed as a definitive checklist or test. The second step mandated that judges decide whether the evidence "fits" or is relevant to the facts at issue. The basis for this requirement rested on Rule 702's dictate that expert scientific or technical testimony must be helpful to those who are to make decisions of fact, that they are to "assist the trier of fact to understand the evidence or to determine a fact in issue" (p. 591). Thus, when a party proffers expert scientific testimony, the trial court must make a preliminary determination of both the (a) reliability and (b) relevance (or fit) of the expert's reasoning or methodology underlying the proposed testimony. The focus on relevance was something unsurprising, given that the established rules of evidence, including practical concerns, expect courts to exclude irrelevant evidence. It was the focus on reliability, and the suggestion that trial courts follow scientific methods, that raised concerns. This increased level of scrutiny is what led *Daubert* to transform the judge's role in cases involving scientific evidence. The *Daubert* Court abandoned the long-standing *Frye* inquiry, which had limited the judge's role and used "general acceptance" as a surrogate for scientific quality. After *Daubert*, a mere finding of general acceptance would not guarantee admission of scientific evidence.

Although *Dabuert* was quite expansive, the Court itself noted two important points that limited its reach. First, the Court stressed that the new test imposed by Rule 702 required a trial court to determine the scientific validity of the "principles that underlie" a proffered expert opinion or scientific evidence and that the focus of the trial court in determining admissibility under the new test "must be solely on principles and methodology, not on the conclusions that they generate" (p. 595). Second, the Court specifically limited its opinion in *Daubert* to scientific evidence because scientific evidence was the only type of expert evidence at issue in *Daubert*. On remand, applying the *Daubert* analysis, the Ninth Circuit ruled again that the district court had properly excluded the plaintiffs' expert testimony, concluding that the testimony of one of the plaintiffs' experts was not reliable and that the testimony of the others was not relevant because they would only testify that Bendectin is "capable of causing" birth defects, not that the drug in fact (more likely than not) caused the plaintiffs' birth defects (*Daubert v. Merrell Dow Pharm. Inc.*, 1995, pp. 1321–1322).

Considered fully, *Daubert* accomplished four transformations. It placed the responsibility of assessing whether proffered scientific evidence was relevant and reliable (i.e., "scientifically valid") on the trial judge (as opposed to the scientific community). As such, *Daubert* established judges as gatekeepers for expert testimony in both civil and criminal trials. It established a framework for the trial court to use in determining reliability (i.e., the application of certain "reliability factors"). It instructed trial courts to focus on the scientific validity of an expert's methodology, and not on his or her conclusions. Finally, it limited the new test's application to scientific evidence and experts. These last two items were clarified, modified and expanded in the next two cases of the trilogy.

The next two cases in the *Daubert* trilogy expanded the trial court's reliability inquiry and made the *Daubert* test far broader than *Frye* ever had been. The second case in the trilogy was *General Electric Co. v. Joiner* (1997), a case that again involved civil litigation. Joiner was a city electrician who worked with electrical transformers that were cooled by a fluid—with which Joiner frequently came in contact—containing polychlorinated biphenyls (PCBs). When he was diagnosed with lung cancer, Joiner sued the manufacturers of the transformers and PCBs, alleging that, although he had been a smoker, it was the PCBs that had "promoted" his lung cancer, and proffering scientific experts to support this allegation. The court granted summary judgment for the defense, stating that the testimony of the plaintiff's experts "did not rise above 'subjective belief or unsupported speculation'" (p. 140). The court did so even though PCBs "are widely considered to be hazardous to human health" (p. 139). The court had rejected expert testimony offered by the plaintiff to show the carcinogenic nature of certain chemicals found in PCBs because the plaintiff had not shown that these substances were contained in the PCBs to which the plaintiff was exposed. On appeal, the decision was reversed, as that court noted that the Federal Rules reveal a preference for admissibility and concluded that appellate courts must apply a very stringent standard of review when expert testimony is excluded. The Supreme Court, however, reversed the judgment of the appeals court. The Court held that evidentiary rulings are to be reviewed by appellate courts under an abuse of discretion standard. The Court noted that although *Daubert* provided a more liberal application of the Federal Rules, *Daubert* did not alter trial judges' gate-keeping role. This led the Court to conclude that no distinction should be made between an exclusion of expert testimony and an inclusion of expert testimony on review by an appellate court and that both of these situations must apply the abuse of discretion standard. In examining the lower court's decision, the Supreme Court held that the district court had not abused its discretion.

*Joiner* held that the studies presented by the plaintiff's experts were so dissimilar to the facts presented in the litigation that it was not an abuse of discretion for the district court to have rejected the expert's reliance on them. The Court emphasized that federal trial courts have wide discretion to exclude expert testimony, holding that such determinations are only subject to a permissive "abuse of discretion" standard of review (*General Electric Co. v. Joiner*, 1997, p. 141). The Court further noted that *Daubert's* direction that courts focus on the expert's methodology in no way precluded a trial judge from scrutinizing the quality of the expert's conclusions.

*Joiner* clarified *Daubert* in two important respects. First, the Court held that abuse of discretion was the proper standard by which to review a trial court's decision to admit or exclude scientific evidence. Second, despite *Daubert's* admonition that a trial court was not to focus on an expert's conclusions in determining reliability and admissibility, *Joiner* supported the view that a trial court could scrutinize the reliability of a scientific expert's conclusions as well as the expert's methodology. In a key passage, the *Joiner* Court stated:

> Conclusions and methodology are not entirely distinct from one another. Trained experts commonly extrapolate from existing data.... Nothing in either *Daubert* or the Federal Rules of Evidence requires a district court to admit opinion evidence that is connected to existing data only by the *ipse dixit* of the expert. A court may conclude that there is simply too great an analytical gap between the data and the opinion proffered. (*General Electric Co. v. Joiner*, 1997, p. 146)

*Joiner's* expansion of the *Daubert* test is noteworthy. Rather than focusing a trial court on the scientific rigor of methodology, *Joiner* allows trial courts to exclude a scientific expert's opinion even if the expert had used reliable and accepted methodology if the trial court determined that the expert's conclusion was not supported by the data produced by the methodology. In short, after *Joiner*, a trial court could scrutinize the reliability of an expert's reasoning process as well as the expert's general methodology. *Joiner* recognized a judge's discretion to scrutinize the reliability of an expert's reasoning process, the expert's general methodology, as well as the expert's conclusions.

The third decision of the *Daubert* trilogy, *Kumho Tire Co. v. Carmichael* (1999), dealt with the extent to which a court's gate-keeping function went beyond scientific evidence to include all expert testimony. In *Kumho Tire*, plaintiffs brought a products liability suit after a tire blowout on their minivan resulted in a fatal accident. The plaintiff's proffered expert, Mr. Carlson, was a tire engineer who wished to tell the jury that a tire defect, not underinflation, caused the blowout (and hence, the accident). Carlson's opinion rested on his visual and tactile examination of the tire, as well as his determination that the tire did not evince at least two of four symptoms of underinflation. The district court reviewed his methodology, which was described as technical, and applied the *Daubert* factors relating to scientific evidence. Even after considering the expert's testimony under a "more flexible" interpretation of *Daubert*, the district court found the expert's testimony unreliable. The appellate court reversed and remanded, stating that *Daubert* applies only to scientific knowledge. The Supreme Court granted certiorari to clarify the confusion among the lower courts about whether *Daubert* applies to nonscientific expert testimony.

In a sweeping decision, the Supreme Court held that a judge's basic gate-keeping function applies to all expert testimony. The Court noted that the language of Rule 702 and *Daubert* suggests that there should be no distinction between scientific knowledge and other knowledge. Furthermore, the Court could not identify a convincing reason to draw such a distinction, as the judge's role as gatekeeper can assist the jury in deciphering all varieties of knowledge. The Court first concluded that the *Daubert*-reliability requirements apply to all experts, not just "scientific testimony" experts. It reasoned that all experts testifying pursuant to Rule 702 must present opinions that are relevant and that are reliably based on the knowledge and experience of the relevant discipline. The Court opined that the trial court's objective:

> is to ensure the reliability and relevancy of expert testimony. It is to make certain that an expert, whether basing testimony upon professional studies or personal experience, employs in the courtroom the same level of intellectual rigor that characterizes the practice of an expert in the relevant field. (*Kumho Tire Co. v. Carmichael*, 1999, p. 152)

The Court also reiterated *Daubert's* flexible approach and noted that the considerations identified in *Daubert* are not a definitive checklist. The Court explained that "the trial judge must have considerate leeway in deciding in a particular case how to go about determining whether particular expert testimony is reliable" (p. 152). The trial court must avoid generalities and instead focus on "the particular circumstances of the particular case at issue" (p. 150). The Court emphasized that trial courts have flexibility in performing the gatekeeper roles. As a result, the *Daubert* factors may be considered, or they may not, depending on the particular expert testimony and the particular issues in the case.

The *Kumho Tire* Court concluded that it agreed with the district court's decision to exclude Mr. Carlson's testimony on the grounds that it was unreliable. To reach this determination, the Court undertook a very detailed analysis of what Carlson did and the manner he reached his conclusions. Briefly stated, Carlson's own method of requiring two out of four abuse symptoms to show underinflation was unreliable because it required accepting Carlson's subjective determination of the presence of signs of abuse. In other words, Carlson created his two-of-four-symptoms test, and then kept his own score, similar to a batter designing his own strike zone and then calling the balls and strikes. The Court found it particularly important that Carlson's method and analysis was not the type of work he would have done had he been still employed at Michelin, the company at which he developed his particular expertise in tires.

In deciding *Kumho*, the Supreme Court resolved an issue that had split the circuits; it ruled that the test it created in *Daubert* applied to all Rule 702 experts and not only to scientific experts. This conclusion makes *Kumho Tire* a significant expansion of both *Frye* and *Daubert* when one considers that the *Frye* test and *Daubert's* holding were both limited to experts who based their opinions on scientific techniques, tests, and experiments. As a result, general acceptance is no longer the most important factor in determining the reliability of expert testimony. Instead, under the *Daubert* trilogy, courts are free to adopt a flexible approach for all expert testimony in analyzing whether the proffered testimony is reliable knowledge. Furthermore, the Supreme Court's jurisprudence insulates lower courts from rigorous review by the abuse of discretion standard, which is applied in all determinations of whether an expert should be allowed to testify and what they should testify about.

This effort to change legal practice eventually was codified to conform to the developing Supreme Court doctrine in December 2000, through extensive amendments to Federal Rule of Evidence 702, Testimony by Experts:

> If scientific, technical, or other specialized knowledge will assist the trier of fact to understand the evidence or to determine a fact in issue, a witness qualified as an expert by knowledge, skill, experience, training, or education, may testify thereto in the form of an opinion or otherwise, if (1) the testimony is based upon sufficient facts or data, (2) the testimony is the product of reliable principles and methods, and (3) the witness has applied the principles and methods reliably to the facts of the case.

Note that the legislature essentially adopted the Supreme Court's two-step approach. Focus centers on reliability and the relevance ("helpfulness") of the proposed testimony. By doing so, the Federal Rules of Evidence adopt the view that judges must play a more active role in enhancing the quality of scientific evidence used to decide legal cases. It is difficult to overestimate this approach. Before *Daubert*, the *Frye* general acceptance test had applied only to limited categories of scientific testimony; decisions to admit all other expert testimony were subjected to a liberal standard that focused on the qualifications of experts. The *Daubert* trilogy expanded the scrutiny to the broader universe of experts and placed them under a narrower view of science based on reliability.

## State Statutory and Judicial Responses

Because *Daubert* involved the interpretation of a federal statute, states are not bound by the opinion and the test it created. Nonetheless, many states have found persuasive *Daubert's* interpretation of the way the Federal Rules of Evidence regulate expert testimony, and a majority of states have adopted *Daubert* or similar tests. On the other hand, several states that have been asked to adopt *Daubert* or a *Daubert-like* test have refused, and some states continue to use the *Frye* test to determine the admissibility of scientific evidence. During the past decade, *Daubert* has transformed judicial decision making on questions of science and law in the federal courts and the thirty states that have adopted *Daubert* in whole or in part. Approximately half of the states have adopted the essential principles of *Daubert*, either expressly or by implication. These jurisdictions include Alaska, Arkansas, Connecticut, Delaware, District of Columbia, Georgia, Kentucky, Louisiana, Massachusetts, Michigan, Mississippi, Montana, Nebraska, New Hampshire, New Mexico, Ohio, Oklahoma, Oregon, Rhode Island, South Dakota, Texas, Vermont, West Virginia, and Wyoming (see Appendix D for citations). These courts can consider a wide range of factors to determine the reliability of expert testimony. In these states, courts hold hearings to determine whether evidence will be admitted. These hearings place the burden on proponents to establish by a preponderance of the evidence that the admissibility requirements have been met. Proponents, however, need not show that their experts' conclusions are correct. Courts need only be persuaded that the science supporting the conclusions is sufficiently valid and relevant. Importantly and as we have learned by the Supreme Court's enumeration of the "*Daubert* court factors," the Frye standard remains quite useful in consideration of these issues. Even in the use of the *Daubert* standards, judges still consider the scientific community's positions.

Importantly, the *Frye* standard (and variations of it) still rules in several states. See Appendix D. Fourteen states reject *Daubert* and continue to apply the *Frye* general acceptance test: Arizona, California, Florida, Illinois, Kansas, Maryland, Minnesota, New York, North Dakota, Pennsylvania, and Washington. Other states have adopted their own standards, or hybrids of the two approaches, and conform to neither *Daubert* nor *Frye*. Eight states apply their own standard for determining the admissibility of scientific evidence, without expressly adopting or rejecting the principles of *Daubert* and its progeny, including Colorado, Hawaii, Idaho, Indiana, Iowa, Maine, Missouri, New Jersey, North Carolina, South Carolina, Utah, and Wisconsin. Some of these courts view the *Daubert* analysis as "helpful" but do not follow it in every case (see, e.g., *Sears Roebuck & Co. v. Manuilov*, 2001; *Leaf v. Goodyear Tire & Rubber Co.,* 1999). In addition, four states (Alabama, Nevada, Tennessee, and Virginia) have adopted a combination of the *Frye* and *Daubert* standards. Tennessee has not expressly adopted *Daubert*, but has adopted a nearly identical approach that could be considered even more stringent than *Daubert* (see, e.g., *McDaniel v. CSX Transp., Inc.*, 1997). States are marked by considerable variation.

As we have seen, however, simply stating that a state is a "*Daubert* state" or has "adopted *Daubert*" only reveals part of the story. It does not reveal whether a particular state has adopted all of the holdings of all of the cases in the *Daubert* trilogy. For example, it does not convey whether the *Daubert* test is applied to experts' reasoning processes and conclusions (*Joiner*) or just their methodology (*Daubert*). Nor does it reveal whether it applies to scientific experts only (*Daubert* and *Frye*) or to all experts (*Kumho Tire*). It also does not tell whether appellate review is under the abuse of discretion standard (*Joiner*) or under the de novo standard (as is required in most *Frye* jurisdictions). It has yet to be determined how many states will wholeheartedly adopt the *Daubert* trilogy.

Regardless of whether a state follows *Daubert*, *Frye*, something in between, or its own unique standard, trial court judges have the ability and duty to guard against unreliable expert testimony. Expert testimony requires a decision on admissibility that is very different from other evidentiary issues, such as hearsay or privilege. General background and experience, in the case of expert testimony, are insufficient bases on which to evaluate admissibility. Each proffered expert presents a unique question as to their qualifications, the reliability of their employed methodology, and the conclusions that they reached. The challenge of some standards is that they may exclude testimony about theories that are reliable and based on sound science, but have not yet gained general acceptance in the field. They can also do so while allowing admission of theories that have arguably gained general acceptance, yet have not been subject to peer review or vigorous testing and may not fit the facts of the case. Clearly, evidentiary standards can make a difference.

## Conclusions: Implications for Addressing Child Maltreatment

Recent developments in the law's approach to expertise potentially have profound implications for responses to child maltreatment. Given how our legal system does not develop through quick and dramatic shifts, the influence of these developments may not be immediate and the eventual outcomes have yet to be determined. The new evidentiary approaches may result in modest developments, or they may be transformative. In the immediate future, the shifting approaches to evidence most likely will influence, for example, the use of various "syndrome" evidence in legal proceedings. This could influence the use of such proffered syndromes as the battered child syndrome, sexual abuse accommodation syndrome, fetal alcohol syndrome, Munchausen by proxy syndrome, parental alienation syndrome, shaken baby syndrome, etc. Courts that have addressed these syndromes often reach different outcomes; and we have yet to see general patterns given the large number of syndromes and jurisdictions (Levesque, 2002a). In the long term, however, the shifting rules may have a much broader influence as they reflect and permeate other legal trends. Current legal responses to child maltreatment do make use of a variety of experts who testify and offer opinions regarding children, such as testimony relating, for example, to what would be in children's best interests. Courts and commentators have yet to use the new evidentiary rules to evaluate these claims systematically. Although the shifts in evidentiary rules may well apply to these cases, it remains to be seen what will be their outcomes. This indeterminacy is of significance as it actually propels our investigation and urges commentators to chart possible directions that recognize the limitations of current legal approaches and understand the benefits of taking emerging trends more seriously.

The lack of clear direction raises important concerns, two of which are particularly worth emphasizing at this juncture. The first concern involves the extent to which applying varying standards inevitably contributes to inconsistent rulings and different results even in similar situations. For example, the same type of evidence that is excluded in a *Frye* jurisdiction can be admissible in a *Daubert* jurisdiction. Relatedly, challenges exist in determining what types of evidence apply to which tests. This makes paramount serious inquiry into the methods used when contemplating the admissibility of evidence in child maltreatment cases and into specific types of evidence offered in recent years. We have yet to see broad evaluations that consider what is admissible, what is not, and what this means for consistently advancing technology and changing rules.

The second concern that emerges from the lack of clear direction involves problems with the type of testimony most often used in child maltreatment cases: mental health testimony. There is no doubt that experts pervasively have good intentions and do seek to do what is best for children in need. Good intentions, however, do not vitiate known limitations of this type of testimony. First, the observations of mental health professionals, while often considered highly reliable, also can be seriously flawed. Second, when such testimony is made in the context of child abuse and neglect cases, concerns arise about bias related to class, race, and gender. Third, psychological tests often are interpreted by courts to provide information beyond their proper scope. Consequently, the shifting rules question the judicial deference afforded to mental health professionals. Together, these concerns go to issues of fundamental fairness in the legal system's response. Although our legal system does permit considerable variation, serious concerns emerge when those variations come closer to arbitrariness and systems do not reach their intended goals.

Despite the lack of clear direction and the concerns that indirection raises, we can detect important benefits in the emerging trends. Critics may have concluded rightly that judges are ill-equipped to evaluate scientific evidence, but taking evidentiary developments seriously still could improve the quality of judicial decisions relating to child maltreatment. The *Daubert* trilogy urges judges, for example, to gain the necessary knowledge and implies that the lack of knowledge about scientific principles provides no excuses for abdication of the evaluative, judicial role. Clear benefits can emerge in judge-decided cases. Holding evidence to a higher standard, such as by requiring evidentiary hearings, is likely to raise previously unasked questions. These additional steps also would help increase judge's knowledge about certain types of evidence and increase the amount of evidence available to judges. More rigorous evaluations of evidence also would encourage those who provide evidence to present higher quality evidence. Together, these processes would help improve the accuracy of information used in legal responses, and hopefully contribute to improved legal outcomes.

We cannot underestimate the potential role that shifting legal rules may have in improving the nature of the information used in the legal system. Child welfare professionals, attorneys, judges and juries cannot effect accurate legal decisions if invalid scientific evidence distorts their understanding of presented facts. The general increase in quality information is of significance not just because judges will evaluate evidence. The increase is of significance because judges actually do not evaluate the evidence in most cases of child maltreatment. It is the prospect that it could be evaluated more rigorously, and what that prospect does to those who make decisions, that is of significance. Knowing, for example, that psychological tests will be admitted into evidence only with discussions of their limitations and supporting methodologies is likely to change professional practice. Not only can it contribute to improved tools, it can help structure guidelines set forth by relevant professions that would discourage overstepping their expertise. We will return to the full importance of this potential in the next chapter. For now, it is important to note that the results of cases may well be the same even without the more rigorous evaluation of evidence. But, as we have seen, the importance of the parent–child relationship requires that decisions interfering with that relationship be based on valid evidence and appropriate interpretations. Given that the new standards seek to establish the scientific nature of evidence, both in terms of actual evidence as well as evidence in the form of testimony, it will be important to see the extent to which legal systems engage these emerging standards and concerns.

# Part IV
# Returning to Child Welfare Law's Foundations

# Chapter 8
# Rethinking Laws Regulating Child Protection

Our legal system increasingly takes seriously the need to protect children from harm. We have seen the enactment of impressive reforms that permit more-aggressive criminal justice system responses. We also have seen the development of a child welfare system devoted to the protection of children believed to have been abused or neglected by their families, a system that permits intervention especially when children are deemed "at risk" of harm. Both of these systems have the power to transform children's relationships, and the systems make full use of this power not only to transform but also to terminate relationships deemed problematic and unremediable. Together, the breadth and depth of laws supporting the state's ability to intervene in children's lives is nothing short of phenomenal.

In the name of child protection, the criminal justice system wields considerable power. That power rests on the basic supposition that society has an interest in protecting children from maltreatment and that society must punish those who abuse children. These dual concerns mean that the system focuses on extreme harms; they also mean that the criminal justice system often waits until children's relationships are no longer remediable and that the system essentially seeks to sever bonds between children and their parents or others who have failed to care appropriately for them. The dual concerns also mean that child protective laws can appear as residuals to other concerns, such as when laws seek to punish caretakers for illegal activities that pose risks to children. For example and, as we have seen, several states now have enacted laws that prohibit the manufacture of specific drugs in the presence of children. These new mandates may reflect the system's concern for extreme risks and harms as well as the urge to punish and control more closely other illegal activities. They do not necessarily reflect, however, concern for rehabilitating individuals' relationships with their families. The system may take some care not to disturb viable relationships, but that care does not reflect the system's primary objectives. That the criminal justice system would operate in a manner that does not focus on protecting relationships is not surprising, given the system's overall mandate. Our criminal justice system focuses on broad societal interests rather than on the needs of individual victims. In doing so, it seeks to assign moral blame and control offenders for their wrongdoing in the name of the state. Given this focus, it is not surprising that much of this area of law aims to protect those accused from erroneous and unfair state actions that would blame them and severely limit their liberties.

The civil child welfare system's mandate differs considerably from that of the criminal justice system, but that difference increasingly wanes even though the child welfare system ostensibly retains very different goals and the legal system has yet to match the criminal justice system's level of protection from erroneous and unfair state intervention. The widely accepted mission of the civil, child protection system is one that seeks to ensure children's well-being by protecting them from maltreatment and providing their families with support. Unlike the criminal justice system, then and under this mandate, civil protective systems seek to strengthen families where children are at risk for abuse and neglect before efforts to sever ties between children and their caretakers. Indeed, that has been the foundational justification for developing the system: the civil child protection system was meant to prevent harm and address the needs of families before the emergence of a severe crisis. Although this constitutes a broad mission that could lead legal systems to focus on a variety of interventions, the system's primary focus has been on the detection and investigation of harms and, when appropriate, placement of children outside of their homes. Despite the system's original protective and rehabilitative orientations, recent reforms provide strong incentives to sever ties with caretakers. These reforms have eased the state's ability to sever ties without even offering remedial or preventative services. Even without these reforms, financial incentives that support state child welfare services inadvertently may encourage the removal of children from their homes. In theory, then, the system seeks to deliver on its promise of being concerned with children's welfare, even if it means severing ties between children and their abusive caretakers. As a result, although the system is guided and molded in a way that is meant to be rehabilitative (as evidenced by decision makers' heightened discretion to intervene, remove children from their homes, and devise treatment plans), reforms increasingly harness the system with incentives and duties that may well be highly punitive and lead to the loss of significant liberties without the concomitant legal protections that individuals would have if the punitiveness and risk of loss were recognized as central possibilities. In many ways, the system's orientation has evolved faster than legal systems have envisioned ways to redefine and adjust themselves to it.

Changes in criminal and civil responses to laws meant to be child protective have been the subject of intense criticisms. The criminal justice system, most notably, has been criticized for not focusing directly enough on individual child victims when it addresses those victims' harms (see, e.g., Levesque, 1995). As we have seen, this criticism may be legitimate, but it simply will not go far given the manner it necessarily challenges the foundation of the criminal justice system's definition of victimization as crimes against the state. The system also has been criticized for not being child-friendly enough when it prosecutes cases. This charge has led to impressive reforms relating, for example, to efforts that accommodate child witnesses' peculiar needs. The extent to which these reforms have been successful has led to another round of criticisms. Child-friendly court accommodations, for example, have led to the criticism that the legal system may fail to protect defendants' rights vigorously enough in cases involving child victims (King, 1992; White, 2003). The manner laws have sought to control offenders who have completed their sentences also continues to attract controversy, as revealed by an increasing number of states that have enacted residency restrictions and require the use of GPS monitoring devices to track released sex offenders (Janicki, 2007).

Importantly, the legal response to children's harms also has been criticized for failing to take crimes against children seriously enough. Child neglect contributing to children's deaths, for example, has a long history of being considered outside of the criminal justice system (Collins, 2006). As we have seen, much of the problems encountered by efforts to use the criminal justice system to address child protection is that, in many ways, those who place children at risk do not have the type of intent with which the criminal justice system typically concerns itself. As a result and although much perhaps could be gained by involving the criminal justice system in child protection, these criticisms highlight well the extent to which the system comes with costs and important limitations when it does address children's harms. In many ways, the criminal justice system cannot become too "child friendly" and cannot address well child victims' needs, which is not surprising given the system's focus on offenders' rights and society's attempt to punish, incapacitate or otherwise control those deemed responsible.

The civil justice, child welfare system's approach also attracts considerable criticisms. Indeed, it most likely has been criticized more harshly than the criminal justice system. Commentators increasingly note that the system fails to serve the interests of parents, children, or the state. Among its alleged shortcomings, the system pervasively fails to address many underlying problems facing families. Many note, for example, poverty's contribution to child maltreatment; yet, our legal system fails to address this issue forthrightly enough (Marcus, 2006; Mangold, 2007). As a result of this failure, as several argue, the child welfare system embraces the removal of children from their homes, and the state too often fails to offer appropriate plans to sustain relationships (Paruch, 2006). The removal of children from their homes comes at a high cost; although it may be appropriate in extreme cases, removal means that children lose their families and suffer significant psychological, educational, and social hardships, especially as evidenced by a surge in research investigating the effects of aging out of foster care (see, e.g., Magyar, 2006). In addition, the child welfare system has been criticized harshly for what many view as rampant and unfair discrimination, either as the result of problematic laws, discrimination in broader society, or the immense discretion granted to those charged with child protection (see Roberts, 2002). Discrimination certainly moves beyond race: the major determinant of children's removal from their parents' custody is not the severity of the abuse or neglect but, rather, unstable sources of parental income (Lindsey, 2003). As many commentators conclude, the system often fails to further the state's interest in building the capacity of children or in preparing them to become contributing members of society.

The complexity of child maltreatment and the deep attachment to what constitutes normal families, coupled by our legal system's own complexities and general orientation to protecting rights, certainly challenge efforts to fashion legal responses that could satisfactorily address a wide panoply of criticisms and failures. Our investigation has uncovered important, recurring issues that reform efforts must consider if they ever can hope to influence the development of child protective systems. Unlike increasingly popular proposals and efforts that seek to remove child protection from formal governmental involvement (and rely, instead, on informal, voluntary assistance), our analysis has highlighted the need to take rights seriously and consider the foundational rationales for child protective systems and our government's very existence. Given that commentators who do examine specific laws regulating child welfare law tend to avoid such analyses in favor of reporting general mandates that focus on the civil aspects of child protective systems (see, e.g., Poecora, Whittaker, Maluccio, Barth, & Plotnick, 2000), we must highlight what more comprehensive efforts must consider when they take seriously the law's foundations and overall response to child protection.

Our next sections enumerate concerns that must be taken more seriously in efforts to consider potential directions in child welfare law. Despite the considerable complexity we have uncovered in legal responses to child maltreatment, the concerns that we have identified distill to one dominant, simple theme: Legal responses to child maltreatment must level the playing field among children, parents, and those who intervene in the name of child protection. We explore key aspects of this concern in light of the constitutional principles and statutory mandates that guide the nature and development of child protection systems. As we will see, there actually exists considerable room for reasonable reforms that could be taken seriously given that some jurisdictions have enacted them and shown that they are practicable.

## Recognize the Ubiquitous Nature of State Intervention

The striking breadth of the state's involvement in families certainly constitutes a fundamental issue fraught with considerable legal implications. Although not part of discussions about the manner the law regulates families, the reality is that the legal system actually always intervenes to varying degrees and in varying ways in the lives of all families. State intervention in the lives of families constitutes an inevitable byproduct of modern, civil society. We have seen several cases, such as *Michael H. v. Gerald D.* (1989) and *Troxel v. Granville* (2000), that rested on the belief that our legal system seeks to protect the ideal of the private family, a family in which individuals within it can freely determine their relationships as long as they do not, for example, become marked by what constitutes maltreatment. In many ways, the dominant belief that the state does not intervene in private families remains a myth largely fostered by the ideal of the private family. As we have seen in chapters 2 and 3, even ideal private families are marked by and supported by laws that regulate the structure and dynamics of families. Most notably, the state still "intervenes" to the extent that it upholds laws reinforcing parental authority over children and protects families from interference from third parties who would seek, for example, to build relationships with children without their parents' consent or provide invasive services to them without their parents' approval. The state broadly establishes a system authorizing parents to make the most important decisions concerning their own children. Even those decisions that we perceive to be made free of state control are made within the legal parameters a state has determined to support rather than prohibit.

For our purposes, the recognition of the state's ubiquitous involvement in family life is of significance for two reasons. Recognizing the state's deep involvement in family life is important to consider when we seek to understand commentators' criticisms of state intervention. When commentators challenge particular interventions, they actually criticize particular policies and manifestations of the manner the state controls family life. Most notably, when commentators challenge particular policies, they have an image of what families are supposed to do, what they are supposed to look like, and how the state should be involved in family life. Remarkably, those images vary considerably, as evidenced by controversies about the proper place of children's rights in family law. Despite these variations, we also have seen that the law supports its own image of families it deems worth protecting over others. Although firmly rooted, the law's image of proper families and appropriate relationships does seem to be changing, a change that provides us with opportunities to consider potential reforms. Recognizing the state's ubiquitous role in family life also gains significance to the extent that intervention matters for the sake of defining the protections individuals have against the state's enormous power to intervene. The typical jurisprudential concerns for family autonomy and privacy oversimplify the complex relationship between families and the state. The state's intervention is both broad and deep. Once we acknowledge the state's inevitable intertwining with families' structures and decision-making, the central concern then becomes how and why the state should involve itself with families, not whether it should do so. Although state intervention is omnipresent, we have seen in all of these chapters that only some forms of intervention count when we consider the rights individual family members have against the state and the rights individuals have to protection from others. That some intrusions count whereas others typically do not provides us with important challenges that also happen to offer opportunities to the extent that we can link the state's relationship to families with broad jurisprudential principles guiding the state's place in modern, civil society.

## Acknowledge the Inherent Limitations of Not Taking Rights Seriously Enough

Taking seriously the position that some forms of state interventions may matter more than others, and that laws regulating interventions are remarkable for their diversity, leads us to consider the types of interventions that are legally permissible yet potentially unproductive or even problematic. By far, the most important legal issue to emerge when we consider the law's current response to child maltreatment deals with the manner the state's broad involvement in child welfare predominantly relies on informal responses. These informal processes rely on the legal system's offering relatively few procedural safeguards, on reduced protections from state actions, and on a lack of a jurisprudence that would foster the development of more laws that would produce more consistent, predictable, and principled interventions.

The lack of formal protections may seem a bit odd, but many rationales currently support the need for a variety of reduced protections from the state's efforts to intervene in families. The most significant rationale for reduced protections from the state's power to intervene widely in families is that the state's intervention to protect children does not seek to be coercive; rather, it seeks to offer assistance through broad discretion and flexibility. Given its benevolent posture, the theory goes, the system need not focus so much on protecting individuals from unwarranted intrusions; the intrusions are assumed to be needed and even wanted. This, as we have seen, is unlike the protections individuals receive against the criminal justice system's interventions. The criminal justice system has an elaborate set of formal rules and procedures that protect individuals from potentially problematic state interventions. Constitutional theory and considerable legislation support these dual approaches to legal regulations, one resting on criminal law and another on civil law. In addition to these statutory and constitutional schemes, significant pressure exists to deformalize child welfare proceedings even more—in the form of family mediation and other alternative dispute resolution mandates (Hehr, 2007). Although several forms of pressure exist to resolve disputes informally and in ways that foster imbalances in power between family members and those acting on behalf of the state, we highlight subtle pressures below and then proceed to examine how and why the legal system typically would view these pressures as problematic and potentially harmful. To the extent that interventions in families are no different from other state interventions in people's lives, this analysis will serve as a basis to reconsider the types of protections our society owes to children and their families.

## *The Nature of the State's Hidden Advantages*

We already have seen that the state still remains the final arbiter of what constitutes proper and appropriate family relationships. Understanding the state's power, however, requires that we move beyond definitions to take a closer look at the system that supports and makes use of those definitions in efforts to intervene in the name of children. The child welfare system's responses to allegations and known instances of child maltreatment involves considerable state power simply because it permits child welfare workers to pressure family members to accept interventions in their lives. These pressures come from numerous sources and raise important concerns.

The most dominant form of pressure to accept intervention involves the type that aims to have cases resolved informally without challenging, for example, the state's interventions. Pressure to address child protection cases in this manner derives from the subtle dynamics of child welfare cases. Those who implement child welfare laws and regulations frame interventions as therapeutic and discourage the formal use of the legal system by, for example, encouraging parents' voluntary transfer of children to the state or the use of informal hearings to address families' needs. This encouraging of informal procedures is not surprising, especially given that even our Supreme Court frames the system as one that is therapeutic. As a result, rather than rest on adversarial litigation and the assertion of rights, the practice of the child welfare's legal system rests on the pressure to cooperate and to resolve cases through compromise and agreement. Although there is nothing inherently suspect about compromises and cooperation, informal responses become problematic when they hide conflict and insert a power imbalance when the law assumes that the very reason for these mechanisms is to reduce conflict and equalize power dynamics.

A close look at the practice of child welfare reveals the ubiquitous potential for unequal power dynamics and, as a result, potential for (hidden) conflict. A first powerful source of imbalance emerges from the extent to which those who intervene in families are professionals who have considerable knowledge of how their own system works and who know key players in the child welfare system. The knowledge and familiarity with other repeat players places those who intervene at an advantage. Among other advantages, those who intervene already have a set of similar assumptions, a common language, and relationships that foster outcomes deemed satisfactory from their perspectives. A second source of imbalance involves the professional training of child welfare workers. Their training centers on developing skills and abilities to enable cooperation, develop trust, and avoid conflict by building nonadversarial relationships. Although effective in therapeutic contexts, this general orientation may cloak the substantial power differential that exists between child welfare workers and the accused caregivers. Caseworkers can wield the law's power to achieve their ends when they disagree with caretakers alleged of placing their children at risk of harm or of having harmed them. Assumptions of mutuality in inherently unequal relationships mask reality.

A third important source of imbalance that may contribute to hidden conflict involves the illusion of shared goals. In chapter 5, for example, we already have seen that concurrent planning formally pushes inconsistent missions. Concurrent planning requires states to plan for the permanent removal of children from their parents while, at the same time, assist parents in their efforts to better care for their children. More subtly, however and as even the Court has recognized, the "best interests of the child" standard is not an objectively determinable absolute; that standard on which state officials make decisions for children remains malleable and subjective (*Troxel v. Granville,* 2000). This subjectivity may mean that case workers and parents may hold entirely different views of what constitutes a particular child's "best interests." If they do hold different opinions, there is no doubt whose matters most. The belief that guides the child welfare system is that the state knows what is best for its children—the state determines what constitutes a child's best interests. Furthermore, the law does assume that parents act in their children's best interests. But parents accused of maltreatment do not necessarily enjoy the benefit of that assumption. They may not do so because of the way the system structures interactions and the way the civil court system is based on decision making that approves the state's position (e.g., the standard for appellate court review in these cases is to view the evidence most favorable to the plaintiff—inevitably the state—and ignore the evidence to the contrary; see Levesque, 2002a). The very standards used in practice and the legal system's response to that practice, then, may not produce shared goals.

Other important sources of systemically imbalanced advantages undoubtedly exist. However, it is clear that preexisting knowledge and relationships, professional norms, potentially conflicting goals, and purposefully vague standards fostering subjectivity create the potential for imbalance and hidden conflict between families and the state. The extent to which these factors remain played down, unacknowledged or ignored reveals the extent to which reform efforts must create systems to address these potential sources of imbalance to the extent that they do not comport with our foundational assumptions of the state's relationship to families. Put simply, parents may be assumed to act on their children's interests, but that assumption dissipates when states intervene simply because the state carries a powerful advantage when it intervenes in families.

## The Law's Typical Concerns About Hidden Advantages

Our legal system typically does not tolerate hidden advantages when the state formally intervenes to limit people's rights. Several general legal principles caution against permitting substantial imbalances of power between the state and caregivers involved in child welfare proceedings. Although many points remain to be developed and applied in this setting, we can decipher several threads of jurisprudence from other areas that do buttress the need to develop responses that would protect the rights of individuals when the state intervenes in their lives, especially when the state does so in ways that may be deemed coercive.

Our legal system has recognized the problematic nature of hidden advantages deriving from informal state responses in both criminal justice and civil contexts. For example, our legal system has recognized informal systems as ripe for coerciveness in the context of power imbalances that exist when the state elicits information from an individual under a palpable threat of a substantial deprivation of liberty. The Court has recognized the implications of this potential for coercion as resulting, for example, in the risk of eliciting inaccurate information that would then contribute to injustices (see *Miranda v. Arizona,* 1966; *Dickerson v. United States,* 2000). Although we tend to think of these concerns as applicable only to the criminal justice system, the same concerns contributed to the jurisprudential groundwork for reforming the juvenile justice system (see, e.g., In re Gault, 1967). The Supreme Court in *Gault* asserted that the state's *parens patriae* power was being overused as a basis for the state's control of children and refuted the doctrine's use almost entirely in the area of juvenile delinquency. Analyses of this area of law typically focus on physical restraints as the necessary deprivation that leads to the need for enhanced legal protections from state interventions, but that was not the sole motivation supporting the rights that were recognized as belonging to juveniles and

that led to reforms of informal juvenile court systems. In *Gault*, families, including parents and children, were granted rights in the juvenile justice system explicitly because the Court reasoned that the state's *parens patriae* power—the same power guiding child welfare cases—must be subjected to checks and balances in the form of basic due process rights that would ensure fundamental fairness in the state's interventions.

*Gault's* jurisprudential underpinnings may be on point, but they have yet to be applied directly to the child welfare system. Yet, no one should be surprised at the argument that the removal of children from families certainly constitutes a potentially grievous loss. Also not surprisingly, the legal system actually has recognized this potential. However, as currently conceived in the child welfare context, legal systems have placed greater emphasis on the end point of the loss (termination hearings) rather than on the beginning of interventions. The lack of focus on initial interactions likely makes alternative, informal approaches problematic in that they remove what would otherwise be available protections from state action. Other systems concern themselves with who gets into and stays in the system much more than the child welfare system does. As we have seen, for example, law enforcement has to carry a heavier burden of proof to intervene and have to abide by rigorous trial procedures. Such protections, as of yet, have not transferred well to the civil, child welfare context.

The potentially unfair disparities that derive from reduced formal protections also may be problematic in child welfare cases to the extent that our legal system recognizes that this type of decision-making may not necessarily produce honest and accurate information when such information is necessary to make critical decisions affecting people's rights. Our legal system has long recognized that vulnerable individuals in relationships marked by imbalances of power, especially against the state, require extra protections. We already have seen that the inherent conflict between a parent and the state (as to who should keep the child) creates a power imbalance. One potential result of this imbalance is that it likely discourages the weaker party from expressing their true position, encouraging them instead to comply. This danger is exacerbated in instances where decisions occur in the absence of formal constraints to the extent that decisions are likely to be susceptible to being swayed by prejudices and stereotypes, as well as innuendo and rumor. The danger that prejudice or incomplete or unreliable information will distort decisions is particularly acute in the emotionally-charged arena of dependency and termination cases. These pressures make especially important the evidentiary constraints and protections against bias and prejudice that would result from a more formal system. Regardless of the criticisms of our criminal justice system, the adversarial system remains our most cherished means of ferreting out legal truth. The system does so by focusing on relevant facts, limiting bias, and reducing prejudice. This would be particularly important in the child welfare system given the manner parties can more easily accept statements uncritically and need not seek out contradictory evidence. Unlike informal systems, trials and judicially administered hearings have formal rules that seek to assure accuracy. Witnesses testify under oath under threat of penalty for perjury. Judges exclude unreliable evidence (like untrustworthy hearsay) as well as

evidence likely to cause unfair prejudice. Judges state the basis for their decisions and the rules governing their conduct, a process that likely encourages impartiality and the appearance of impartiality. Of course, these mechanisms are far from perfect. However, the system directly concerns itself with ways to control biases and prejudices. This is very much unlike informal responses that largely proceed without standards or that, when they do have standards, may be either very low, or very difficult to enforce, or both. Methods to resolve disputes that embrace reduced protections and informal resolutions, then, may not lead to the open, accurate, and just outcomes in cases that are necessarily fraught with power struggles and open to unfair biases and discrimination.

Another concern that arises from the push toward reduced rights and greater informality is the threat to ensuring uniformity among cases and to adhering to collective norms, both of which constitute fundamental concerns for any system of justice. Formal processes require the application of formal rules and standards, which helps to promote consistency, both among cases and with collective norms. Unlike informal systems, formal ones with rules and legal standards provide mechanisms for articulating a collective standard through legislative and judicial action. These standards are applied to decisions in individual cases to ensure consistency of individual outcomes with the collective norms reflected in those standards. In the child welfare context, for example, the collective judgment about the balance between individual liberty and social welfare generally requires a showing of parental unfitness and harm to children before they can be removed from their families. Rather than reflecting collective or democratically determined norms, informal proceedings produce results that reflect the disparity of power between the parties. Decisions are based on the extent to which each side exhibits a willingness to compromise rather than on a neutral evaluation of evidence and arguments. Although not perfectly effective, formal processes do seek to equalize power disparities between the parties. Each party (theoretically) has an attorney, versed in the language and rules of the forum, and formal rules that equally limit both side's introduction of evidence and arguments. Informal proceedings provide no equivalent check on power imbalances and may not provide those already vulnerable with needed protections that would increase their chances of having their voices heard and their circumstances determined by facts rather than unfair biases, prejudices, and innuendos.

Other concerns may exist, and informal mechanisms may have their place, but in the context of child welfare cases, informal procedures appear unlikely overall to be as effective as formal ones in producing predictable outcomes and achieving the goals of procedural due process. The substantial power disparity between the parties, the emotionally charged nature of the subject matter, the lack of a shared set of interests and values between the parties, and the absence of mechanisms ensuring the use of accurate information, all permit distortions of decision making processes. Traditional formal adversarial processes have mechanisms that, while far from perfect, are designed to reduce distortions caused by such conditions. Informality generally offers no equivalent protections and actually discourages families and children from taking advantage of procedural protections. This is not to say that all informality can be erased and that informality necessarily causes con-

cern in responses to all allegations of child maltreatment. However, such concern arises when informality operates in the context of an imbalance of power (as the result of emotional attachments, knowledge, values, resources, etc.) between family members and those who act on behalf of the state. This imbalance is of significance because it provides the foundational rationale for providing individuals with rights against the state's efforts to interfere unjustly in their lives. It is to the nature of those rights that we now turn.

## Take Jurisprudential Developments Seriously

Opportunities for revising child protective laws, especially those based on the civil justice system, through reconsidering the nature of state intervention derive from the manner our legal system determines the appropriateness of the government's intervention in the name of child protection. Developments certainly have not gone in one linear direction. Rather, developments have been haphazard and often outside of the civil child protection system. Nevertheless, we have seen that legal developments framing the nature of rights, and the methods used to determine the relative weight given to rights, transfer to the child protection context. In addition, we have seen that the extent to which the legal system deems particular approaches appropriate rests on their relative effectiveness in reaching broad policy objectives. We revisit these two conclusions here to highlight how jurisprudential and broader policy concerns counsel a turn away from current trends that seek more informal and intrusive governmental intervention in families in the name of child protection.

### Recognize Significant Developments in Family-Related Liberties

As we have seen, family-related liberties, such as the right to marry or to bear and raise a child, are said to be zealously guarded through the strict scrutiny that courts will give to state mandates that infringe on fundamental constitutional rights. This bestowal of fundamental status carries considerable legal significance. Fundamental rights garner a particularly high degree of protection because an alleged encroachment on a fundamental right requires the government to meet a particularly high burden that would justify the intrusion. Under strict scrutiny, the regulation at issue will withstand judicial review only if it serves a compelling government interest and is tailored narrowly to serve this interest. Courts have interpreted the narrowly tailored condition to require that the governmental regulation be necessary for, not merely rationally related to, the accomplishment of the compelling interest, and that the intrusion not interfere unjustifiably on rights in the name of serving the state's interests. In practice, this requirement means that the regulation or statute must provide the least restrictive means for achieving the government's interest. When properly applied, the necessity requirement of the narrowly tailored inquiry mandates that a court weigh the regulation against any proffered alternatives. In practice, government regulations rarely survive a court's strict scrutiny analysis; this is likely because the rights are deemed so important and in need of utmost protection from state intrusions.

Recent developments reveal the extent to which the Court seeks to protect parents, intimate relationships, and children's rights from inappropriate infringement from governmental actions. If any general jurisprudential and legislative trend exists, it actually is toward increased protection. As reported in chapters 2 and 3, the Court has announced important legal developments in this area. Three developments are worth highlighting as they point the development of jurisprudence in directions away from perceived popular trends that would reduce protections. Instead, these developments reveal the need to move toward formal, rights-based approaches when governments interfere in families and relationships.

The first recent development takes the form of a decision, *Troxel v. Granville* (2000), that offers the Supreme Court's latest pronouncement on the constitutional status of parental rights. *Troxel* emerges as the latest in a long line of cases that has recognized the fundamental nature of parental rights. In *Troxel*, the Court unabashedly noted that the due process clause of the Fourteenth Amendment includes a "substantive component that 'provides heightened protection against government interference with certain fundamental rights and liberty interests'" and that the interest of parents in the care, custody, and control of their children is "perhaps the oldest of the fundamental liberty interests recognized by" it (p. 65). Although prior cases dealing with parental rights often skirted the nature of parental rights, or actually did not even deal directly with parents, *Troxel* clearly stands for the notion that the Constitution firmly protects the right of parents to make decisions about their children. This, of course, is not to say that the constitutional rule treats parents' parental rights as an isolated one to be exercised arbitrarily. Parents' liberty interests are based not on isolated factors but, instead, within the context of their impact on particular families as a whole, as exemplified most recently by the Court's refusal to permit a probable biological father from even attempting to prove his paternity when the putative fathers' rights were balanced against those of family members (*Michael H. v. Gerald D.,* 1989). The explicit and high attachment bestowed on parental rights, however, necessarily means that our legal system must grant it the highest protection, even when it seeks to infringe on those rights in the name of a compelling state interest like child protection.

*Lawrence v. Texas* (2003) highlights the second area of development. In that case, the Court examined the right to engage in and maintain relationships. The Court reaffirmed the right to constitutional protection for personal decisions relating to marriage, procreation, family relationships, and child-rearing as the Court extended the right to nonheterosexual relationships. The Court did so in a now famously ambiguous manner as it failed to mention the typically pivotal words—privacy, fundamental right, and compelling interests—that would situate the case in the Court's established substantive due process framework of either strict scrutiny or a more rational basis to determine the law's constitutionality. Rather, the Court spoke of emergent rights and the construction of intimate lives that were protected by the Fourteenth Amendment's Due Process Clause. Even in the absence of using traditionally accepted methods of analysis, the Court held the state to a very high standard when the government sought to infringe even in rights that are deemed "emergent" rather than explicitly firmly rooted in judicial doctrine. In addition to this mode of analysis that resulted in protecting rights to relationships, the case stands as an important statement on the extent to which the law can protect nontraditional families, even though it is unclear how these families will gain protection when courts need to balance those interests with those dealing directly with child protection.

The third development deals with the Court's announcement that children do have rights that move beyond their need to protections from harm. The history of children's rights has been one that has focused on shielding children from potential harms by granting parents the right to control children and to control how children would exercise their rights when they did have them. We have seen this in *Wisconsin v. Yoder* (1972), in which the court affirmed its commitment to offering parents the power to control their children's educational environments. The history of children's rights also includes a focus on ensuring that the state retained the freedom to act benevolently, even when it did not in practice. These conceptions of children's rights have evolved.

In contrast to the protectionist strain of children's rights, a preservationist strain of children's rights has evolved and reflects the view that unnecessary state intervention in the family violates children's right to remain with their parents. In this conceptualization, family preservation reflects both parents' rights (not to have a child removed unnecessarily) and children's rights (not to be removed unnecessarily). The Supreme Court already has recognized this preservationist view of children's rights. For example, in *Santosky v. Kramer* (1982) the Court began its analysis of the burden of proof required by the Fourteenth Amendment in a proceeding to terminate a parent's rights by recognizing the right of a parent to the care and custody of a child. The Court then stated that, until the state demonstrated parental unfitness, "the child and his parents share a vital interest in preventing erroneous termination of their natural relationship" (p. 753). Similarly, in *Parham v. J.R.* (1979), the Court addressed the procedural due process requirements necessary when a parent commits a minor to an institution for mental health treatment. The Court addressed a concern with a formalized, adversarial hearing reviewing the parent's decision, noting that "requiring a formalized, factfinding hearing ... poses significant intrusion into the parent–child relationship. Pitting the parents and child as adversaries often will be at odds with the presumption that parents act in the best interests of their child" (p. 610). The Court evinces considerable concern for preserving families, for not permitting the legal system to intervene unreasonably in parent–child relationships.

Despite concern for protecting families from formal state intervention, the Court does provide children with some independent rights when there may be conflicts with their caretakers. The cases we have just reviewed also stand for the position that our legal system now recognizes that children's rights can be separate from those of their parents. The Court recognizes a need for increased due process protections, especially when family members face potential conflict (see, e.g., *Parham v. J.R.,* *1979; Planned Parenthood of Central Missouri v. Danforth, 1976; Belotti v. Baird,* *1979*). Equally importantly, significant developments seek to ensure that children, even those not deemed mature enough to exercise their own rights, necessarily retain basic due process rights when the state intervenes in their lives. As *In re Gault* (1967, p. 28) properly noted, the condition of being a child does not justify a "kangaroo court." Before *Gault,* it was generally thought that juveniles had no right to liberty when the state interfered in their families, in this instance, to institutionalize them. Rather, children had a right to custody, the right to have someone take care of them. If the parents could not care for them, the state would. *Gault* modified that traditional rule as it found that youth deserved protections from state actions, even those the state deemed beneficial. These cases, and others like them, have yet to be taken seriously enough. The Supreme Court, most notably, has yet to develop a coherent conception of children's own rights beyond the right to protection through being in an adult's custody (see, e.g., Levesque, 2007). Most importantly for our purposes, the implications of these developments for the child welfare system have yet to be addressed and remain quite uncharted.

## Address Uneven Developments in Child Protection Laws

Despite the recognition that interventions in families involve intrusions in the fundamental rights of parents (and in some instances the rights of their children), the child welfare system operates in ways that previously have avoided more demanding levels of analysis. This continues despite the important developments in conceptions of rights that we have noted above. Presumably, the system has continued in this manner for important reasons. Those reasons help explain why the rights family members have against state intrusions vary considerably and do not always hold the state to high standards. Equally importantly, those reasons reveal what reform efforts must address if they wish to be taken seriously.

### Challenge Reasons for Treating Child Protection Cases Differently

The first major reason that the child welfare system has avoided a greater level of judicial scrutiny involves the manner child welfare systems (including some criminal justice approaches to protecting children from harm) deal with risk to children. As we have seen in *Prince v. Massachusetts* (1944), the state retains a compelling interest in child protection. As we also have seen, however, this compelling interest does not grant the state a *carte blanche* to enter into families and disturb relationships. The need to balance protection from state action and the need for the state to act raises complex issues that eventually distill to determining when and how a state should intervene, and when that intervention is deemed the type of intervention that requires the legal system to grant family members protections from governmental actions. Regrettably, this area of jurisprudence remains underdeveloped to the extent that states have adopted a variety of responses to deal with similar decision points in legal processes that regulate intervention in families in the name of child protection.

The second major explanation for the extent to which laws regulating child welfare tend to escape closer judicial scrutiny is that the vast majority of intrusions involve the civil, child welfare system. Intrusions from this system are seen as different, as less intrusive and less potentially damaging than intrusions from the criminal justice system. As a result, the intrusions are deemed in need of lesser protection from the state's actions and states have more flexibility to the extent that the law holds them to a lower standard. A look at leading cases reveals a clear trend toward recognizing the need for protection but nevertheless offering reduced protections from state actions. In *Ferguson v. City of Charleston* (2001), for example, hospital personnel used urine screens designed to prove their suspicion that pregnant women were using illegal narcotics. The Court ruled the Fourth Amendment applicable because the staff's motives were not benign since the policy involved law enforcement and the threat of punishment. Absent the possibility of criminal prosecution, protections from searches and seizures would have been reduced. This approach follows the general rule that administrative searches need not adhere to the usual warrant or probable cause requirements of the Fourth Amendment. We have seen these relaxed protections exemplified most clearly in *Wyman v. James* (1971), a case that reduced protections from a law that conditioned receipt of welfare benefits on a home visit to assure that funds were used appropriately by parents for food and clothing for the children. The state's actions were deemed reasonable, and therefore permissible. Despite these cases, the practice of caseworkers' investigations have gone largely unimpeded by the courts: The United States Supreme Court has yet to decide a case involving the constitutionality of child maltreatment investigations, and in particular, the Fourth Amendment's applicability to those investigations. Because we are not dealing directly with criminal justice systems that are more directly controlled by constitutional mandates, this area of law remains undeveloped.

The lines of cases reducing protections from state intervention obviously deal with a multitude of complexities. They do, however, reveal important themes emerging from this area of law. The first theme involves the general conclusion that individuals' claims to protections from state intrusions yield to the societal imperative to assist children in need. This is particularly the case in the civil, child welfare system when children need protection from their own families. It now also is even the case in the criminal justice system when the legal system permits reduced evidentiary standards in the prosecution of crimes against children and the control of those deemed to have offended against children. Yet, parents still have rights in child welfare systems; and defendants and those deemed criminal also still have rights against the state's efforts to punish and control them. The second theme that these cases reveal involves the need to address issues relating to the state's compelling needs when it interferes in families and the level of protection the state should grant families from state intervention. Regrettably, no system currently exists that could serve as guide for a system that would place increased weight on the rights of parents and children when the state claims an interest to intervene. As we have seen, legal systems tend to operate between extremes based on the typical protections granted in civil or criminal justice systems. The significance of parental rights and the potentially significant intrusion in family dynamics leave us without a clear system from which to determine the nature of the protections from state actions.

Regardless of the systems used to intervene in the name of child protection, the attachment to child protection does not remove the need to protect individuals and families from state interference. We have seen that those offering policy reforms may properly highlight the need for increased governmental assistance for families with children in need of better care. Our look at legal responses to maltreatment, however, also points to the equally pressing need to protect families and individuals in them from inappropriate interventions done in the name of child protection. Neither of the reasons for treating children's cases differently—the fact that we are dealing with children and that civil cases received reduced protections—now support the minimal protections from intrusions that were designed for a system that has dramatically changed and by a system that lags behind in adopting protections embraced by other systems.

## Recognize the Limits of the Rapid Hybridization of Child Welfare Law

We have seen that the civil justice system often does not provide enough protection from state intervention. We also have seen that the typical criminal justice system's protections cannot be imported wholesale into the civil, child welfare system. Indeed, the criminal justice system increasingly uses the traditional rationales of civil law to control offenders. In many ways, the child welfare system has been in the process of becoming a hybrid. It is unclear how this hybrid system will develop, but we have seen hints of potential directions. These directions regrettably reveal the fundamental limitations of current trends toward hybridization.

The most important and obvious example of the legal systems' hybridization of child protection laws involves the manner the civil, child welfare system has granted individuals rights against a state's action that deal directly with the termination of parental rights. We have seen that the Court, in *M.L.B. v. S.L.J.* (1996), borrowed significantly from criminal cases as it eventually ruled that an indigent parent facing termination of parental rights has a right to a free transcript on appeal. Similarly, in *Santosky v. Kramer* (1982), the Court ruled that the constitutionally required standard of proof in a termination of parental rights proceeding is the intermediate clear and convincing evidence standard rather than the lower standard (a preponderance of the evidence) typically used in civil systems. In that case, the Court was unwilling to go so far as to require the standard used in criminal justice cases: beyond a reasonable doubt. But the Court certainly took seriously the need to recognize that the child welfare system should not rest on the reduced standards customary for typical civil cases. As we already have noted, however, these protections deal with the end results of interventions, not initial interventions in families and not the services provided. Current constitutional jurisprudence focuses on the severing of relationships rather than the processes that lead to the state's intrusion.

Consistent with this line of jurisprudence, state statutes and case law interpreting constitutional due process protections direct trial courts to conduct dependency and termination proceedings at an intermediate level of formality. These proceedings include most of the standard aspects of traditional adversarial models of dispute resolution. The state must set forth its allegations in a petition and serve it on the parent. Judges hear the cases. Witnesses testify under oath and a court reporter transcribes the proceedings. Rules of evidence apply, with some exceptions. The parties may be represented by lawyers and may appeal adverse decisions. At the adjudicatory phase, the state must show parental unfitness by proving acts or omissions on the part of the parent that bring the child within the statutory definition of a "dependent" child or a "child in need of assistance." This increased formality, an increase that receives greater and greater support by the courts and legislatures, certainly reveals that there are some aspects of the child welfare system that benefit from taking rights more seriously.

The above protections provide more than examples of the progress made in protecting the rights of family members. They also offer strong examples of how difficult it will be to recognize rights fully enough to offer protection from erroneous state actions. An indigent parent may have a constitutional right to appeal but, as we have seen, that right remains limited precisely because we are dealing with a hybrid system. Two examples of the limitations are illustrative.

The first example of the limited protection involves states that provide a right to appointed counsel by statute. This certainly is an important right, but it becomes limited to the extent that states typically fail to address whether the right includes effective assistance of counsel. Federal Constitutional law provides no real assistance in this matter. Largely because an indigent parent in a dependency or termination case has no constitutional right to appointed counsel (*Lassiter v. Dep't of Social Services*, 1981), the standard on which to determine the effectiveness of counsel's representation remains uncharted. As a result, parents in dependency and termination proceedings do not receive many of the procedural rights enjoyed by criminal defendants facing minor charges. One of the most cherished rights—the right to effective assistance of counsel—simply has no current relevance in the civil, child welfare context.

A second example of the limited rights deals with the burden of proof used in dependency and termination of parental rights cases. It is true that the state has a higher burden in the child welfare than in the typical civil cases. But, it is unclear what that burden actually is if we consider the type of evidence permitted in child welfare cases. For example, civil child welfare systems apply relaxed evidentiary standards. Thus, termination and dependency cases generally provide some basic due process protections that help ensure that the state will prove its case. For example, parents have an opportunity to confront and cross-examine witnesses (with exceptions for child witnesses). But, many jurisdictions admit into evidence social workers' hearsay reports. There is no prohibition against self-incrimination contained in the Fifth Amendment. The Supreme Court has yet to address and develop many of the due process rights of parents and children in dependency and termination proceedings; it remains to be seen the extent to which the rights include many other rights that would be analogous to those in the criminal justice system. This area of law has been left largely unexamined by courts that could develop a broad, coherent jurisprudence.

The reduced rights parents and children have in child welfare systems do not only occur during actual adjudications. Investigations of allegations of child maltreatment provide some of the clearest examples of reduced protections. Courts do not require social workers investigating reports of child abuse to comply with the Fourth Amendment's warrant and probable cause requirements before searching a home, and no exclusionary rule limits the admissibility of improperly obtained evidence. This way of investigating child maltreatment allegations is consistent with the government's compelling need to address the nation's maltreatment problem. Yet, despite compelling needs, the investigation may not be as meritorious from the perspective of the investigated child. Despite best intentions, the process can be harmful in the manner investigations can undermine the types of Fourth Amendment fundamental values our society seeks to protect: privacy, dignity, personal security, and mobility. This is especially problematic, given that the Court has interpreted the Fourth Amendment to guard the child's own individual interest in these values, by protecting the child's right also to be free from unreasonable searches and seizures both inside and outside the family home. This also is especially problematic given recent reports that, nationally, 71% of cases the states investigated for suspected child maltreatment ultimately did not result in substantiated reports (National Clearinghouse on Child Abuse & Neglect Information, 2006). Permitting the state to infringe in families by using a system that does not protect significantly individuals from futile intrusions remains one of the most peculiar aspects of our constitutional system.

The hybrid system not only permits reduced rights during investigations, it also permits reduced rights to the extent that courts support, as we have seen in chapter 4, a system that actually fosters intervention. All states currently have broad legal definitions of abuse and neglect and broad screening criteria that permit investigations. All states also have statutory or regulatory provisions that mandate the investigation of all screened-in reports, and related provisions that allow state officials to compel compliance with investigations. These broad mandates would be problematic in criminal law; but they currently pass constitutional muster because they rest on the justification that they are part of an administrative, civil system. There is no doubt that agencies caution investigators to respect children's dignity and the sanctity of families; and agencies protect investigators who act in good faith. However, respecting privacy while still conducting comprehensive investigations runs the risk of producing inherently irreconcilable objectives. The objectives permit parties to seek conflicting ends: the parent can seeks to preserve family unity and privacy, whereas the investigator necessarily infringes in the family's privacy, the child's privacy and, if necessary, disrupts the family unit. The parent–investigator relationship is likely to be adversarial, not mutually supportive. And, as we have seen, parents and children need not have increased protections if the system uses acquired information to launch a full-scale intervention. That law enforcement also typically is involved in the investigatory scheme or in the conduct of the investigation itself necessarily increases the process' intrusiveness; it also increases the chances that evidence will be used that otherwise would not be deemed permissible if law enforcement had acted alone. The legal system has the tendency to ignore these potential legal harms. The system does so even when we know that investigations can result in emotional and psychological harm, ranging from temporary discomfort to significant long-term harm. A criminal justice system would recognize and seek to prevent these harms, but that is less the case in the current hybridization of child welfare. These potential sources of harm may counsel against reducing the rights of family members against state actions presumed to be for their own benefit, but the reduced protections continue. These reduced protections continue even though, as we have seen, our legal system has yet to develop fully a right to treatment or services that would be needed to address the reasons for the state's intervention in the first place. This, of course, remains less of an issue in the criminal justice system, where the system clearly need not focus on rehabilitation. Thus, the degree of interconnectedness between civil and law enforcement authorities and motivations that underlie investigatory schemes preclude the usefulness of doctrine designed for the civil system; they also preclude the appropriateness of doctrine designed explicitly for the criminal justice system. We must return to broad constitutional principles that serve as the foundation for both systems if we are to address the balance between family privacy and aggressive intervention programs in a way that best reflects the children's need for protection against both private (familial) and public (state) violence.

## Accept the Need to Treat Different Stages of Legal Intervention Differently

Hybridization may have its limitations, but current limitations need not dissuade us from envisioning a hybrid system that could be more consistent with the constitutional values that envision a society free of unwarranted state involvement. Hybridization and the need to protect rights more vigorously need not necessarily mean that we must rely entirely on formal legal proceedings and the removal of discretion governed by informality. Legal responses to child maltreatment, as we have seen, operate in different systems, and those systems vary in terms of the protections they offer partly based on the point of the intervention (investigations or service delivery). This diversity provides us with opportunities to fine-tune the legal protections offered to family members.

One of the most important phases to distinguish most likely would include postadjudicatory phases of a dependency case. Unlike initial proceedings, the characteristics of these phases may warrant a more informal approach. These phases involve judicial determinations of where the child should be placed given that courts already have determined the presence of abuse or neglect. These phases also require subsequent periodic review hearings. During these decision points, cases shift from a retrospective, fact-based inquiry to a prospective inquiry into what steps parents must take and what services agencies must provide to alleviate the conditions that led to intervention. The preservation of the relationship between the parent and the state's service providers becomes a legitimate goal at the dispositional and review phases of a dependency proceeding and, indeed, an important factor in ensuring the success of prospective rehabilitative plans. Although disparities in power and potential for differences of opinions on norms and values persist, the shift in the relative importance of retrospective fact-finding in terms of the preservation of relationships may warrant a shift to less formal procedures at these stages of a dependency case. Unlike an adjudicatory hearing, the dispositional and review hearings proceed on the assumption that the families need state intervention.

The proposal that child welfare systems still could embrace informality at appropriate places is not entirely unlike current jurisprudence regulating the criminal justice system. We have seen similar developments in the manner the state treats those determined guilty of crime. The criminal justice system has adopted relaxed rules that guide the post-adjudication of guilt. The sentencing of those deemed criminals involves relaxed rules of evidence. For example, evidence of prior crimes can be used to shape a sentence but not (necessarily) adjudications of guilt. Similarly, protections from the state are again relaxed when offenders are released, such that, for example, the state is granted more power to control those who have been found criminal. We have seen these developments in new laws that deal, for example, with released sex offenders. Even legal protections from searches and seizures can be reduced in the criminal justice system. For example, jurisprudence governing the need for probable cause for searches and seizures is marked by numerous exceptions, such as exigent circumstances that permit the need to obtain a warrant. Incidentally, the focus on voluntariness and informality before the person becomes an accused also is permissible in the criminal justice system. This is so mainly because it is a reasonable response and because the system has protections in place (e.g., to determine whether defendants' actions were voluntary; see Levesque, 2006). This level of protection that ensures voluntary, noncoercive actions is very much unlike the current child welfare system. There are no reasons indicating that these rules should not apply vigorously in the child welfare context so that we could announce a general rule that we prefer to have neutral fact finders, rather than case workers, determine whether cause exists to intervene in families. This is especially relevant given the potential involvement of law enforcement in child protection cases and their need to abide by their own standards.

We end with the principle that intrusions in family life call for greater procedural protections than are normally available in civil proceedings and in what traditionally has been granted families involved in the child welfare system. Greater procedural protection implies greater formality, more stringent standards, and more limits on state action. Despite strong hesitance by commentators to recognize this approach, we have seen that courts actually have followed this path when addressing some phases of child protection's legal processes. The current state of the law has provided us with several important examples of areas that can benefit from increased formal protections. The recurring theme that emerges from the above analysis is that informalism remains particularly ill-suited to meeting due process goals in situations involving gross disparities of power between the parties. It also appears that formality better leads to accurate factual determinations and helps assure consistent and just outcomes in an environment of moral and cultural diversity, whereas informality better preserves ongoing relationships between disputing parties. In other words, informal processes work best under conditions of relative social equality, in communities with consensus about norms and values, and where preserving relationships in the future is more important than reaching accurate factual understandings of the past. If these conclusions make sense, they reveal a need to reconsider the protections families have against the state.

## Support More Empirical Research Focusing on Legal Processes

As we have seen in chapter 1, the study of child maltreatment has produced enormous amounts of research. We now understand why it may not be taken seriously enough. The immense progress in the study of child maltreatment does not address directly enough the fundamental concerns that arise when the legal system intervenes in families in the name of child protection. Research may have established that society has a compelling state interest that provides the rationale for intervention. And researchers may have examined how the legal system responds to child welfare (see Levesque, 2002a; Kendall-Tackett & Giacomoni, 2005; Haksins, Wulczyn, & Webb, 2007). But, we need much more research to determine the extent to which the state's actions are narrowly tailored, to determine the extent to which governmental actions constitute the appropriate response to achieving the state's compelling interest.

Our investigation has revealed numerous potential areas of research that would provide useful information for legal analyses. We need research that examines perceptions of what constitutes privacy within families. We also need research investigating what constitutes healthy family life, particularly in terms of diverse family styles that deserve protection. We need to know more about the nature of biases in perceptions of appropriate relationships and how to control unwarranted biases. We need research to help us understand the nature of informal responses to allegations of child maltreatment. Also needed is research on what would lead parents to act voluntarily when states intervene. We need basic research that would help us deal with thorny issues involved in adopting more precise definitions of maltreatment. We need more research on risk assessment and the decision making capacities of those who provide evaluations, especially including those who do so outside of formal legal responses. We also need research on evidentiary rules, especially in terms of judges' abilities to evaluate evidence and the effects of experts' proffering evidence. We also need research on the results of using exceptions to hearsay rules. Also important would be research on the effectiveness of efforts that seek to control and incapacitate offenders. Researchers also could work to reconcile the current conflict among experts about how to define abuse and neglect, to eliminate definitions that are so broad that they give officials on the ground unfettered discretion to define maltreatment, and to make sure that the definitions that remain include real instances of maltreatment that society currently prefers to ignore. Thus, we need research on perceptions of maltreatment. We also need organizational research to determine how best to hire, train, and retain officials to work in the field who are given an appropriately sized caseload, sufficient support, and clear guidelines to reduce the extent of their discretion, so that they can perform their duties with due care and precision, and with respect both for the privacy of the family and for the health and safety of those subjected to their programs and procedures. We need to know more about what we could expect from citizens and professionals when they allege maltreatment. These needed areas of research certainly require that we move research in ways that capitalize on our legal understandings of responses to maltreatment. These concepts are conceptually, politically, and legally complicated. These complications, however, should not deter us from developing a system that respects the values that shape our society's commitment to fostering a just society that protects our most cherished relationships.

## Conclusions: Recognizing the Law's Transformative Power

Violence against children rouses our passions, and much can be achieved in the name of children. That passion, coupled by our growing understanding of the nature of violence against children, has contributed to unprecedented legal responses. Society has long recognized that the need to protect children reaches to the core of what most of us view as central to our lives and, as our jurisprudence reveals, remains central to the smooth functioning of our society. As a result, legal mandates broadly structure our families and relationships within them; and our legal system assumes greater power to transform our relationships. Trends in legal responses fostering increased interventions in family life may be well-intentioned and even appropriate. They do, however, raise important questions about the role our government plays in our lives. In this area of law, legal reforms are being grafted onto a system that seeks to maintain its original mission while it adopts new roles and supports new trends. These changes, regrettably, largely have gone unnoticed and have escaped the type of scrutiny typically given to the legal system's efforts to control and direct our behavior. The lack of scrutiny is, in many ways, not surprising. Much of the legal system we have examined essentially remains stealth.

A primary reason the system remains obscure is that responses to violence tend to involve the criminal justice system. When we think of the state's obligations to protect us from violence, we think of law enforcement. Relatedly, when we think of the state's infringing on our rights for wrongdoing, we readily think of law enforcement and the risk of being punished. The focus is intuitively understandable. Criminal law and criminal procedure law provide the paradigmatic arena in which we frame much of our debate about the relationship between individuals and the state. For example, criminal procedure law largely has set the gold standard for our due process rights when states intervene in our lives and accuse us of wrongdoing, as evidenced by the rights to remain silent, retain an attorney, not incriminate one-self, and other basic rights when state officials would seek to incriminate us. These are important protections. Yet, states need not provide these protections when they intervene in families in the name of child protection.

Our society has developed a child welfare system that remains strikingly differ-ent from the criminal justice system and that likely has an even deeper impact on individuals, their private lives, and their relationships. The system has developed ways that permit broad mandates and discretion to guide interventions in our lives. Despite reduced protections from the system, the system's power remains much like the criminal justice system: it can bring us into court against our will, accuse us of acts that ignite severe social reprobation, and deprive us of important liberties. Like the criminal justice system, the child welfare system can reach the very core of our identities and destroy our sources of purpose, fulfillment, and happiness. The two systems also share massive failures, including unwarranted intrusions in our per-sonal lives and unwarranted discrimination. Despite the indisputable importance of the interests at stake, relatively little attention has been paid to the principles and the procedures the child welfare system embraces to determine what the state can do in the name of child protection.

The lack of focus on child welfare systems is not something that is spurred by fundamental legal principles. The Constitution, most notably, guarantees pro-cedural rights to more than just criminal defendants. It accords a right of "due process of law" to all citizens whom the government deprives of life, liberty, or property. As we have seen, this right encompasses ideals that seek to promote ac-curate and fair decision-making and provide people a voice in decisions that will affect them. Both of these goals are particularly compelling in cases involving children's welfare. The gravity of allegations demands that courts provide those with involved interest ample opportunity to be heard. We know that tragic results can come from courts' inaccurate decisions and when children are wrongly re-moved or left with harmful families. Yet, in practice, we have seen that the child welfare system operates by granting reduced protections to those subjected to its processes.

Although broad protections may not apply fully to child welfare law, our Con-stitution strives to protect us from inappropriate state actions. That these protec-tions, to varying degrees, do apply to all legal responses confirms the need to pay closer attention to an increasingly wide variety of legal approaches that fall under the umbrella of child welfare law. The nature of the multiple systems that now encom-pass child welfare law continues to change. These changes provide us with oppor-tunities to identify inadequacies and reconsider our approaches to child protection. As we have seen, the seemingly haphazard development of legal responses appear to have moved in some directions that no longer respect what our legal system has recognized as important rights: the right to protection from unwarranted intrusions by those who act on behalf of our government and even on our own behalf. In the absence of broad social welfare reform efforts challenging ingrained social values relating to how we care for one another, our efforts must turn to design, research, and refine the development of systems that limit intrusions in families, respect diverse social values, and ensure that our efforts achieve their goal: fostering healthy human development in a just society.

# Appendix A
# Defining Child Maltreatment

## State Provisions Regulating Child Psychological Maltreatment

Alabama, §26-14-1(1)-(3); Alaska, §47.17.290; Arizona, §8-201; Arkansas, §12-12-503; California, Penal Code §11166.05; Colorado, §1901-103; Connecticut, §46b-120; Delaware, tit. 16, §902; Georgia (none explicitly); Florida, §39.01; Hawaii, §350-1; Idaho, §16-1602; Illinois, Ch. 325 §5/3; Indiana, §31-34-1-2; Iowa, §232.68; Kansas, §38-1502; Kentucky, §600.020; Louisiana, Ch. Code Art. 603; Maine, tit. 22, §4002; Maryland, Family Law §5-701; Massachusetts, ch. 119, §51; Michigan, §722.622; Minnesota, §260C.007; 626.556; Mississippi §43-21-105; Missouri, §210.110; Montana, §41-3-102; Nebraska, §28-710; Nevada, §432B.070; New Hampshire, §169-C:3; New Jersey, §9:6-8.9; 9:6-8.21; New Mexico, §32A-4-2; New York, Family Court Act §1012; North Carolina, §7B-101; North Dakota, §50-25.1-02; Ohio, §2151.011; Oklahoma, tit. 10, §7102; Oregon, §419B.005; Pennsylvania, tit. 23, §6303; Rhode Island, §40-11-2; South Carolina, §20-7-490; South Dakota, 26-8A-2; Tennessee, §37-1-602; Texas, Family Code §261.001; Utah, §62A-4a-402; Vermont, tit. 33, §4912; Virginia, §63.2-100; Washington (none specified); West Virginia, §49-1-3; Wisconsin §48.02; Wyoming, §14-3-202

## State Provisions Regulating Child Physical Maltreatment

Alabama, §26-14-1(1)-(3); Alaska, §47.17.290; Arizona, §8-201; Arkansas, §12-12; California, §Penal Code §11166.6, 11166.5, 11166.3; Colorado, §19-1-103; Connecticut, §46b-120; Delaware, tit. 16, §902; Florida, §39.01; Georgia 19-7-5(b); Hawaii, §350-1; Idaho, §16-1602; Illinois, Ch. 325 §5/3; Indiana, §31-34-1-2; Iowa, §232.68; Kansas, §38-1502; Kentucky, §600.020; Louisiana, Ch. Code Art. 603; Maine, tit. 22, §4002; Maryland, Family Law §5-701; Massachusetts, ch. 265, §13J; Michigan, §722.622 §722.628; Minnesota, §626.556; Mississippi, §43-21-105; Missouri, §210.110; Montana, §41-3-102; Nebraska,

§28-710; Nevada, §432B.020, 432B.090, 432B.150; New Hampshire, §169-C:3; New Jersey, §9:6-8.9; 9:6-8.21; New Mexico, §32A-4-2; NY CLS Soc Serv §1012; North Carolina, §7B-101; North Dakota, §50-25.1-02; Ohio, §2151.011; Oklahoma, tit. 10, §7102; Oregon, §419B.005; Pennsylvania, tit. 23, §6303; Rhode Island, §40-11-2; South Carolina, §20-7-490; South Dakota, 26-8A-2; Tennessee, §37-1-102; Texas, Family Code §261.001; Utah, §62A-4a-402; Vermont, tit. 33, §4912; Virginia, §63.2-100; Washington §§26.44.020, 26.44.030; West Virginia, §49-1-3; Wisconsin, §48.02; Wyoming, §14-3-202

## State Provisions Regulating Child Neglect

Alabama, §26-14-1; Alaska, §47.17.290; Arizona, §8-201; Arkansas, §12-12-503; California, Penal Code §11165.2; Colorado, §19-01-103; 19-3-102; Connecticut, §46b-120; Delaware, tit. 16, §; Florida, §39.01; Georgia 19-7-5(b); Hawaii, §350-1; Idaho, §16-1602; Illinois, Ch. 325 §5/3; Indiana, §§31-34-1-1, 31-34-1-9, 31-34-1-10, 31-34-1-11; Iowa, §232.68; Kansas, §38-1502; Kentucky, §600.020; Louisiana, Ch. C. Art. 603; Maine, tit. 22, §4002; Maryland, Family Law §; Massachusetts, ALM GL ch. 119, §51A; Michigan, §722.622; Minnesota, §626.556; Mississippi, §43-21-105; Missouri, §210.110; Montana, §41-3-102; Nebraska, §28-710; Nevada, §432B.140; New Hampshire, §169-C:3; New Jersey, §§9:6-8.9; 9:6-8.21; New Mexico, §32A-4-2; New York, CLS Soc Serv, §371; North Carolina, §7B-101; North Dakota, §§50-25.1-02; 27-20-02; Ohio, §§2151.031; Oklahoma, tit.10, §7102; Oregon, §419B.005; Pennsylvania, tit. 23, §6303; Rhode Island, §40-11-2; South Carolina, §20-7-490; South Dakota, §26-8A-2; Tennessee §37-1-102; Texas, Family Code §261.001; Utah, §62A-4a-402; Vermont, tit. 33, §4912; Washington §26.44.020; West Virginia, §49-1-3; Wisconsin, §48.981; Wyoming, §14-3-202.

## State Provisions Regulating Child Sexual Maltreatment

Alabama, §26-14-1; Alaska, §47.17.290; Arizona, §8-201; Arkansas, §12-12-503; California, §Penal Code §11165.1; Colorado, §19-01-103; Connecticut, §46b-120; Delaware, tit. 16, §902; Florida, §39.01; Georgia 19-7-5(b); Hawaii, §350-1; Idaho, §16-1602; Illinois, Ch. 325 §5/3; Indiana, §31-34-1-2; Iowa, §232.68; Kansas, §38-1502; Kentucky, §600.020; Louisiana, Ch. C. Art. 603; Maine, tit. 22, §4002; Maryland, Family Law, §5-701; Massachusetts, ALM GL ch. 119, §51A; Minnesota, §626.556; Mississippi §43-21-105; Missouri, §210.110; Montana, §41-3-102; Nebraska, §28-710; Nevada, §432B.100, 432B.110; New Hampshire, §169-C:3; New Jersey, §§9:6-8.9; 9:6-8.21; New Mexico, §32A-4-2; New York, CLS Soc Serv, §371; North Carolina, §7B-101; North Dakota, §50-25.1-02; Ohio, §§2151.031; Oklahoma, tit. 10, §7102; Oregon, §419B.005; Pennsylvania, tit. 23, §6303; Rhode

Island, §40-11-2; South Carolina, §20-7-490; South Dakota, 26-8A-2; Tennessee, §37-1-602; Texas, Family Code §261.001; Utah, §62A-4a-402; Vermont, tit. 33, §4912; Virginia, §63.2-100; Washington §26.44.020; West Virginia, §49-1-3; Wisconsin §48.02; Wyoming §14-3-202.


# State Provisions Relating to Child Endangerment, Contributing to Delinquency or Dependency of a Minor and Similar Offenses

Alabama, §13A-13-5, 13A-13-6; Alaska, §§11.51.100-11.51.110; §11.51.130; Arizona, §§13-3623, 13-361; Arkansas, §§5-27-203, 5-27-205, §5-27-206; California Penal Code §273a; Colorado, 18-6-401; Connecticut, §53-21; Delaware, tit. 11, §1102; Florida, §§827.03, 827.04; Georgia, §16-5-70; Hawaii, §709-903.5; Idaho, §18-1501; Illinois,720 ILCS 5/12-21.6; Indiana, §35-46-1-4; Iowa, §726.6; Kansas, §§21-3608, 21-3609, 21-3604; Kentucky, §530.060; Louisiana, 14:92, 14:93; Maine, 17-A M.R.S. §554; Maryland, Criminal Law, §3-204; Massachusetts, ch. 265, §13L; Michigan, §750.136b; Minnesota, §§609.377, 609.378 (2006); Mississippi, §97-5-39; Missouri, §568.060; Montana, §45-5-622; Nebraska, §28-707; Nevada, §200.508; New Hampshire, 639:3; New Jersey, §2C:24-4; New Mexico, §§30-6-1, 30-6-3; New York, CLS Penal, §§120.20, 120.25; North Carolina, §§14-316.1, §14-318.2; North Dakota, §§14-07-15, 14-09-22; Ohio, §§2919.21, 2919.22, 2919.24; Oklahoma, ch 21 §852, ch 10, §7115; Oregon, §§163.205, 163.575, 163.577; Pennsylvania, Ch 18, §4304; Rhode Island, §11-9-5; South Carolina, §20-7-50; South Dakota, §26-10-1; Tennessee, §§39-15-401, 39-15-402; Texas Penal Code §22.04; Utah, §§76-5-112.5, 76-5-109; Vermont, ch 13, §§1301, 1304; Virginia, §18.2-371; Washington, §9A.42.035; West Virginia, §§61-8D-1, 61-8D-4; Wisconsin, §948.03; Wyoming, §§6-4-403, 6-4-405.


# State Provisions Providing Exemptions from Definitions of Maltreatment

Alabama, §26-14-7.2; Alaska, §47.17.020(d); Arizona, §8-201; Arkansas, §12-12-503; California, Penal Code §11165.2; 11165.6; Colorado, §19-01-103; 19-3-103; Connecticut, §46b-120; Delaware, tit. 16, §913; 29, §9002; Florida, §39.01; Georgia 19-7-5(b); Hawaii, 32-11(22); Idaho, §16-1602; Illinois, Ch. 325 §5/3; Indiana, §31-34-1-12, 31-34-1-14, 31-34-1-15; Iowa, §232.68; Kansas, §38-1502; Kentucky, §600.020; Louisiana, Ch. C. Art. 603; Maine, tit. 22, §4010; Maryland, 5-313(d)(2); Massachusetts (none specified); Michigan, §722.634; Minnesota, §626.556; Mississippi, §43-21-105; Missouri, §210.110 210.110; Montana, §41-3-102; Nebraska (none specified); Nevada, §432B.020; New Jersey, §9:6-8.21; New Mexico, §32A-4-2; New York Penal Law 260.15; North Carolina (none specified);

North Dakota, 50-25.1-05.1(2); Ohio, §§2151.03(B); 2151.031; Oklahoma, tit. 10, §7103(E); 7106(A)(3); Oregon, §419B.005; Rhode Island, 40-11-15; South Carolina, §20-7-490; South Dakota, 26-8A-2; Tennessee, 37-1-602; Texas, Family Code §261.001; Utah, 76-5-109(4); Vermont, tit. 33, §4912; Virginia, §63.2-100; Washington, §26.44.015; 26.44.020; West Virginia, §49-1-3; Wisconsin, §48.981; Wyoming, §14-3-202.

# Appendix B
# Removing Children from Their Families

## Examples of State Provisions Regulating Rescues

Alabama, §12-15-56; Arkansas, §9-27-313(a)(1)(c); Arizona, §§8-303, 8-821; Connecticut, §17-101g; Florida, §39.401; Georgia, §15-11-45; Hawaii, §587-22, §524; Illinois, §5/5; New York, Court Acts Law, §1024(a); Idaho, §16-1612; Iowa, Iowa §232.79; Kansas, §38-1527(b); Kentucky, §620.040(5)(c); Maryland, Family Law, §5-709(d); Michigan, §712A.14; Mississippi, §43-21-303; Montana, §210.125.2; §41-3-301(1); North Dakota, §27-20-13; Pennsylvania, tit. 42, §6324; Nevada, §432B.390.1(a); Oklahoma, tit.10, §7003-2.1.A.1; Oregon, §419B.150(1)(a); Utah, §62A-4a-202.1(1)(b); Rhode Island, §40-11-5(b); Tennessee, §37-1-114(a)(2); Wisconsin, §48.19(d)

## State Provisions Regulating Reasonable Efforts Requirements

Alabama, §12-15-65(m); Alaska, §47.10.086; Arizona, §8-801; Arkansas, §9-27-303; California, Welf. & Inst. Code §361.5; Colorado, §19-1-103(89), §19-1-115; Connecticut, §46B-129, §17a11b; Delaware, tit. 29, §9003, tit. 13 §1103; Florida, §39.521(1)(f), §39.806(1); Georgia, §15-11-58; Hawaii, §587-26, §587-2, §587-71; Idaho, §16-1615, §16-1610, §1619(6)(d); Illinois, Ch. 325, §5/8.2, Ch. 20 §505/5, Ch 705, §405/2-13.1; Indiana, §31-34-21-5.5, §31-34-21-5.6; Iowa, §232.102; Kansas, §38-1563; Kentucky §620.020, §610.127, §600.020; Louisiana, Ch. Code Arts. 603(17), 626, 684, 672.1; Maine, tit. 22 §4041(1-A), §4036-B, §4041(A-2), §4002(1-B); Maryland, Family Law §5-525(b), §5-525(d) and, Maryland, Courts & Jud. Prod. §3-812(d); Massachusetts, 119, §29C; Michigan, §712A.18f, §712A.19a, §722.638; Minnesota, §260.012; Mississippi, §43-15-13(2), §43-15-13(8), §43-21-603(7); Missouri, §211.183; Montana, §41-3-423; Nebraska, §43-532(2), §43-283.01; Nevada, §432B.393; New Hampshire, §169-C:24a; New Jersey, §30:4C-15.1, §30:4C-11.1, §30:4c-11.2, §30:4c-11.3; New Mexico, §321-4-21, §32A-4-2, §32A-4-22, New York, Social Service Law §384-b, §385-a; North Carolina,

Roger J.R. Levesque, *Child Maltreatment and the Law*
© 2008 Springer Science+Business Media, LLC

§7B-101, §7B-507; North Dakota, §27-20-32.2, §27.20.02; Ohio, §2151.419; Oklahoma, tit. 10, §7003-5.3, §7003-5-5(E), §7003-4.6; Oregon, §419B.340; Pennsylvania, tit. 23, §6373, tit. 42, §6351, tit. 42, §6302; Rhode Island, §40-11-12.2; South Carolina, §20-7-736, §20-7-763; South Dakota, §26-8A-21, §26-8A-21.1; Tennessee, §37-1-166, §36-1-102(9); Texas, Family Code §262.001, §262.2015; Utah, §78-3a-311, §62A-4a-203; Vermont, tit. 33 §5515, §5531; Virginia, §16.1-281; Washington, §13.34.30, §13.34.132; West Virginia, §49-6-5; Wisconsin, §48.355; Wyoming §14-3-440, §14-2-308(c).

## State Provisions for Concurrent Planning

Alabama, §12-15-65(n); Alaska, §47.10.086(e); Arizona, §8-845(D); Arkansas, §9-27-303; California, Welf. & Inst. Code §706.6(k); Colorado, §19-3-608(7); Connecticut, §17a-110a; Florida, §39.601(3)(a); Georgia, §15-11-58(a)(6); Idaho §16-1610; Illinois, Ch. 20 §505/5(l-1); Iowa Ann. Stat. §232.2(4)(h); Louisiana, Ch. Code Arts. 615(C); Maine, tit 22 §4041(1-A)(D); Maryland, Family Law §5-525(b), (d)(3); Massachusetts, Ch. 119, §26; Minnesota, §260.012(k); Mississippi, §43-15-13(2)(f); Missouri, §211.183(9); Montana, §41-3-423(6); Nebraska, §43-283.01(6); Nevada, §432B.393(2); New Hampshire, §169-C:24a (ll); New Jersey, §30:4C-15; New Mexico, §32A-4-29(f); North Carolina, §7B-507; North Dakota, §27-20-32.2(5); Oklahoma, tit. 10, §7003-5.5(B); Oregon, §419B.342; Rhode Island, §40-11-12.2(g); South Carolina, §20-7-763(D); Tennessee, §37-1-166(g)(6); Texas. Family Code §263.102(e); Utah, §78-3a-311(2)(c); Washington, §13.34.136; West Virginia, §49-6-5(a); Wisconsin, §48.355(2); Wyoming, §14-3-431, §14-3-440(c).

## State Provisions Regulating the Termination of Parental Rights

Alabama, §26-18-7; Alaska, §§25.23.180(a), 25.23.180(c), 47.10.011, 47.10.080(c)(3), 47.10.080(o), 47.10.088(a)-(k); Arizona, §§8-533, 8-846(B); Arkansas, §9-27-341; California, Welf. & Inst. Code §§361.5(b), (h), (i), 366.26(c)(1); Colorado, §19-3-604; Connecticut, §§17a-112(j)-(k), 45a-717; Delaware, tit. 13 §1103; Florida, §39.806; Georgia, §§15-11-58, 15-11-94; Hawaii, §§571-61; 587-2; Idaho, §§16-2005, 16-1608(e); Illinois, tit. 750, §50/1 et. seq.; Indiana, §§31-35-2-4.5, 31-35-3-4, 31-35-3-8; Iowa, §§232.111, 232.116; Kansas, §§38-1583, 38-1585; Kentucky, §§600.020(2), 610.127, 625.090; Louisiana, §101; Maine, tit. 22 §§4002, 4055, 4041(A-2); Maryland Family Law, §§5-313, 5-525.1(b)(1); Massachusetts, ch. 119, §26(4), ch. 210, §3(c); Michigan, §§712A.19b(1), (3), (6); Minnesota, §§260.012, 260C.301; Mississippi, §93-15-103; Missouri, §§211.183(6)-(7), 211.447(2)-(7); Montana, §§41-3-609, 41-3-423(2)-(3); Nebraska, §§43-283.01(4), 43-292, 43-292.02; Nevada, §§128.105-128.107, 128.109, 432B.393(3); New Hampshire, §§170-C:5, §169-C:24-a; New Jersey, §§30:4C-15, 30:4C-15.1(a)(b), 9:2-19, 30:4C-11.2; New Mexico, §§32A-4-28(B)(E), 32A-4-2(C),(D), 32A-4-29(K); New York, Social Service Law, §384-b,

358-a(3)(b); North Carolina, §§7B-101(2), 7B-1111; North Dakota, §§27-20-02(3), 27-20-20.1(2)-(4); Ohio, §2151.414; Oklahoma, tit. 10, §7006-1.1-1.6; Oregon, §§419B.500, 419B.502, 419B.504, 419B.506, 419B.508; Pennsylvania, tit. 42, §6302; Rhode Island, §§15-7-7(a)-(c), 40-11-12.2(e); South Carolina, §§20-7-1572, 20-7-763(C),(F); South Dakota, §§26-8A-21.1, 26-8A-26, 26-8A-26.1, 26-8A-27; Tennessee, §§36-1-113(g)-(h), 37-1-166(g)(4); Texas Family Code §161.001, 161.003(a); Utah, §§78-3a-311(2)-(4), 78-3a-402(2), 78-3a-403(2), 78-3a-407, 78-3a-408; Vermont, tit. 15A, §3-504(a), (b), (d); Virginia, §16.1-283(A), (B)-(E), (G); Washington, §§13.34.180, 13.34.190, 13.34.132; West Virginia, §§49-6-5(a)(1), (b), 49-6-5b; Wisconsin, §§48.415, 48.355(2d); Wyoming, §14-2-308, 14-2-309.

# State Provisions Regulating Determinations of Children's Best Interests

Alabama, §12-15-1.1; Alaska §47.10.082, §47.05.065(4)-(5); Arizona, §8-847(C); Arkansas, §9-27-102; California, Welf. & Inst. Code §16000; Colorado, §19-1-102(1), (1.5); Connecticut, §451-719; Delaware, tit. 13, §722; Florida, §39.810; Georgia, §15-11-1; §15-11-94(a); Hawaii, §587-73(a)(3); Idaho, §16-1601; Illinois, tit. 705, §405/1-3(4.05); Indiana, §31-34-19-6; Iowa, §232.104(1)(c); Kansas, §38-1584(a), b(4); Kentucky, §620.023; Louisiana, Ch. Code Art. 675(A); Maine, tit. 22 §4055(2)-(3); Maryland, Family Law, §5-525 (e)(1); Massachusetts, ch. 119 §1; Michigan, §722.23; Minnesota, §260C.193; Mississippi, §43-21-103; Missouri, §211.433; Montana, §41-3-101; Nebraska, §43-533; Nevada, §128.005(2) (c); New Hampshire, §169-C:2(l); §169-C:2(ll); New Jersey, §30:4C-11.1(a); New Mexico, §32A-4-28(A); §32A-1-3 (2006); New York, Social Service Law, §384-b(1); §358-a(3) (c); North Carolina, §7B-507(d); North Dakota, §14-09-06.2(1); Ohio, §2151.414(D); Oklahoma, tit. 10, §7202(2), (5), (10)(a) (2006); Oregon, §107.137(1); Pennsylvania, tit. 42, §6301(b)(1), (1-1), (3), (4); Rhode Island, §15-7-7 (c); South Carolina, §20-7-20(D); South Dakota, §26-7A-56; Tennessee, §36-1-113(I); §36-1-101(d); Texas, Family Code §263.307 (a) - (c); Utah, §78-3a-402(2); Vermont, 33, §5540; 15A §3-504 (c); Virginia, §20-124.3; Washington, §13.34.020; West Virginia, §49-1-1(a)(1)-(a)(8), (b); Wisconsin, §48.426(2)-(3); Wyoming, §14-3-201.

# Examples of State Provisions Regulating the Appointment of Counsel for Parents

Alabama, §12-15-63; Alaska Children in Need of Aid Rule, 12; Arizona, Juvenile Procedure, 52; Arkansas, §9-27-316; Colo .R.S. 19-3-602 (2); Connecticut, §45a-716; Delaware (not provided); Florida, §39.013(1); Georgia, §15-11-98(b); Idaho, §16-2009; Illinois, ch 705, §405/1-5; Indiana, §31-32-4-1; Iowa, §232.89; Kansas, §38-1505(b); Kentucky, §625.080; Louisiana Ch. Code Art. 608; Maine, tit.

22, §4005(2); Maryland, Courts and Judicial Proceedings, §3-813(a)-(b); Massachusetts, ch. 119, §29; Minnesota, §260C.163(3) (a)-(b); Missouri, §211.462(2); Montana, §41-3-425; Nebraska, §43-279.01; Nevada, §128.100(2); New Hampshire, 170-C:8; New Jersey, §30:4C-15.4; New Mexico, §32A-4-10; New York, Family Court Act, §262; North Carolina, §7B-602(a); North Dakota, §27-20-26; Oregon, 2151.352; Pennsylvania, tit. 23, §2313; Rhode Island Juvenile Procedure Rule, 18; South Carolina, §20-7-110(2); South Dakota, §26-7A-31; Tennessee, §36-1-113; Texas Family Code §107.013; Utah, §78-3a-913; Virginia, §16.1-266; Washington, §13.34.090; West Virginia, §49-6-2; Wisconsin, §48.23; Wyoming, §14-2-318, §14-3-211(b).

## Examples of State Provisions Regulating the Appointment of Representation for Children

Alabama, §12-15-1; Alaska, §47.10.050; Arkansas, §9-27-316; Arizona, §8-221(A)-(I); California, Welf. & Inst. Code §317; Colorado, §19-1-111(I), §19-1-103; Connecticut, §17a-103(2); Delaware, tit. 10, §925 (14); Florida, §39.822, §39.820(1); Georgia, §15-11-55(b), §15-11-30(b); Hawaii, §587-34(a), 34(c); Idaho, §16-1618(a) (1999); Illinois, Ch 705, §405/2-17(1)(a); Indiana, §31-33-15-1, §31-9-2-50; Iowa, §232.71C(3), 232.89(4); Kansas, §38-1505; Kentucky, §620.100l; Louisiana, Ch. Code, tit. VI, art. 697, 607; Maine, tit. 22 §4005; Massachusetts, Ch. 119, §29(1999); Maryland, Courts and Juvenile Procedure, §3-834; Michigan, §722.630(10); Minnesota, Juvenile Procedure Rule 40.01; Mississippi, §43-21-121, §43-21-201; Missouri, §43-272; Montana, §41-3-303, §41-3-401; Nebraska, §43-272; Nevada, §432B.500, §432B.420; New Hampshire, §169-C:10(I)-(II) (1999); New Jersey, Juvenile Court Rules, 1969 R.5:B, 9:6-8.23; New Mexico, §31A-4-10(C); New York, Family Court Act, §242; North Carolina, §7B-1202; North Dakota, §50-25.1-08; Ohio, §2151.281, Ohio Juvenile Procedure Rules, 4; Oklahoma, tit 10, §7003-3.7; Oregon, §419B.195; Pennsylvania, §6333, §6382; Rhode Island, §40-11-14; South Carolina, §20-7-110; South Dakota, §26-8A-9, §26-8A-18; Tennessee, §37-1-149; Texas, Family Code §107.011; Utah, §78-3a-912; Vermont, tit. 33, §5525, and Family Court Rules, 6; Virginia, §16.1-266 (1999); Washington, §26.44.053, §13.34.100(6); West Virginia, §56-4-10, §49-6-2; Wisconsin, §48.235; Wyoming, §14-3-211.

# Appendix C
# Criminal Justice System Responses

## State Statutory Provisions Regarding Alternative Means of Providing Children's Testimony

Alabama, §15-25-1; Alaska, §12.45.046; Arizona, §13-4253; Arkansas, §16-43-1001; California, §1347; Colorado, §16-10-402; Connecticut, §54-86g; Delaware, tit 11, §3514; Florida, 92.54; Georgia, §17-8-55; Hawaii, §616; Idaho, §9-1801; 725 Illinois, §5/106B-5; Indiana, §35-37-4-8; Iowa, §915.38(1); Kansas, §22-3434; Kentucky, §421.350; Louisiana, Ch. Code Art. 329; Maryland, Crim. Pro. Code Ann., §11-303; Massachusetts, Ch. 278, §16D; Minnesota, §595.02(4); Mississippi, §13-1-401 et seq.; Missouri, §491.680; Nebraska, §29-1926; Nevada, §50.500 et. seq.; New Hampshire, 517:13-a; New Jersey, §2A:84A-32.4; New York, Crim. Proc. Law, §65.00 et seq.; North Dakota, §31-04-04.1; Ohio, §2945.481; 10 Oklahoma, §7003-4.3(for non-criminal cases only); Pennsylvania, tit. 42,§§5985, 5982; Rhode Island, §11-37-13.2; South Dakota, §§26-8A-30, 26-8A-31; Tennessee, §24-7-117; §24-7-120; Texas, Code Crim. Proc., §38.071; Utah, Crim. Proc. 15.5; Virginia, §18.2-67.9; Washington, §9A.44.150; Wisconsin, §908.08.

## State Provisions of "Tender Years" Exceptions to Hearsay Rules

Alabama, §§15-25-31 to 15-25-37; Alaska, §12.40.110(pertains only before a grand jury); Arizona, §13-1416; Arkansas, §16-41-101, R. Evid. 803(25); California, Evid. Code. §1228; Colorado, §§13-25-129, 18-3-411(3); Delaware, tit. 11, §3513; Florida, §90.803(23); Georgia, §24-3-16; Hawaii, 804(b)(6); Idaho, §§19-809A, 19-3024; Illinois, ch. 725, §5/115-10; Indiana, §35-37-4-6; Kansas, §60-460(dd); Maryland, tit. 15, §1205; Courts & Jud. Proc., §9-103.1; Massachusetts, ch. 233, §81; Michigan, R. Evid., 803A; Minnesota, §595.02; Mississippi, §13-1-403; Missouri, §491.075; Nevada, §51.385; New Jersey, R. Evid., 803(c)(27); Ohio, R. Evid., 807; Oklahoma, tit. 12, §2803.1; Oregon, §40.460, R. Evid., 803(18a); Pennsylvania, §5985.1; Rhode Island, §11-37-13.1 (pertains only in front of a grand jury); South

Roger J.R. Levesque, *Child Maltreatment and the Law*
© 2008 Springer Science+Business Media, LLC

Dakota, §19-16-38; Texas Crim. Proc. Code P38.072; Utah, §76-5-411; Vermont, R. Evid., 804a; Washington, §9A.44.120.


## State Provisions Known as "Sexually Violent Predator Laws"

Fifteen other states have passed laws substantially identical to the Kansas Act Kan. Stat. Ann., §§59-29a02(a) (2005): §Arizona, 36-3701; California, Welf. & Inst. Code §6600; Florida, ch. §394.910; Illinois, tit. 725, §207/1; Iowa, §229A.1; Massachusetts, ch. 123A, §1; Minnesota, §§253B.185; Missouri, §632.480; New Jersey, §30:4-27.25; North Dakota, §25-03.3-01; South Carolina, §44-48-100; Texas Health & Safety Code §841.081; Virginia, §37.1-70.6; Washington, §71.09.010; Wisconsin, §980.01.


## State Provisions "Containing" Released Sex Offenders through Registration and Notification

Alabama, §§15-20-20 to -38; 13A-11-200; Alaska, §§12.63.010, 12.63.020, 12.63.030; Arizona, §§13-3821 to -3827; Arkansas, §§12-12-901 to -920; California, Penal Code 290; Colorado, §§16-22-101 to -114; Connecticut, §§54-250 to -261; Delaware, tit. 11, §§4120; Florida, §§775.21; Georgia, §§42-1-12; Hawaii, §§846E-1 to 846E-9; Idaho, §§18-8301 to -8326; Illinois, tit. 730, §§150/1 to /12; Indiana, §§5-2-12-1 to -14; Iowa, §§692A.1 to .16; Kansas, §§22-4901 to -4912; Kentucky, §§17.510, 17.520, 17.530, 17.578; Louisiana, §§15:540-549; Maine, tit. 34-A, §§11221 to 11228; Maryland, Criminal Procedure, §§11-701-11-721; Massachusetts, ch. 6, §§178D-178Q; Michigan, §§28.721 to .732; Minnesota, §§243.166; Mississippi, §§45-33-21 to -57; Missouri, §§589.400- et. seq.; Montana, §§46-23-501 to -513; Nebraska, §§29-4001 to -4013; Nevada, §§179D.460; New Hampshire, §§651-B; New Jersey, §§2C:7-1 to -19; New Mexico, §§29-11A-1 to -8; New York, Correct. Law, 168; North Carolina, §§14-208.5, 14-208.6 to 14-208.6c; North Dakota, §§12.1-32-15; Ohio, §§2950.01 to .11; Oklahoma, tit. §§57, 581 to 589; Oregon, §§181.592 to 181.607; Pennsylvania, tit. 42, §§9791 to 9792, 9795 to 9799; Rhode Island, §§11-37.1-1 to -20; South Carolina, §§23-3-400 to 23-3-530; South Dakota, §§22-22-31 to 22-22-41; Tennessee, §§40-39-101 to 40-39-111; Texas, Criminal Proc. Code §§62.01-62.14; Utah, §§77-27-21.5; Vermont, tit. 13, §§5401 to 5414; Virginia, §§9.1-900 to 9.1-920; Washington, §§9A.44.130, 9A.44.135, 9A.44.140; West Virginia, §§15-12-1 to -10; Wisconsin, §301.45; Wyoming, §§7-19-301 to 7-19-307.

# Appendix D
# Expert and Scientific Evidence

## States' cases dealing with the *Daubert* and *Frye* approaches to scientific evidence

### States Expressly Adopting the *Daubert* Standard

Alaska: State v. Coon, 974 P.2d 386 (Alaska 1999); Connecticut: State v. Porter, 698 A.2d 739 (Conn. 1997): Delaware: Bell Sports, Inc. v. Yarusso, 759 A.2d 582 (Del. 2000); Idaho: State v. Trevino, 980 P.2d 552 (Idaho 1999); Kentucky: Mitchell v. Commonwealth of Ky., 908 S.W.2d 100 (Ky. 1995); Louisiana: State v. Ledet, 792 So. 2d 160 (La. 2001); Maine: State v. McDonald, 718 A.2d 195 (Me. 1998); Montana: State v. Moore, 885 P.2d 457 (Mont. 1994); New Mexico: State v. Anderson, 881 P.2d 29 (N.M. 1994); North Carolina: State v. Goode, 461 S.E.2d 631 (N.C. 1995); Ohio: Miller v. Bike Athletic Co., 687 N.E.2d 735 (Ohio 1998); Rhode Island: State v. Quattrocchi, 681 A.2d 879 (R.I. 1996); South Dakota: State v. Hofer, 512 N.W.2d 482 (S.D. 1994); Tennessee: McDaniel v. CSX Transp., Inc., 955 S.W.2d 257 (Tenn. 1997); Texas: E.I. du Pont Nemours & Co. v. Robinson, 923 S.W.2d 549 (Tex. 1995); Vermont: State v. Brooks, 643 A.2d 226 (Vt. 1993); West Virginia: Wilt v. Buracker, 443 S.E.2d 196 (W. Va. 1993); Wyoming: Bunting v. Jamieson, 984 P.2d 467 (Wyo. 1999).

### States Retaining the *Frye* Standard

Arizona: Logerquist v. Mcvey, 1 P.3d 113 (Ariz. 2000); California: People v. Leahy, 882 P.2d 321 (Cal. 1994); Illinois: Donaldson v. Cent. Ill. Pub. Serv. Co., 767 N.E.2d 314 (Ill. 2002); Indiana: Sears Roebuck & Co. v. Manuilov, 742 N.E.2d 453 (Ind. 2001); Kansas: State v. Canaan, 964 P.2d 681 (Kan. 1998); Maryland: Hutton v. State, 663 A.2d 1289 (Md. 1995); Mississippi: Gleeton v. State, 716 So. 2d 1083 (Miss. 1998); Missouri: Callahan v. Cardinal Glennon Hosp., 863 S.W.2d 852 (Mo.

1993); Nebraska: Sheridan v. Catering Mgmt., Inc., 566 N.W.2d 110 (Neb. 1997); New York: People v. Wernick, 674 N.E.2d 322 (N.Y. 1996); North Dakota: City of Fargo v. McLaughlin, 512 N.W.2d 700 (N.D. 1994); Pennsylvania: Commonwealth v. Arroyo, 723 A.2d 162 (Pa. 1999); Washington: State v. Copeland, 922 P.2d 1304 (Wash. 1996).

## States Adopting Variations or Not Explicitly Changing or Not Fully Adopting *Daubert*

Alabama: So. Energy Homes, Inc. v. Washington, 774 So. 2d 505 (Ala. 2000); Arkansas: Moore v. State, 915 S.W.2d 284 (Ark. 1996); Colorado: People v. Shreck, 22 P.3d 68 (Colo. 2001); Iowa: Leaf v. Goodyear Tire & Rubber Co., 590 N.W.2d 525 (Iowa 1999); Massachusetts: Commonwealth v. Senior, 744 N.E.2d 614 (Mass. 2001); Nevada: Dow Chem. Co. v. Mahlum, Inc. 973 P.2d 842 (Nev. 1999); New Hampshire: State v. Cort, 766 A.2d 260 (N.H. 2000); New Jersey: State v. Harvey, 699 A.2d 596 (N.J. 1997); Oklahoma: Torres v. State, 962 P.2d 3(Okla. Crim. App. 1998); Taylor v. State, 889 P.2d 319 (Okla. Crim. App. 1995); South Carolina: State v. Council, 515 S.E.2d 508 (S.C. 1999); Utah: State v. Butterfield, 27 P.3d 1133 (Utah 2001); Virginia: Spencer v. Commonwealth, 393 S.E.2d 609 (Va. 1990); Wisconsin: State v. Peters, 534 N.W.2d 867 (Wis. Ct. App. 1995).

## States Rejecting or Not Applying *Daubert* Despite Recognizing It

Florida: Brim v. State, 695 So. 2d 268 (Fla. 1997); Georgia: Jordan v. Ga. Power Co., 466 S.E.2d 601 (Ga. 1995); Hawaii: State v. Fukusaku, 946 P.2d 32 (Haw. 1997); Minnesota: State v. Klawitter, 518 N.W.2d 577 (Minn. 1994); Oregon: State v. Brown, 687 P.2d 751 (Or. 1984); State v. O'Key, 899 P.2d 663 (Or. 1995).

# References

Abel, R. (Ed.). (1982). *The politics of informal justice*. New York: Academic Press.

Addington v. Texas, 441 U.S. 418 (1979).

Adoption Assistance and Child Welfare Act, Pub. L. No. 96-272, 94 Stat. 500 (1980).

Adoption and Safe Families Act, Pub. L. No. 105-89, 111 Stat. 2115 (1997).

Bartholet, E. (1999). *Nobody's children: Abuse and neglect, foster drift, and the adoption alternative*. Boston, MA: Beacon Press.

Bellotti v. Baird, 443 U.S. 622 (1979).

Board of Education v. Earls, 536 U.S. 822 (2002).

Bowers v. Hardwick, 478 U.S. 186 (1986).

Child Abuse Prevention and Treatment Act, Pub. L. No. 93-247, 88 Stat. 5, 42 U.S.C. §§5101–5107 (1974).

Child Abuse Prevention and Treatment and Adoption Reform General Program, 42 USCS §§5101–5107 (2007).

Child Victims' and Child Witnesses' Rights Act, 18 U.S.C. 3509 (1990).

Collins, J. (2006). Crime and parenthood: The uneasy case for prosecuting neglectful parents. *Northwestern University Law Review, 100,* 807–855.

Coleman, D. L. (2005). Storming the castle to save the children: The ironic costs of a child welfare exception to the Fourth Amendment, *William & Mary Law Review, 47,* 413–540.

Commerce, Justice, and State, the Judiciary, and Related Agencies Appropriations Act, 42 U.S.C. 14071 (1998).

Connecticut v. Doe, 538 U.S. 1 (2003).

Coy v. Iowa, 487 U.S. 1012 (1988).

Crawford v. Washington, 541 U.S. 36 (2004).

Cross, T., Walsh, W. A., Simone, M., & Jones, L. M. (2003). Prosecution of child abuse: A meta-analysis of rates of criminal justice decisions. *Trauma, Violence and Abuse, 4,* 323–340.

Dandridge v. Williams, 397 U.S. 471 (1970).

Daubert v. Merrell Dow Pharmaceuticals, Inc., 509 U.S. 579 (1993).

Daubert v. Merrell Dow Pharm. Inc., 43 F.3d 1311 (9th Cir. 1995).

Delgado, R. (1985). Fairness and formality: Minimizing the risk of prejudice in alternative dispute resolution. *Wisconsin Law Review,* 1359–1404.

DeShaney v. Winnebago County Department of Social Services, 489 U.S. 189 (1989).

Dickerson v. United States, 530 U.S. 428 (2000).

Dwyer, J.G. (1994). Parents' Religion and children's welfare: Debunking the doctrine of parents' rights. *California Law Review, 82,* 1371–1447.

Eisenstadt v. Baird, 405 U.S. 438 (1972).

Elk Grove Unified School District v. Newdow, 542 U.S. 1 (2004).

Ferguson v. City of Charleston, 532 U.S. 67 (2001).

Foster, E. M., & Kalil, A. (2005). Developmental psychology and public policy: Progress and prospects. *Developmental Psychology, 41,* 827–832.

Frye v. United States, 293 F. 1013 (D.C. Cir. 1923).

Gelles, R. (1996). *The book of David: How preserving families can cost children's lives.* New York: Basic Books.

General Electric Co. v. Joiner, 522 U.S. 136 (1997).

Gideon v. Wainwright, 372 U.S. 335 (1963).

Griswold v. Connecticut, 381 U.S. 479 (1965).

Guggenheim, M. (2005). *What's wrong with children's rights.* Cambridge, MA: Harvard University Press.

Haksins, R., Wulczyn, F., & Webb, M. B. (Eds.). (2007). *Child protection: Using research to improve policy.* Washington, DC: Brookings Institution Press.

Hehr, A. M. (2007). Child shall lead them: Developing and utilizing child protection mediation to better serve the interests of the child. *Ohio State Journal on Dispute Resolution, 22,* 443–476.

Helfer, M. E., Kempe, R. S., & Krugman, R. D. (Eds). (1997). *The battered child* (5th ed.). Chicago: University of Chicago Press.

Idaho v. Wright, 497 U.S. 805 (1990).

In re Gault, 387 U.S. 1, 55 (1967).

Ingraham v. Wright, 430 U.S. 651 (1977).

Jacob Wetterling Crimes Against Children and Sexually Violent Offender Registration Act, 42 U.S.C. 14071 (2004).

Janicki, M.A. (2007). Better seen then herded. Residency restrictions and global positioning system tracking laws for sex offenders. Boston University Public Interest Law Journal, 16, 285–311.

Jenkins, P. (1998). Moral panic: Changing concepts of the child molester in modern America. New Haven, CT: Yale University Press.

Kansas v. Crane, 534 U.S. 407 (2002).

Kansas v. Hendricks, 521 U.S. 346 (1997).

Kendall-Tackett, K. A., & Giacomoni, S. M. (2005). *Child victimization.* New York: Civic Research Institute.

Kennedy v. Mendoza-Martinez, 372 U.S. 144 (1963).

King, R. H. (1992). The molested child witness and the Constitution: Should the Bill of Rights be transformed into the bill of preferences? *Ohio State Law Journal, 53,* 49–99.

Klevens, J., & Whitaker, D. J. (2007). Primary prevention of child physical abuse and neglect: Gaps and promising directions. *Child Maltreatment, 12,* 364–377.

Kumho Tire Co. v. Carmichael, 526 U.S. 137 (1999).

Lassiter v. Department of Social Services, 452 U.S. 18 (1981).

Lawrence v. Texas, 2 539 U.S. 558 (2003).

Leaf v. Goodyear Tire & Rubber Co., 590 N.W.2d 525 (Iowa 1999).

Lehman v. Lycoming County Children's Services 458 U.S. 502 (1982).

Lchr v. Robcrtson, 463 U.S. 248 (1983).

Levesque, R. J. R. (2007). *Adolescence, media and the law.* New York: Oxford University Press.

Levesque, R. J. R. (2006). *The psychology and law of criminal justice processes.* Hauppauge, NY: Nova Science Publishers.

Levesque, R. J. R. (2002a). *Child maltreatment and the law: Foundations in science, policy and practice.* Durham, NC: Carolina Academic Press.

Levesque, R. J. R. (2002b). *Not by faith alone: Religion, adolescence and the law.* New York University Press.

Levesque, R. J. R. (2001). *Culture and family violence: Fostering change through human rights law.* Washington, DC: American Psychological Association.

Levesque, R. J. R. (2000). *Adolescents, sex, and the law: Preparing adolescents for responsible citizenship.* Washington, DC: American Psychological Association.

Levesque, R. J. R. (1995). Prosecuting sex crimes against children: Time for "outrageous" proposals? *Law & Psychology Review, 19,* 59–91.

Lindsey, D. (2003). *The welfare of children.* New York: Oxford University Press.

Loving v. Virginia, 388 U.S. 1 (1967).

M.L.B. v. S.L.J., 519 U.S. 102 (1996).

McDaniel v. CSX Transp., Inc., 955 S.W.2d 257 (Tenn. 1997).

Magyar, K. A. (2006). Betwixt and between but being booted nonetheless: A developmental perspective on aging out of foster care. *Temple Law Review, 79,* 557–605.

Mangold, S. V. (2007). Poor enough to be eligible? Child abuse, neglect, and the poverty requirement. *St. John's Law Review, 81,* 575–600.

Mangold, S. V. (1999). challenging the parent-child-state triangle in public family law: The importance of private providers in the dependency system. *Buffalo Law Review, 47,* 1397–1456.

Marcus, J. E. (2006). The neglectful *parens patriae*: Using child protective laws to defend the safety net. *New York University Review of Law & Social Change, 30,* 255–297.

Martell, D. R. (2005). *Criminal justice and the placement of abused children.* New York: LFB Scholarly Publishing.

Maryland v. Craig, 497 U.S. 836 (1990).

Mathews v. Eldridge, 424 U.S. 319 (1976).

Mattox v. United States, 156 U.S. 237 (1895).

Maynard v. Hill, 125 U.S. 190 (1888).

Medina v. California, 505 U.S. 437 (1992).

Meyer v. Nebraska 262 U.S. 390 (1923).

Michael H. v. Gerald D., 491 U.S. 110 (1989).

Miller v. Albright, 523 U.S. 420 (1998).

Mills, L. G. (1999). Killing her softly: Intimate abuse and the violence of state intervention. *Harvard Law Review, 113,* 550–613.

Miranda v. Arizona, 384 U.S. 436 (1966).

Moore v. City of East Cleveland, 431 U.S. 494 (1977).

Morao, K. (2006). Domestic violence and the state. Georgetown *Journal of Gender and the Law, 7,* 787–817.

Morse v. Frederick, 127 S. Ct. 2618 (2007).

Myers, J. (2006). *Child protection in America.* New York: Oxford University Press.

National Clearinghouse on Child Abuse & Neglect Information. (2006). *Child Maltreatment 2004: Summary of key findings.* Washington, DC: US Department of Health and Human Services.

New Jersey v. T.L.O., 469 U.S. 325 (1985).

Newton v. Burgin, 414 U.S. 1139 (1974).

Nguyen v. INS., 533 U.S. 53 (2001).

Ohio v. Roberts, 448 U.S. 56 (1980).

Pam Lyncher Sexual Offender Tracking and Identification Act of 1996, 42 U.S.C. 14072–73 (2004).

Parham v. J.R., 442 U.S. 584 (1979).

Parratt v. Taylor, 451 U.S. 527 (1981).

Paruch, D. (2006). The orphaning of underprivileged children: America's failed child welfare law & policy. *Journal of Law & Family Studies, 8,* 119–165.

Pecora, P. J., Whittaker, J. K., Maluccio, A. N., Barth, R. P., & Plotnick, R. D. (2000). *The child welfare challenge: Policy, practice, and research* (2nd ed.). New York: Aldine de Gruyter.

Pelton, L. (1989). *For reasons of poverty: A critical analysis of the. American child welfare system.* Westport, CT: Praeger.

Pierce v. Society of Sisters, 268 U.S. 510 (1925).

Planned Parenthood of Central Missouri v. Danforth, 428 U.S. 52 (1976).

Prince v. Massachusetts, 321 U.S. 158 (1944).

Reynolds v. United States, 98 U.S. 145 (1878).

Roberts, D. (2002). Shattered bonds: The color of child welfare. New York: Basic Books.

Santosky v. Kramer, 455 U.S. 745 (1982).

Schall v. Martin, 467 U.S. 263 (1984).

Sears Roebuck & Co. v. Manuilov, 742 N.E.2d 453 (Ind. 2001).

Seling v. Young, 531 U.S. 250 (2001).

Sinden, A. (1999). "Why won't Mom cooperate?": A critique of informality in child welfare proceedings. *Yale Journal of Law and Feminism, 11,* 339–396.

Skinner v. Oklahoma, 316 U.S. 535 (1942).

Smith v. Doe, 538 U.S. 84 (2003).

Smith v. Organization of Foster Families for Equality and Reform, 431 U.S. 816 (1977).

Stanley v. Illinois, 405 U.S. 645 (1972).

Storrow, R. F. (2006). Rescuing children from the marriage movement: The case against marital status discrimination in adoption and assisted reproduction. *U.C. Davis Law Review, 39,* 305-370.

Suter v. Artist M. 503 U.S. 347 (1992).

Terry v. Ohio, 392 U.S. 1 (1968).

Troxel v. Granville, 530 U.S. 57 (2000).

Turner v. Safley, 482 U.S. 78 (1987).

U.S. Advisory Board on Child Abuse and Neglect. (1993). Neighbors helping neighbors: A new national strategy for the protection of children. Washington, DC: U.S. Government Printing Office.

Waldfogel, J. (1998). The future of child protection. Boston, MA: Harvard University Press.

White, P. J. (2003). Rescuing the confrontation clause. *South Carolina Law Review, Spring, 54,* 537–622.

White v. Illinois, 502 U.S. 346 (1992).

Wisconsin v. Yoder, 406 U.S. 205 (1972).

Wolf, M. P. (2007). Proving race discrimination in criminal cases using statistical evidence. *Hastings Race and Poverty Law Journal, 4,* 395–427.

Wyman v. James, 400 U.S. 309 (1971).

Youngberg v. Romeo, 457 U.S. 307 (1982).

Zablocki v. Redhail, 434 U.S. 374 (1978).

# Index

Printed in the United States of America